# ARCHES OF THE YEARS

# THE ARCHES
# OF THE YEARS

By

HALLIDAY SUTHERLAND

WILLIAM MORROW AND COMPANY
NEW YORK                    MCMXXXIII

COPYRIGHT 1933

by Halliday Sutherland

PRINTED IN THE UNITED STATES OF AMERICA
BY THE DE VINNE PRESS, NEW YORK

To
My Daughter
JANE

# CONTENTS

# CONTENTS

# CHAPTER I

# THE TERROR OF THE GLEN

"WANTED, a detective—to arrest the flight of time."
These strange words, heard by me as a boy of eight,
were spoken by a man who lodged one summer at the farm-
house in the Highlands of Scotland, where my father, mother
and sister, three years my junior, usually spent our holidays.
The name of the man was Mr. Cox. His bedroom was over
our sitting-room, and, on fine mornings, Ellen, the farmer's
daughter, a woman of twenty-five, carried his wicker arm-
chair out into a field near the house—and there the tall,
silent man, with white and often unshaven face, would sit
with a rug over his knees and a deer-stalker cap on his
head. At meal-times Ellen went out to fetch him, and he
followed her back into the house like a tame animal.

Once, when crossing the field, I passed near to his chair
and heard him mutter: "Wanted, a detective—to arrest the
flight of time." I asked my mother why he said it, and she
told me that Mr. Cox was not quite well. My father, who
was a doctor, said: "He has no right to be here," and also
told me that once Mr. Cox had won his blue for boxing at
a great English university.

There was fishing in the river below the house and in the
mountain burns, rabbits to be shot on the farm, and game
to be poached. Mr. Cox did none of these things; he never
even went for walks, nor, so far as I knew, did he ever read
books or newspapers. He sat in the field all day looking
down at the grass, but if any of the wandering barnyard
fowls came near he would rise, waving his stick and shouting
words which I knew to be oaths. All the dogs about the
farm avoided him and horses grazing in the field never
approached his chair.

I

The house stood on a small plateau on the south bank of the swift-running river that flowed down the glen, and from the other bank there rose a barrier of rugged hills and volcanic rocks. On the hills were large purple patches of heather and smaller green patches of bracken and grasses, and here and there little woods of birch and of fir scrambled up the slopes. High and solitary above the crags was a silver birch—the tree that grows at greater heights than all other trees—and on sunny days pieces of quartz sparkled in the rocks. On the other side of the hills was an inland loch, very long, very narrow, and very deep, and from its farther shore rose the side of a great mountain crowned by a precipice. In clear weather the top of this crag could be seen from the house.

The great inland loch was out of sight and also the little steamers that passed through it on their way from one shore of Scotland to the other along the Caledonian Canal. Behind the house were rising moors, glens, and mountains where the mists of morning linger. Over these mountains and under the clouds was a wild country, where in late autumn the glens echoed to the roaring of stags. There I once found a great stone, and on the top, as on a savage altar, the skin and bones of a sheep picked clean by eagles.

Down the glen westwards ran the river in a series of broad shallows, narrow rapids, and deep pools. Just below the house was a salmon pool through which the water ran black and swirling. On our side of the pool was a sandy beach, and at the top end a little sandy bay of still, shallow water. Between the bay and the entrance of the rapids into the pool was a small plantation of bushes and trees. In dry weather this was a peninsula jutting into the pool, but when the river was in spate it was an island, and the water poured round it into the sandy bay. At the end of the peninsula was a withered ash with smooth trunk and branches, which was easy to climb naked. I would walk along a branch overhanging the place where the rapids poured into the pool, and from there dive into the stream. It was a very deep pool, and not always did I manage to reach the smooth rocks at the bottom. When I did, it seemed a long time before I got back to the surface and found that the moving wall of water had carried me to the tail end of the pool. What did I hope to find at the bottom? A salmon lying quiet, to be seized by the gills and dragged to the surface after a desperate struggle. The other thing I dreamt to find was the under-water entrance to a secret cave into which I could swim and find myself in a cavern under the rocks on the farther bank. These were animal instincts, in childhood not altogether lost.

In the depths of the pool I found neither the salmon nor hidden caverns. The light was so dim that all I could see was the blurred outline of rocks past which the current carried me.

The water of the river and of the burns which feed it was peaty, but in the woods on either side were many springs clear as crystal on a floor of glistening pebbles.

Up and down the glen were farms and crofts, a mile or more apart, and beside each was a field or two of corn and a small walled-in garden, flanked at each corner by rowan trees, which kept away certain evil things that dwelt in the mountains. On calm days blue smoke from peat fires in the houses rose in the still air, and the silence of the hills was broken by the sound of running water, and now and then by the bleating of sheep, the crowing of the cock on a distant farm, the sharp, startled cry of the grouse—"Go-o back, go-o back"—or by the wail of a curlew.

On each side of the river was a road. The one on the other side was a real road with milestones, and the mail-coach passed by every day. But the road on our side was a peaceful, moss-covered road overhung by bracken on either side. There were no milestones here, but you knew the distances

3

by the houses you passed or by the burns which ran across the road at the foot of little gullies.

Cameron was the name of the farmer with whom we lodged. He was sixty-five years of age; a short, white-bearded man with gnarled hands. His wife was ten years younger, and the family consisted of Ellen, Alec, Davy and Donald, a lad of sixteen. Their features were rough cast, but the men had rosy faces and the women quiet eyes. In expression they looked serious, as do those who win their daily bread by tilling an unfertile soil and think deeply because they are very near to the three great mysteries of life: he was born; he begat children; he died.

One evening we were having "high" tea: fried trout— caught by me that day in one of the mountain burns—home-made oatcakes and scones, fresh butter, strawberry jam, heather honey in the comb, and tea with cream.

Around the table sat my father, mother, sister and myself. There were two windows in the sitting-room. The front window looked on to the rough lawn and the back window on to a kitchen-garden. It was daylight, although near sunset, but even at night there were no blinds or shutters to close. My father sat with his back to the kitchen-garden, my mother sat opposite, and on either side were my sister and myself.

My father was of medium height, broad shouldered, with strong features, black hair and brown moustache. He had large brown eyes, well set apart, and bushy eyebrows—they were honest eyes.

In the midst of our meal we heard the slight clatter of plates as Ellen went upstairs with Mr. Cox's supper. Suddenly there was a scream and the high falsetto of a woman shrieking for help. From the kitchen old Mr. Cameron rushed along the corridor, shouting: "I'm coming, lass," followed by his two elder sons and three barking collies. The house shook as men and dogs ran up the narrow stairs.

My father had risen and reached the door, where he turned to say: "Stay here, every one of you." Then he left us and went upstairs too. There was a minute or two of silence followed by a thud which shook the ceiling. Something heavy had fallen on to the floor upstairs. My mother moaned: "Your father will be killed." Next moment came the tramp of heavy feet, the piercing screams of Ellen, the crash of falling furniture, and then another and heavier thud on the floor. Again a moment of silence, broken by my father's voice ɔhouting from the top of the stairs: "Ropes! bring ropes, I say. Donald, bring ropes."

Ellen ran down the stairs to help her youngest brother to find the rope, and from the kitchen came the cries of Mrs. Cameron: "Oh, woe is me!" From the room above all that we heard was the snarling of dogs and the oaths of Mr. Cox. It seemed a long time before Ellen and Donald went upstairs with ropes trailing behind them. After another long interval those who had rushed upstairs came down slowly, and when my father re-entered the sitting-room blood was streaming down his face from a cut over the left eyebrow.

He had been the last to enter the room upstairs, where he found Mr. Cox holding Mr. Cameron by the neckband of his shirt and brandishing a razor at the old man's throat. The two sons, dull-witted in emergency, were standing inert, while the three dogs snarled and snapped round the legs of Mr. Cox. My father stepped forward: "How dare you threaten an old man with a razor. Put it down, sir!" Mr. Cox released Mr. Cameron, placed the open razor on the dressing-table, squared up, boxer that he was, and next moment sent my father to the floor with a blow that cut open his left eyebrow. That was the first thud on the ceiling. Then Mr. Cameron and his two sons closed on Mr. Cox and the struggle began. My father rose to his feet and went to their aid. Again there was a crash as four men and a

5

madman fell together on the floor. When the ropes arrived, Mr. Cox was tied hand and foot, lifted on to his bed, and there bound down again.

My father sat down in the arm-chair, and my mother brought two handkerchiefs which made a pad and bandage for the cut. Then she found pen, ink and paper, and my father wrote a note to the doctor who visited Mr. Cox from time to time. The doctor's house was eight miles away, and Donald had to ride there that night with the note. "Your patient," wrote my father, "is a homicidal epileptic. We leave here in the morning. You must arrange for his immediate removal to the county asylum." We then resumed our high tea, now cold and unattractive, and awaited Donald's return. This was not a night on which children could be sent to bed early. Soon after ten o'clock Donald was back. The doctor would come in the morning with a wagonette and three men to take Mr. Cox away.

Having given Donald's news, Mr. Cameron asked if Ellen might give Mr. Cox a drink of milk. "Yes, if she feeds him," said my father. Ellen went upstairs with the glass of milk. She was there some time, and, as she came down, father opened the door and asked: "Is he all right?"

"Yes, doctor, yes," she answered, and ran along the corridor to the kitchen. The door of our sitting-room had not been closed for more than a moment when there was a thud on the ceiling and sounds of movement in the room above.

"My God," said my father, and Mr. Cameron rushed along the corridor shouting:

"Doctor, doctor! she's loosed the ropes. Will ye no' go up again?"

"The fool!" shouted my father. "Never again. Back to your kitchen and barricade yourselves in. We will stay in this room."

There was no lock on the door, but we dragged a little

bookcase from the wall and made it lean against the panels. Behind the bookcase we placed a small harmonium. Such was the barricade. My mother cleared the table, putting the dishes into the larder.

"You and the children had better go in there," said my father, indicating the little room under the stairs, "and lock the door. I stay here." I wished to stay with him, so he said: "Very well."

Once my mother and sister were in the little room my father moved the lamp from the table to the mantelshelf and drew the table nearer the back window. On the table he laid his twelve-bore gun and beside it a box of cartridges. Then he sat down, facing the door, and loaded his gun. As he did this he looked carefully at the number on the outer wad of the cartridges, and I noticed that he chose No. oo. That was buckshot, the heaviest charge. He laid his loaded gun on the table.

The horse-hair arm-chair stood by the hearth, and I was told to rest there.

From the room above came sounds of someone fumbling about in the dark, for the lamp had been removed from Mr. Cox's room. Just then the door of the little bedroom opened. My mother came out and saw the gun on the table.

"Jack, you're not going to—to——?"

"Stay in that room, and lock the door. I take no risks."

As I watched my father sitting quietly at the table, I could have cried, because blood was trickling down from beneath the bandage, making a dark, black stain on the front of his Harris-tweed jacket. But there were times when he hated tears. This was such a time—and on his deathbed was the last. And yet he and I had shed tears over the sorrows of *Les Misérables*, which he had read aloud to me.

I began to think of the great criminal, Jean Valjean, of Gavroche, the boy who slept with the rats inside the belly of the stone elephant, of cruel Inspector Javert who rubbed the snow down poor Cosette's back, and of kind Bishop Myriel whose door was never locked. Had my father been a bishop, I felt sure he would have been like Bishop Myriel. He was kind to criminals. There was the burglar he had saved from pneumonia in the Glasgow prison. On leaving jail the man had thanked him. One morning the police found a sack of stolen silver outside our front door. Had my father any idea who had left it there? The detectives thought it must be some thief whom he had treated in prison. A grateful thief? No; my father had no recollection of anyone likely to leave silver at his door. But at breakfast he made a cryptic remark: "Gratitude is very rare." And, musing thus, I dozed in the arm-chair.

It was past midnight when I awoke. There had been a crash upstairs. My father was sitting at the table as before, but now he held the gun in his hands. "Is he coming down?" I asked.

"Hist, I think so."

The stairs creaked; Mr. Cox was coming down very quietly. Intent on listening, we could scarcely hear a sound when he reached the foot of the stairs. Very gently the handle of our door was turned, the door was forced open an inch, and the little barricade moved slightly. My father's voice rang clear and steady: "Go back to your room, or I shoot."

There was no reply, but the footsteps moved away from our door. Next came the crash of broken glass, falling flower-pots, and a fumbling with the lock of the front door.

"In the porch. He's going out of the house! Put the lamp out, or he'll see us through the window."

I turned down the wick and pressed the extinguisher. My father moved to the wall opposite the fireplace, where he could watch both windows, and there I stood beside him. We heard the front door open. Mr. Cox was outside. Again there was silence.

8

"Can you see where he is?" asked my father.

I moved to the middle of the room. "He's standing in the middle of the grass. Now he's coming to the window." In a moment I was back beside my father. It was moonlight and the moon was over the mountains on the other side of the river. As Mr. Cox approached the window the light of the moon threw a dark shadow on the carpet. Then his body almost occluded the window, and through the upper pane I saw his face and staring eyes peering in—and above the face the outline of a deerstalker cap. I was afraid, although I knew that I was safe. My father had raised the gun to his right shoulder and its barrels were levelled at the figure outside the window. It seemed quite natural that Mr. Cox was going to be shot. He was a wild animal who would kill us all if he could; but my greatest sense of security came from the homely peat-smoke odour from my father's Harris tweed. Suddenly Mr. Cox turned from the window, rushed back through the porch, and fled upstairs to his room. His door was slammed, and then began a new noise of snarling and tearing. My father sat down again and put the gun on the table. "He'll soon tire himself out. Then he'll sleep for hours. He's tearing up his bedding."

When I awoke in the arm-chair it was daylight. My mother was packing up our luggage, and the farmer's gig stood on the lawn. It was seven o'clock, and after a hurried breakfast we set off on a two hours' drive up the glen and round the hills, to a pier on the long inland loch where the steamer called. We were going farther west, to friends. Before we left, words passed between Mr. Cameron and my father.

"It's hard, doctor, for me to be losing all my summer visitors in a day. And yon Mr. Cox, with all his faults—his lawyers paid me well."

"Lose your visitors!" said my father; "last night you nearly lost your life."

On board the steamer my mother and sister went down to rest in the cabin, while my father and I walked the deck. He wore a cap, and under the clean handkerchief round his forehead his left eye was black and swollen. It was not a pleasant sight, and one or two people looked at him as we passed. One man on deck might have been going to a funeral. He was dressed in black and wore a black trilby hat. His waistcoat was cut low at the neck showing an expanse of white front—an imitation white shirt with a single brass stud in the centre. He wore a low white collar and a black bow tie. He was pale, with watery blue eyes and had a short, square, yellow beard. Crossing to our side of the deck, he stood directly in my father's way and smiled as he held out a leaflet. "May I offer you a tract, brother?"

"No, thanks," said my father. "I'm not interested," and turned to walk off.

But the man walked alongside him and continued to talk, although my father ignored him. "Brother, when I saw you coming on board I said to myself: a brand to be plucked from the burning. You must think of your wife and children, brother. Last night the devil gained a victory. Thank God the injury was no worse! Strong drink, brother, is like a raving——"

"Be off," shouted my father. "Be off, you damned scoundrel, or I'll put you overboard."

The man shook his head sadly, and left us, saying as he went: "I'll pray for you, brother."

There are people who walk about the earth asking to be murdered and there are times when homicide is justifiable.

# CHAPTER II

## ARCADIA

ALL the summers of childhood and boyhood were passed in the Highlands, and so even in the desert-places of later life a mirage has always appeared. There was the mossy road that went between woods of birch, sloes and hazel trees, and through little fragrant forests of pine where roedeer sheltered. It was there that I shot my first roebuck. I went out to shoot rabbits on the farm, but the twelve-bore gun which I carried called for better things than rabbits, and I wandered through the woods in search of them. It was one of those days when nothing goes wrong. I knew I was poaching, and that was an added thrill. Two miles below the farm I waded across the river in a shallow reach to explore a field of corn. I walked through the corn and against the wind. In the middle of the field two birds rose, one on either side—a wood-pigeon and a wild duck. I fired at each and both came down. My thrill of satisfaction was turned to fear when I heard behind me a stentorian shout: "Well done, boy; a right and a left." I turned round and fear left me when I saw our minister from Glasgow, who was staying in a farm near by. He was a tall, bearded, and most cheerful man, and held liberal views on poaching, especially on an estate over which neither the proprietor nor his friends ever fired a gun. It was a kindness to thin down the game that swarmed on the moors and in the woods. The minister himself did not shoot: he was content to fish the river for trout and to land a large number of grilse and salmon. The water-bailiff, Mr. Coutts, was old and deaf, and but for this the minister would assuredly have been caught red-handed. When he was killing a fish it had to be gaffed by his daughter Minnie, aged twenty, and the voice of the father shouting to his daughter could be heard half a mile away.

I had tea with him, his wife and his daughter, and they refused to accept either the duck or the pigeon. Afterwards, with both birds in my bag, I recrossed the river and made for home through the woods below the road. I was climbing down the bank of a gully, through bracken that almost reached to my shoulders, when I heard a noise that made me stand quite still. Then I saw him bounding down the gully—a roebuck with three points on each antler. He passed within twenty yards. I fired both barrels and he fell in the bracken. I clambered down and found him dead, shot through the heart. He was so beautiful that for a moment I felt remorse. But there were other things to think about— to hide the carcass and to arrange for getting it home after dark. I cut great stalks of bracken with my knife, and soon the dead deer was hidden. Then I crept up to the edge of the gully and looked out to see if my shot had attracted attention.

I could see the road, which crossed the top of the gully, and on the road was a policeman coming my way. Once a month he did this lonely beat. Would he pass the gully, or would he come down to see who had been shooting? I lay flat on my stomach in the bracken and held my breath, which increased the thumping of my heart. The minutes of suspense seemed like hours. Then a new danger arose. Quite near me I heard the sharp sniff-sniff of what sounded like a dog seeking a scent. Was it the keeper's dog or a friendly collie? If it found me or the buck would it bark and bring its master, who must be near? If it found me first—yes, I thought of my knife. Even if the deed were done in silence its master would look for it. The sniffing seemed nearer to me now. Very slowly I raised my head and looked into the bracken on either side. There was no sign of a dog. Then I could have shouted when I remembered what made the sniffing noise—the ferret that I carried in a bag in my pocket.

Gone were all qualms of conscience. Gun in hand I walked openly across the fields to a farm. There I was with friends. I told them of my quarry and they arranged to bring it to our farm after dusk in a cart. They were doubtful when I said that all I wanted was the head, and that they could have the venison. Then I showed one of the lads where the deer was hidden, and walked home by the road.

My father was pleased when I told him of the "right and left," and of the deer. But it was nonsense, he said, to have promised all the venison—half was quite enough for the farm people. We needed some for ourselves, and it was folly to be quixotic.

At ten o'clock that night a cart rumbled up to the door. The lad who drove it, my father and I, dragged out the deer and skinned and dressed it by the light of a stable lantern on the rough lawn in front of the house. This took some time and we made little noise. The horse stood patiently, tethered to a gate-post. Every one else was in bed and the house was in darkness.

The following afternoon the water-bailiff paid us a visit. He sat at the sitting-room table, and my father gave him a glass of whisky. This the old man sipped neat. He had white hair, and some days' growth of stubble on his chin, because in that country men only shaved on the Saturday—in preparation for the Sabbath. Mr. Coutts may have paid other visits that day. He was very garrulous and told us all about the plan of the house. The part we occupied had once been the dower-house of the castle.

"This room was the old dining-room, and that in there" (pointing to a door which opened into a little room under the stairs) "was a store-room. Maybe it's noo a bedroom."

He was right. I slept there. Then he looked at the oppo-

13

site corner of the room, where another door gave entrance to the lower part of a circular turret.

"It was a queer thing to build that turret. Maybe it was to remind the dowager of the castle. Ye see, it's no' a real turret—no stair up it; only yon wee place in there. But it's cool in there. They used it for the larder: that's why all the great hooks are round the walls. Aye, I mind the day when that place was full of game. An' there's a big hook in the roof where many a time I've hung the roedeer." (He looked at my mother.) "I'd like to show you, mum, which one it was. There'll only be a few rabbits hanging there now."

My heart was thumping. But my father rose. "When you've finished your whisky, Coutts." And he poured more into the old man's glass. Then my father talked of fishing. "Did the distillery seven miles up the glen hurt the fish?"

"No, no, doctor. The fush get drunk where the used barley gets into the river. Aye, ye'll see them floating belly-up downstream for a mile. After that ye'd no' see them. They get owre it. An' noo I maun be going."

When Mr. Coutts had gone my father said: "That old man is no fool." I thought of the larder and of my roedeer. If Mr. Coutts had only known, the present contents of that larder were no disgrace to the spacious days of the dowager! Perhaps he did know. Then my father said: "The wind is right; we'll try the ducks to-night."

At dusk we walked down to the pool, along a stubble field, and then entered a wood which overhung a long shallow reach of the river. Here we had made a path for ourselves along the slippery bank of the river, and we knew every foot of the way, especially those places where the path, three feet above the river, was very narrow. My father went first and I followed with Leo, a black spaniel, on a lead. Our other dog, Wasp, a Scotch terrier, was not to be trusted to refrain from barking on these occasions, and was at home in the stable.

14

This reach of the river was overhung by an avenue of trees on either side, but in places between the trees it was possible to see a space of sky. My father's tree was old, with broad roots which made a seat for him, so that he could lean back against its trunk. My tree was twenty yards down the river and had none of these comforts. Sitting beside it I could see the sky, but my feet dangled over the three-foot bank of the river. In my left hand I held the twelve-bore, because I shoot from the left, and with my right hand I stroked Leo as I told him to keep quiet. Night was falling. The sky was becoming dark. Not a sound was heard and, but for the occasional movement of a twig, my father might have ceased to be. Then came the soft whirr of wings, a double blaze of red fire from my father's tree, the same from mine, and then the glorious smell of black gunpowder amongst trees. "One down," called my father. "Let him see it before he goes in." Leo was now standing whining, his large brown eyes centred on the river. I held him by the collar. Then he saw the duck and lurched forwards. I let go my grip and he jumped three feet into the river, retrieved the duck and returned to the bank. As the bank was fairly steep I had to hang head down, holding on to roots and shrubs by my feet, get the duck from Leo, throw it up on to the bank, and then help the dog to regain the path. Sometimes Leo failed to retrieve, and followed the duck downstream towards the rapids. There was no retrieving to be done there, as the dog had enough to do to get out of the river when it rushed over rocks and stones. Then I would race downstream to the deep pool and wait there for the duck. Sometimes an eddy would bring it inshore, where it could be got by wading. But once I saw the duck being carried past on the other side. I took off my shoes and swam across the pool in my clothes! When my father and Leo found me on the bank I was dripping wet, but had the duck. During that swim I wondered

15

if otters were abroad that night. The pool at that time seemed full of danger. Night alters the appearance of even familiar things, and by night the pool looked more sinister than it ever was. Once I fished there all night for salmon. Our minister from Glasgow had given me the three-hooked tackle, which I baited with worms. He had told me what to do.

"You will feel a big tug, boy: then you will see your line move across the pool. Do nothing. Then you will feel one, two, three tugs. That means he's swallowing the bait. At the third tug, but not before, strike. Then play him. When he's tired, draw him into the sandy bay and kick him out of the water with your foot."

No better advice was ever given by one poacher to another. In the darkness I fished for an hour. Then came the first tug, and in a moment I had whipped the bait clean out of the lips of the salmon. I fished on, but once warned he was twice shy. But I was glad to have stood all night by the pool. There was the sound of the river, a rising and falling cadence. Once abed, there is no greater soporific than the music of the stream. But when you are awake and on its bank at night you wonder if it is a cadence. You think you hear unusual sounds and are nervous until you hear them recur with regularity. Then you know it is only another note of the river that you had not heard before.

That night, also, I discovered the hour before the dawn, and I was afraid. In the starlit sky it was not possible to tell east from west. But things happened. In the woods birds twittered and moved on their perches. Even in the grass there seemed to be movement, as if the creeping things that live at night were going home. In the field behind me I heard horses and cattle rise, stir about, and then lie down again. It is the hour when those who sleep in bed wake and turn on the other side, to sleep again. It is the hour when most of us will die, because at that hour the tide of life is at its

16

lowest ebb: we are waiting for the dawn to revive us, and one day the dawn will never come.

In boyhood I learned the superstitions of my race. Old Mr. Cameron, the farmer, told me of witches riding on their brooms across the dark waters of Loch Awe. He had also known a witch, and had killed her. She had lived three miles up the glen in a small croft, now in ruins, and at night had gone about in the form of a hare. One moonlight night he had seen this hare running away from the door of the byre, and in the morning one of the cows stopped giving milk.

The next night he loaded his gun and over the charge rammed down a sixpence, because a silver bullet is the only bullet that will kill a witch. Then he waited behind a wall overlooking the byre, and in the moonlight saw the hare coming back. He fired. She gave a scream and fled on three legs, trailing a broken right hind-leg behind her. On the following day no smoke was rising from the house of the witch, and when neighbours entered they found her groaning on her bed. When the doctor came he said her right thigh was broken below the hip-joint. The witch explained that she had fallen in her room. Mr. Cameron knew better, and in a few days she was dead. If the doctor had cut into her he would have found a sixpence in her thigh!

Mr. Cameron had never seen a warlock, the male of the species, but one was once said to have been seen in a neighbouring glen. When a warlock and a witch mated they did not breed, or, if they did, their offspring were fearful monstrosities that died after birth. The initiation of a warlock or a witch included ceremonies too dreadful to be told. Within a magic circle, which became a part of hell, was a boiling cauldron with a brew of toads and other evil things, and within this circle the devil and his pupil sealed their eternal bargain by drinking the blood of a new-born child.

17

A lesser bargain could be made with the devil to obtain the Horseman's Word. That is a magic word, and, if spoken aloud, you can bring down a horse ridden by your enemy in any part of Scotland. To obtain this word you must sit up alone all night in an empty house or loft. No other person must be within call. You must eat half a loaf of bread and drink a bottle of whisky. Then the devil appears, points to the hour on his watch, and gives you the word. The hour on his watch is the number of years you will serve in hell in return for knowing the word. Mr. Cameron had not yet seen the devil, but his eldest son, Alec, aged twenty-three, had seen him. Alec was riding home one night along the moss-covered road. Suddenly his horse stopped, shivered, and refused to go on. Then from behind a tall figure passed alongside. The horse broke into a sweat. The figure took long steps and was soon out of sight: his footsteps made no noise. Alec dismounted and examined the ground over which he had passed, and found the imprints of the cloven hoofs.

Apart from the devil and his pupils, other evil things, less easily recognised, were out at night. When masons were rebuilding the wall round the churchyard up the glen, the stones they set up during the day were always thrown down at night. Then the minister took the business in hand. In a tree overlooking the wall he sat up all night with an open Bible in his hands. At midnight he heard the first stone thrown down, but saw nothing. Then he called out in a loud voice: "In the name of the Father, and of the Son, and of the Holy Ghost, I abjure ye, whoever ye be." No more stones were thrown down and the building of the wall was completed. Against all these things there was one sure protection —the recital of the Lord's Prayer.

It was also possible to gratify hatred without making a direct bargain with the devil. You moulded a little image of your enemy in clay, stuck nails into it, and then placed

it in a stream of running water which wasted away the clay.
The position of the nails decided in which part of the body
your enemy would be afflicted by disease. Running water
has magic powers to destroy or create, and the hair from
the tail of a horse turns into an eel if placed in a stream.
And yet the truth about eels is more wonderful than magic.

All the eels in Western Europe which breed travel
thousands of miles on the bed of the ocean to the Sargasso
Sea, where they spawn. From that place the young eels
—elvers—travel back to the rivers and streams of Europe,
and the journey occupies three years. What guides them?
It is not that current of warm water which flows north-east
from the Equator and gives Western Europe an equable
climate. That current is on the surface, and the eels travel
on the bottom. The American eels also breed in the Sargasso
Sea, and their offspring return to America!

In the woods were fairies. They were mostly neutral
beings who did not hurt you unless you hurt them. If you
did offend them they could be vindictive. They would take
a baby out of its cot and put a changeling in its place. Mr.
Cameron had once seen a fairy funeral crossing the road
from one wood to another. There was the little hearse,
about a foot high, drawn by four little horses, and followed
by a long procession of the little people. His friend, Angus
Macdonald, had once seen the same thing, and had thought
it was all his imagination. He drove his horse and cart
through the procession, and, as he passed over it, the procession faded from the road, although he could still see the
little people in the wood on either side. When he reached
home his wife said to him: "That stairway is very narrow.
I couldna' get the arm-chair out of the kitchen up to the
bedroom." A week later he was dead, and his coffin had
to be taken out of the window because the stairs were too
narrow.

Then there was Donald Grant's boy, aged eight. He

found a cheese in the woods and brought it home. "Take it back where ye got it," said his father. "It's a fairy cheese." The boy took the cheese away, but hid it in an outhouse, where he ate it in secret. In the hayfield a week later he fell on the scythe, cut the main artery in his thigh and bled to death in a few minutes.

Some fairies are capricious, and that is why you never name another person when walking in the woods at night. The fairies might overhear the name, and, once they knew it, could entice the person away. Fairies also dislike to hear humans boasting, so you never said: "That's a fine field of corn," but always, "That corn is no' so bad," because they have power to put a blight on crops. There was only one way in which crops could be protected: if a virgin walked naked round the fields at midnight, but none must see her walk.

Out of the unseen world another Thing sometimes appeared—the Forego. Only a few have the power to see it, and of these Mr. Cameron was one. Coming home through the woods in daylight he passed his youngest boy, Geordie, aged ten. He called to him, but the boy did not answer and walked on towards the hills. On reaching home he found Geordie in the kitchen—the boy had been about the house all day. But his Forego had been seen and a week later the child was dead. Were all these Things fantasies woven by the human mind amidst the solitude of mountains, and was the void of the unseen peopled by the imagination of man? You may not believe in these things, but you have no right to laugh at them—unless you are so modern as not to believe that a mascot made in Birmingham will protect you and your motor car from harm. I think the bunch of rowan berries carried by horses in their harness is a more beautiful charm.

These people of the mountains had a dual faith to which they gave equal credence. They believed in these things, and also in the Christian faith as modified by Luther and Calvin. Their code of morality was no worse than that of other peasants, although their illegitimate birth-rate was the highest in Scotland. This was not the result of general promiscuity, but the natural consequence of an economic law. They had to earn their living on a hard soil, and to cultivate that soil the aid of a family was a necessity. No childless married couple could manage the work alone. The man must marry a woman who could bear him children, and the woman knew it. Pre-nuptial congress was therefore not uncommon, followed by marriage after the birth of the child.

Religion and superstition are not identical, although both are beliefs. In true religion there is nothing repugnant to reason, and when Rome failed to eradicate pagan super-stitions she Christianised them.

My earliest memory of religion concerns a girl of sixteen, who, in the Catholic Church, might have been allowed to try her vocation in a convent. In the Free Church of Scotland she taught a lads' class in the emotional manner of Moody and Sankey. Being then aged seven, I was too young to attend this class, of which I was somewhat jealous. The class met once a week at the house of an uncle with whom I was staying. I used to keep awake in my bed upstairs waiting for the class to finish. After their last hymn there was always a pause: the lads were handing over their pennies, which she banked for them. Then she would come upstairs to take an interest in my spiritual welfare. She knelt by my bed and prayed, and when she prayed I felt religion to be as good and beautiful as herself. After this prayer she tucked me into bed and kissed me good night. That was what I really wanted, because as a child of seven I yearned for a woman's love. In the language of that time, I was saved. Across the years I know better. Love and religion— love for a creature and love for the Creator—are two powerful emotions which may dominate mind and conduct. Each has its place in our well-being, but when these two emotions are so interwoven as to be indistinguishable in the mind of man or woman, or even in the mind of a child, this confusion may be a psychological disaster.

The next memory is of a grand-uncle who was a Calvinist of the Free Church in the far north of Scotland. I recall the Sabbath day, against which I then revolted. The morning service, first in Gaelic, then in English, lasted three mortal hours. Communion services were even longer. It was then that the minister called from the pulpit: "Jeanagh, the Lord has been very merciful to you: approach His table." At this the oldest woman in the parish would shuffle forward a few yards down the aisle and then sit down in another pew, groaning the while. Again came the exhortation from the pulpit, and old Jeanagh would creep a few pews nearer the table, where eventually she partook of the bread and wine. Three times was the exhortation given, and only after the third did the old woman's strange journey end. How I scoffed in later years at this simple episode enacted between bare, whitewashed walls! And yet it was only a vestige of the faith of Europe, and of the words well-spoken thrice: *Domine, non sum dignus.*

On Sabbath afternoons my grand-uncle would summon his household to the dining-room, where, seated at the head of his table he read aloud for an hour or more whole chapters from enormous commentaries such as Jenkins on *Jude*. At this I also revolted. The discipline of the morning service was as much as God had any right to expect, and revolt took a practical form of inducing my sister to play draughts under the table at which the old man was reading. Being short-sighted and a little deaf, he never missed us from the audience until one afternoon I so bullied my sister about her bad play that she wept aloud. Hearing this unwonted noise from the region of his feet, the old gentleman stopped reading, and, on looking under the table, beheld the recusants. We were not upbraided, but he expostulated with his wife concerning her obvious connivance, while she maintained that the bairns could not be expected to understand the works of so learned a writer as the Reverend Dr. Jenkins. "Maybe not," said the old man, "but they could listen."

Apart from the walks to church we did not walk on the roads on the Sabbath, but only in the grounds of the house. Once, when walking with my grand-uncle past a plantation, I saw a rabbit in a trap and went forward to kill it. "Stop," cried the old man, "would you desecrate the Lord's Day?" The cruelty of that came as a shock, and yet the old man, had he broken his leg on the Sabbath, would probably have refused to have had a doctor until the Monday. There was something to admire about these old Calvinists. They believed in an appalling doctrine invented at the Reformation, namely, that millions of people are predestined to hell for the glory of God—irrespective of their conduct on earth. Unless you were one of the elect, and there was no means of knowing, you went to hell no matter whether your life on earth had been good or bad. In such a doctrine there was no incentive to good conduct or self-denial. Had I ever believed it I would have taken as an exhortation the words of Luther: "Sin and believe." And yet these Calvinists lived good lives. It was a faith that bred bigots but not cowards.

There were many taboos in that old religion. Once another uncle found me on a Sunday afternoon with a book in my hand and tears of laughter in my eyes. His displeasure was great, and, on taking the book away from me, he remarked: "That is not a proper book for Sundays." The book was *Don Quixote*! And thus the older generation of Protestants sought to honour God by the practice of self-denial on the Sabbath.

The religion of my parents was more liberal, although I resented the learning of the Shorter Catechism and eight

23

lines of Psalms on Sundays. But I liked the family worship when my father, with understanding in his voice, would read a chapter from the Gospels, and then a prayer which began: "Father of Light." But the hymns I hated. They were all in the minor key which made me feel miserable, as indeed they would do now were I to sing or hear them.

The differences between the various sects in Scotland were not, for the most part, differences in doctrine. The Free Church was allied to the Liberal Party, whereas the Presbyterian Church of Scotland, "as by law established," was allied to the Conservative Party. The three bones of contention were Disestablishment, Home Rule for Ireland, and what was then called the Temperance Question. This alliance introduced me to the first Catholic priest I ever met, a Passionist Father who was then Catholic chaplain to the Glasgow prison of which my father was medical officer. The two were agreed upon Home Rule, and the priest was often in our house, especially about the times of general elections. Indeed, it was said by their enemies that priest and doctor saw to it that every jailbird in Glasgow voted Liberal. That was a slander, but the presence of a priest in our midst led to questions on my part. I learnt that he was a very good man, a shining light in a somewhat dubious community; that he himself did not worship images, but that other persons with whom he was associated did so. It was all rather confusing.

My visualisation of the Creator was as a stern old gentleman with a grey beard, who did not wish people to be happy. Once, as quite a young child going out for a walk with my nurse, I shouted: "Three cheers for the Holy Ghost." Whereupon she told me I had committed the unforgivable sin and could never be pardoned. That news rather depressed me until I told my father, and learned that the nurse had been talking rubbish.

# CHAPTER III

## EXILED

MY father had made a career for himself in medicine. The son of an exciseman, he was educated in the village school of Lybster in the north of Scotland. As a boy he won county scholarships, medals in classics and a small bursary to Edinburgh University, where he graduated M.D. —the Gold Medallist of his year. There was no free education in those days. The village schoolmaster earned a meagre living, and the brighter boys and girls were coached *con amore* by the minister, who was usually a scholar. The minister who coached my father in classics and mathematics afterwards became my grandfather. It was a small bursary that my father won, and, to pay his fees at the University, he spent his summer holidays in tutoring the sons of wealthier people. A long struggle—but when he died his obituary occupied half a column in *The Times*.

My earlier life was cast on easier lines. At the age of thirteen I was sent to Merchiston. To that school I owe such physique as comes from playing compulsory games. In my first term I suffered the usual bullying which was then regarded as almost necessary if every boy was to be beaten more or less into a common mould. Then I found my feet and the way to an easier school life. I was not good at games, and never rose higher than the second fifteen at rugger, but without any great effort I excelled in writing essays and in mathematics. At the age of fourteen my first article appeared in the Press. It was entitled "Training in Rugby Football," was signed by *nom de guerre*, and was published in the Saturday Sporting Edition of the Glasgow *Evening Citizen*. A week later a friend, the son of a New York publisher, and I, having obtained an afternoon's leave from school, travelled from Edinburgh to Glasgow. There I interviewed an astonished editor and asked for payment. He thought a master of the school had written the article, explained that the paper paid monthly, and then gladly advanced ten shillings out of his own pocket. At school I became an apt pupil in English literature and mathematics, and was permitted to slack in every other subject in the curriculum—Latin, French and German. I ought to have been made to take more trouble over these subjects, although I did not think so at the time.

After school came the University and freedom. Here again success in non-essentials was too easily won. In my first term I spoke in a Union debate, in the next seconded a motion, and in the third led the Union in a Parliamentary debate. To accomplish this I spent energy which should have been applied to the study of botany, zoology, physics, and chemistry. These were the days when life was like the trial trip of a newly-launched ship, when mistakes could be rectified, and when the wreckage was not beyond salvage. There also I discovered that I possessed the dangerous faculty of learning enough in three weeks to pass examinations for which three months' preparation was rightly required. Then came disaster—I failed in the second professional.

On a dull afternoon the lists were posted up inside the University gates. I did not expect to see my name amongst the others, and waited until the crowd round the notice-board had dispersed. Then I went up, just to make certain that my name was not there, and discovered that it was. I had passed in one subject—physiology—and failed in anatomy. That was a bit of luck, and I could enter for the next examination in anatomy in four months. I could also pass, then, in materia medica. That night I went home very late and did not see my father until the next morning at breakfast. From the set expression on his face it was obvious that he knew the worst. The lists had been published in that morning's *Scotsman*. After breakfast our interview began.

"You have failed in anatomy. To me the surprise would have been had you passed. That would have been worse, because you haven't worked. You've been wasting your time."

"I've done other things. Last week, when you heard me lead that Union debate, you said you never knew I had it in me."

"Are you studying for Medicine or for the Bar? Even at the Bar oratory only counts if the man knows Law, which is more difficult than anatomy—much more difficult and less interesting."

"I'd rather be an advocate."

"Too late. When you began to get on in your school debating society, I told you the way to the Bar—hard work at school and a scholarship to Oxford. You never worked. You needed extra coaching to pass the 'Prelim.' in medicine, equal to four Lower Grade Leaving Certificates. Many a boy in a Board School takes them as a matter of course."

"You didn't send me to a Board School; you sent me to a school where nobody worked—only one or two, and they were called 'swots.' You sent me to school with boys who had rich fathers; boys who had no need to work."

"Would you have done better at any other school?"

"I can pass in anatomy and materia medica in four months from now."

"Yes, if you work. So I've arranged for you to go out to your uncle in Spain for the next three months. He's a surgeon, knows his anatomy, and can supervise your reading."

"I could work as well here."

"Rubbish. In addition to your debating and literary activities—no one would object to these in reason—you have also formed some undesirable friendships with wasters

27

who will never be any good to themselves or to anyone else."

"I am not going to Spain."

"Why?"

"The disgrace. Every one will know I have been taken away from the University."

"Better to leave the University for three months, or even for a year, than to leave it without a degree."

"I am not going to Spain."

"Very well. Then from this moment you earn your own living. You can have board and lodging in this house, but you will pay for it out of your earnings."

"You know that I can't earn my living."

"Rubbish. Gilbert of the *Scotsman* is a friend of mine. For the past three months you have been writing a weekly column of 'University Notes' for the *Evening Dispatch*. They have been paying you thirty shillings a week. And you never told me!"

"I'm sorry, father."

"Be a journalist by all means, but they'll make you learn shorthand. As a profession it will suit you. It's the only profession in which irregularity of conduct and of hours does not matter—provided your copy is delivered in time. I hear that the editor of the *Evening Dispatch* last week spoke to you about unpunctuality. You delayed the first edition of the paper for half an hour. You would have been fired, but that Gilbert is my friend."

"I don't want to be a journalist."

"Are you going to Spain?"

"Yes."

"Well, you had better start packing. The steamer sails from Cardiff next week. Go to that shop on the Mound and get a steamer-trunk, and when you are there get a pair of leggings. Your uncle will give you a horse to ride."

On arriving in the south of Spain I found that my uncle

had arranged that I should have a three weeks' holiday with Spanish friends of his who lived in a village on the Low Sierra. Not a word of English was understood in that village. On the first morning I was wakened by loud cheepings and twitterings from a nest of swallows under the eaves above my window. Waiting patiently in my bed for early tea I watched their doings. The young birds were learning to fly. One of the parents would seize a cheeper and push it out, sending it flopping to the ground. If the cheeper did not fly back, a parent would go down and return with the young bird in its beak; then the youngster would be thrown out again. Swallows are said to return to the same nesting-place every year, but the wherefore and the why of migration remains a mystery.

At eight o'clock I went down to breakfast and found a cup of coffee and a roll. A poor breakfast, but probably merely to replace the morning tea and to be followed by a real breakfast at nine. At nine o'clock the dining-room table was occupied by the señora with her sewing-machine and by some of her daughters, who were dressmaking—healthy girls, who looked well fed. There was sure to be a good lunch at one. The family consisted of a grandmother, an unmarried son and daughter, a married son and his wife with their five children aged from eight to sixteen, and a niece of twelve who was staying with them on a short visit. They all appeared to live in harmony and were ruled by the grandmother.

The men worked in the family vineyard outside the village and the housework was done by the women. They had no servant. At eleven o'clock the women and children sat down to a meal of meat and fish. This, no doubt, was their late breakfast, which I declined as it was now getting near lunch time. One of the girls came and spoke to me, but not a word did I understand. They left me alone, thinking, maybe, I was ill or home-sick. I was not home-sick, being eighteen years of age, but was suffering from hunger caused by obstinacy. At one o'clock there was no lunch, only more sewing and dressmaking. I tried to speak about food to the girl who had spoken to me, and our second attempt at conversation was a little better than the first, because it ended in her bringing me a glass of water.

After a walk in the country I returned in good time for afternoon tea. There was no tea, nor was it possible there could have been tea, because tea was unknown in the village. At five o'clock the men returned and we all sat down to an excellent meal: a cold, vinegary soup with pieces of meat, fish, potatoes and beans in it, followed by meat, fish, cheese and fruit. It was possible to live, and live well, on two meals a day: *desayuno* in the forenoon, and, in the late afternoon, *la comida*. Even the flesh of horses and goats may be tender if stewed in white wine, and there is a wonderful ham smoked over an enormous acorn fire (*jamon crudo*) which can be eaten raw. Their *bacalao* (dried ling or cod), some of which comes from the Shetland Isles, is tough and needs a sauce of butter with grated cheese and chopped raw onion. The *olla podrida* (a stew of mutton, bacon, chicken, with chick peas, potatoes, beans and garlic) is good. Olives are eaten between each course, and the green medium-sized ones are the best. The small, darker ones are too hard and the very large ones too bitter. There is also a cheese made from fruit (quince) which is really a sweetmeat eaten with bread. The ordinary red wine and the light sherry called Manzanilla are more acid than the *vin ordinaire* of France. In a *fonda* two men once disputed which was better, the vinegar or the wine. The landlord was called in to decide. "Señores, it is impossible for the vinegar to be better than the wine because they were drawn this very day from the same cask."

In the winter months there is a brazier with charcoal under the dining-room table. A charcoal fire may be unhealthy because of the fumes, but under the dining-room table is the best place for a fire. The warmth spreads equally through the room, and there is no wasted heat going up a chimney—as those who possess an electric fire may easily prove for themselves. In many houses the bedrooms opening off the *patio* (an open, central court), have no windows and are pitch dark to keep out the heat of summer, and those who are wise sleep under mosquito nets.

In the evening the family sat at garden-tables in the street, where friends joined them. The street was of cobblestones— and of all roads the cobbled road is the most enduring. The one to Jerusalem has lasted since the time of Constantine; the military roads of France since the time of Napoleon; and, if the stones are well laid, they are good motoring roads.

During these evenings a girl with her guitar would sing narrative songs of twenty or thirty verses. Their songs are the *coplas*, handed down from generation to generation. Years later in London I heard a Russian gypsy song, and the tune seemed the same as the one to which the girl had sung in the Sierra. The singer was now an exiled prince, and he told me that the gypsy tunes were very old and had travelled all over Europe.

There were no newspapers and few books in the Sierra, and the stories told by the old men sometimes lasted for an hour. One of these was of an English bank clerk who robbed his bank and fled to Spain, bringing with him his loot of sovereigns. He reached the village San Juan del Puerto, on the banks of the Rio Tinto, and married the daughter of the man with whom he lodged. Then rumours came of civil guards inquiring in neighbouring villages as to the source of the English gold in circulation. The father-in-law sheltered the man, and, when the civil guard arrived, the clerk and his gold were hidden for eight days and nights in an empty wine vat. Then, tired of hiding, he decided, unbeknown to his wife or to her father, on another dash for freedom. One morning at dawn he went down to the river, which is there half a mile wide, and stole a boat to row across. But the civil guard were watching, and manned another boat. Half-way across they overtook him and called on him to stop. He fired his revolver and they replied with rifles. He stood up wounded in the boat, seized the box of gold, and dived overboard. His body was found downstream but the gold they never found.

One old man often tried to talk to me because I came from England, which he described as "Un pais muy barbaro." When I knew this to mean "a most barbarous country," and had enough of the language to contradict him, I said: "Señor, you are mistaken. It is not a barbarous country." He replied: "No, señor, I am not mistaken. It is a most barbarous country. I speak the truth."

He went away and in ten minutes returned with a paper. It was an English newspaper, and in front was a full-page illustration of a half-dressed, dishevelled girl lying across a bed with her throat cut. On the back page was the picture of a pinioned man, a white hood over his head, standing on the scaffold, and around him warders, a surpliced clergyman with his prayer-book, and the executioner about to pull the drop. I had not the words to explain that this was not our leading daily newspaper, or to ask how a copy of the *Police Budget* had found its way to the Sierra. As a medical student in Edinburgh I had found this periodical, which is not generally read by policemen, to be a cure for depression on Sabbath afternoons. It taught one lesson—that things might be worse.

These simple people were living in a civilisation that differed little from that of the thirteenth century, but when we speak of civilisation we seldom give the word its proper meaning—the Art of Living. We rather imply that our own particular method of combining mental culture and bodily comfort is the highest, noblest and best way to live.

That is by no means certain, and there are other ways in which the art of living has been and is practised. The old man had never been in England, but certain aspects of our social life have brought tears to eyes undimmed by the industrial traditions of the last century.

On Saturday and Sunday afternoons we had picnics in the *campo*, to which I rode on a donkey with a girl sitting behind, keeping her balance by holding my waist. The girl who usually rode behind me was the little niece. Her name was Inés. With her arms round my waist, she held in her hands in front of me a basket of provisions and fruits, and amused herself by holding up things out of the basket and asking me to name them in Spanish. She knew by touch what she was holding, and it was funny when I could not say what it was, although I could see it. At the end of my visit the grandmother asked if I liked Spain.

"Yes, señora, and I like the people of Spain."

"Young man," said the old lady, "you have been well brought up."

This holiday over, I went to my uncle's house and devoted three months to the more or less intensive study of anatomy and materia medica. I then returned to England with a young girl who had lived her twelve years of life on the plains of Andalusia. She had been placed in my charge for the voyage by her uncle, the manager of the Rio Tinto mines. That was the highest testimony ever offered to my character at the age of eighteen.

She was going to a convent at Wimbledon, and may have pictured London as a city with walls of amethyst and streets of gold, for, when the train passed through that district which lies south of Waterloo, the girl wept. "Look at these houses," she sobbed. "*Dios mio*, they have no view."

# CHAPTER IV

## THE PROFESSOR

AT Edinburgh I passed the examination in anatomy and materia medica, but my father was taking no risks. The next subject was pathology, and this I was to study at Aberdeen under a professor who had been a fellow-student at Edinburgh with my father. I did not like the new arrangement. I could work equally well in Edinburgh, and if I spoke once in the Union I was certain to be chosen to represent Edinburgh that winter in the debate with Cambridge. There was ample time for Cambridge, said my father, and he had made all arrangements for Aberdeen.

Professor Hamilton, under whom I was to study, had a brilliant record as a student at Edinburgh. After graduating, he had won the Astley-Cooper prize of three hundred pounds for his essay on the spinal cord. This enabled him to travel and study pathology at Paris, Vienna and Strasbourg. On his return to Edinburgh he began to teach, and opened a class on pathology. It was the only one in Scotland, and although it was not a compulsory class, his lecture-room was crammed with students who wished to learn a new science. Then a Chair of Pathology was founded at Edinburgh University, and Hamilton applied for the appointment. He was not appointed. In academic circles his wife was not *persona grata*. A professor from London was appointed. So there were now two teachers, one inside and the other outside the University. At first very few students attended the class of the London professor, and most of them learnt from the man who taught outside. Then came the examination. Hamilton's students failed to pass, even his medallist was "ploughed." It was inevitable: the teaching of the two men was so different. It was also inevitable that next session

34

Hamilton's class should be deserted for that of the London professor. Between the two men seeds of bitterness had been sown. Then Sir Erasmus Wilson gave a gift of ten thousand pounds to found a Chair of Pathology at Aberdeen, and Hamilton was invited to be the first professor.

Such was the early history of the man under whom I was to study. His first wife was now dead and he was married to a charming lady, whom I was to meet. My father had written to the professor about me, and now gave me a card of introduction.

On arriving at Aberdeen I went to the University office and enrolled as a student in the class of pathology. That night, in the haunts of students, I made discreet inquiries about Professor Hamilton.

"Oh, you mean The Bull."

"Why is he called The Bull?"

"You'll soon find out! He's got the neck of a bull, the head of a bull, and little eyes like a shorthorn. He charges like a bull; he bellows like a bull; and there's another thing, he stands no damned nonsense."

This intelligence was most disconcerting, but there was no reason why I should present my card of introduction. With any luck I could pass through his class without personal contact with a man who was apparently a holy terror.

Next morning I took a seat at the back of the lecture theatre. There were about forty students, men and women, in the room, and they talked in low tones. As the minute-hand of the clock pointed to ten there was silence. Behind and to the right of the rostrum a door opened, The Bull marched to the centre of the low platform and placed his notes on the desk. He was a short, white-haired man with a high forehead, a red face, and fierce blue eyes shining through gold spectacles. His bushy moustache and the little tuft of beard from the lower lip to the centre of the chin were also white. He had a short neck and sloping shoulders,

35

and was wearing a black stuff gown open at the front. Under his low collar was a black tie, held by a large gold pin. The gown was worn loosely and did not hide his Norfolk jacket and grey flannel trousers. Such was the man whose reputation was European, who had discovered the causes of two diseases in sheep (braxy and "loupin' ill") and was now reputed to be working on a vaccine that would save British agriculture a quarter of a million a year. He gave one swift glance round the room and began to lecture. In front of him, running the whole length of the rostrum, was a broad bench covered with large models in wood and plaster, to illustrate his lecture. These models he himself had made.

At the end of five minutes I knew myself to be in the presence of a born teacher, with clear incisive style and command of words. Already he was putting life into one of the driest theories of immunity. Why were none of the students taking notes? I searched for my notebook, but another new-comer to the class had begun to write, and the lecture was suddenly interrupted.

"Stop writing. Put that notebook away. No one shall attempt to take notes. The taking of notes was a practice that was of value in the Middle Ages, before the discovery of printing. You can borrow my textbook from the library or buy it new or second-hand, but notes you shall not take. I am here to teach, and I cannot teach unless I have the undivided attention of your eyes and ears for an hour."

A most sensible professor! At the end of the lecture he walked to the end of the rostrum and held the class spellbound as he paid a tribute to his own teacher.

"Theories will come and go, our views of things will change as they must change in a science not seventy years old, but the work of Rudolf Virchow—the pathology of the cell—will endure for all ages to come."

And now I had to wait for twenty-three hours before I could hear this man again. Within a week I presented my

36

card of introduction and asked the Professor if I might work in his laboratory.

"Do you wish to be paid?"

"No, sir."

"Oh, dear me! The average student arrives and asks to be paid. And now a man from Edinburgh—my own University—asks to be allowed to work. Yes, Mr. Sutherland, you may work, but if your aim be research, you must begin at the beginning."

Next day I began work in the Department of Pathology— as a bottle-washer, under the direction of Ray, the laboratory attendant.

The great teachers! How rare they are, and how slender their reward! There was one other I had known as a small boy attending Glasgow High School. He was an old man with a long white beard, and we called him "Daddy Barker," but he was also a Doctor of Literature and of Law. I was always in a hurry to set out for school and to miss nothing of his class. This interest in school made my parents a little apprehensive, and I think they doubted whether Daddy Barker was really qualified to teach. You will find the great teachers here and there in every class of school, even in public schools. They are content with their vocation. Their greatest reward is to see their pupils in after-life gain honours, wealth and power. There is no envy when the boy or girl they taught has far excelled his teacher. They are content to remember that it was they who once

> Blew on the drowsy coal,
> Held still the target higher,
> Chary of praise, and prodigal of counsel.

And how rare are the great writers on medicine! Much time, trouble and money would be saved on medical education if medical textbooks were better written. It is insufferable that a sentence should have to be read half a dozen times before its meaning can be discerned by an intelligent person reading his native language. There are brilliant exceptions, such as the late Charles Mercier, who wrote firm English. Too many medical writers are merely assiduous compilers of the writings of other men. And there are others who, when they do make an effort, cultivate that imitative prose called "precious"—which is even more irritating than bad syntax because it is less original.

In that year the Professor was investigating for the Board of Agriculture the prevention of braxy in sheep. None of us knew the results, but the rumour was that he had prepared a vaccine. Meanwhile, the *Aberdeen Free Press* had published three of my articles on Spain, and one Saturday morning I had a note from the editor asking for a column about the Professor's work on braxy. That afternoon I went to the Professor's house. I had to wait half an hour, because the Professor was having his *siesta* and his wife would not wake him before the hour. He appeared, blinking, and I told him my business and that the article would mean a guinea for me.

"Impossible," said the Professor. "If this research concerned only myself I would allow you to make it known. But I have a grant from the Board of Agriculture, and nothing must be published until the Blue Book with my report is laid on the table of the House of Commons. After that you may publish your article. But, Mr. Sutherland, you don't know anything about this research? No? Then I must tell you about it before we have tea."

The Professor had simplicity—the only attribute of mind common to genius and to fools. Lesser men often excel genius in the acquisition of honours and of wealth. They never leap, and always look before they walk. Behind their most apparently disinterested kindnesses and courtesies is a motive of self-interest. Their interest is not in the battle but in the intrigues of life. Without these party manners their minds would be unmasked, naked, petty and incompetent. The professor lacked these adjuvants, and some of his friends thought that had he been less outspoken he would have been knighted. At the time of the operation on Edward VII for appendicitis, the Professor had made a pungent comment. His comment was unwise and unjust because it was based on speculation. He had made it to two doctors, but so pungent were his words that they travelled far—perhaps farther than he anticipated. It may have been so, but in all probability the lack of a knighthood never troubled the Professor. In his simplicity he had the mind of a child.

Unlike the Church at Corinth, the Professor did not suffer fools gladly. One day, as we sat with our microscopes in the practical class, he told us to put on the low-powered lens. The man next to me put on the high power. He was detected. Up and down the room went the Professor, shouting: "L-O-W, low; P-O-W-E-R, power." The offender looked at his lens, but made no change. "Stand up, sir," bellowed the Professor. "My God, has it come to this, that I teach a kindergarten! Do you know your alphabet—can you spell simple words? Then spell low, L-O-W; and spell power, P-O-W-E-R. Now say both words together—low power. Do you know what the words mean? Then look at your microscope and do as you are bidden."

Soon afterwards a test-tube containing live cholera vibrios was handed out to each of us. We were to examine these germs under the high power. The unhappy wretch beside me dropped his tube on the bench. The glass broke and there was a little pool of cholera germs on the bench. This he mopped up with his handkerchief, which he replaced in his pocket. In this act he was detected. For a moment the Professor was speechless; the veins stood out on his neck and forehead, and he looked on the verge of an apoplectic fit. Then he found speech.

"Ray, Ray, Ray!" he bellowed.

And from outside the room came the answering shout of his faithful attendant: "I'm coming, sir."

"Ray, Ray, Ray! Bring me carbolic one-in-forty. A Winchester of carbolic, one-in-forty, Ray, at once. Carbolic!" The Professor seized the bottle of carbolic and rushed for our bench. He came with such speed that his gown floated behind him in the air, and he looked like a large and angry bird about to attack. He sluiced the bench with carbolic, then turned to the culprit. "Hold out your hands." Carbolic was poured over them. "Hold out your handkerchief." It was soused. "Hold out your pocket." Carbolic was poured into the pocket and over the jacket. "If you have no respect for your own life, you shall respect the lives of your fellow students. And now, you most damnéd fool, leave my class and go back to the plough from whence you came."

The Professor knew how to let himself go in anger. But he never bore malice, and if to-day he stormed at a student or assistant, none would have been more surprised or grieved than the Professor if the offender had not appeared on the morrow. His house was a pleasant home, and there I once found him on his knees with a pair of boxing-gloves teaching two little nieces to box. He could paint, play the violin, and was also a classical scholar. How disappointed he was to find I could not follow eight lines of Virgil which he quoted from memory. "Oh, dear me, what is education coming to!" His one grievance against the people of Aberdeen was that they would not follow his advice in architecture: if only they would roof their granite buildings with red tiles they would have the most beautiful city in Northern Europe. He was never satisfied with second best.

One forenoon I was going to assist him in examining a sheep that was said to have died of braxy. This meant a railway journey, and we had ten minutes to wait for the train.

"Would you like some beer?" He led the way into the refreshment room. "Two beers in tankards."

"We've no tankards," answered the girl.

"Oh, dear me, what is beer without its tankard!" And out he marched, followed by me, to whom the girl remarked:

"Huffy old man your Pa is, ain't he?"

From his wife I learnt something that otherwise I would never have known. She dreaded the time of examinations, because then, if his students were doing badly, the Professor would pace his study half the night going over and over his lecture-notes to find where he might have failed in imparting knowledge.

The Professor was a conscientious teacher. He supervised all post-mortems, and students were required not only to attend but also to make these examinations. At the time Aberdeen was the only University in Britain where students had this experience. To the novice it was a strange experience. We sat on tiers of benches around the post-mortem theatre. In the centre of the floor was a marble table on which lay the stark, dead body. We were allowed to smoke. The Professor would make the first necropsy, lecturing on what he found. The next post-mortem was made by a student. Sometimes there were scenes. One day, on entering, the Professor glared at a lad sitting on the back bench. "Take off your cap! If you have no respect for me, at least you shall respect the dead." One student, who had removed the heart from the body, was told to demonstrate the mitral valve. He did not know the left from the right side of the heart, and handled it gingerly. The Professor became impatient. "Don't fiddle with it like a schoolgirl." The student became nervous and rapidly turned the heart over and over. "Oh, dear me!" shouted the Professor. "Don't worry it like a dog."

Once I had to face his anger, and pride preceded the fall. I had begun research on the prostate gland, and had planned experiments on male cats. Before applying to the Home Office for a licence, I had to learn the anatomy and physiology of the cat. I dissected dead cats, and for this the Professor lent me his instruments, which I had to clean, polish and return to his room after using them.

I could not afford to buy cats and had to—hunt for them. My best preserve was in the grounds of the fever hospital, where I set traps. They were humane traps: an empty soap-box turned upside down and raised above the ground at one end by a stick inside; a piece of fish was attached to the top of the stick; the cat walked under the box, seized the fish, displaced the stick, and was captured. After dark I visited the traps and carried away any male cats in a sack. The thought of stealing never troubled me. I was benefiting the fever-stricken patients whose sleep would be less disturbed by the most hideous sound on earth. Yet in that hospital were some nurses who loved cats, and between these nurses and myself was a silent feud. They visited my traps and upset them, and I was forced to go there before the friends of the cat came off duty. I have no ill-will towards cats, but do not love them. Even Maeterlinck, whose devotion to animals is almost blasphemous, writes of their "cold, contemptuous eyes." Hilaire Belloc has also written a terrible indictment about them: "They will eat the dog's biscuits, but never upon any occasion will they eat anything that has been poisoned, so utterly lacking are they in simplicity and humility, and so abominably well filled with cunning by whatever demon first brought their race into existence."

The friends of the cat in this world are also powerful. After some weeks these nurses complained to Authority, and the Medical Officer of Health sent for me. He said that he was an old friend of my father and was therefore pained to know that I had been using the grounds of the fever hospital, the property of the Corporation of Aberdeen, for the purpose of stealing cats. He regretted that it was impossible to use any other word except stealing. This was a criminal offence. He was quite sure that the Professor had not the slightest idea of the methods I had chosen to adopt for the purpose of obtaining cats. (This was true, because the Professor had never asked.) In the circumstances he did not propose to report this most regrettable occurrence to the chief constable provided I undertook to abandon this method of obtaining cats. To this ultimatum I readily agreed, because, for the time being, I had obtained all the cats I required.

At ten o'clock one night I was dissecting a cat in the laboratory. In his private room the Professor was also working late. Then his door opened and he passed through the laboratory on his way out. He usually departed without speaking to anyone, but on this night he stood behind me and watched what I was doing. After a time he spoke:

"Mr. Sutherland, you remind me of my youth." Without another word he marched to the door, where he turned to say "Good night." He left me in the seventh heaven—I would soon be doing real research.

There was no lecture next morning, and I reached the main entrance to the department at ten o'clock. On the steps I met the senior assistant on his way out. He had lost his usual cheerfulness.

"Taking a day off?" I inquired.

"You will be off for good," was the answer.

"What's the matter?" I asked.

He opened the main door and said: "Listen!"

From the depths came the voice of the Professor. He was bellowing. Some of the words I could hear: "Rack and ruin —slackness all round. . . . Department going to the devil. . . . No order . . . no method. . . . As soon as he arrives. . . ."

I nodded. "It's another attack of gout."

"Gout! Nothing of the kind. It's *you*. Why the devil did you leave that cat on the bench last night, with all his

43

instruments covered with blood and fur. Nobody could clean up the mess. The old man was first here this morning. At seven o'clock! We've all had to suffer—but he wants to see *you* as soon as you arrive. Ray is the only one left downstairs."

My heart sank, but the longer I delayed the worse it would be. I went in and waited in the corridor until the tumult had subsided and the Professor had retired to his room. Then I cleaned up the mess, polished his instruments, and knocked on his door. The answer was a shout: "Come in." I entered, and without a word, walked to the instrument case and replaced the instruments as if nothing had happened. My back was towards the Professor, who sat at his desk, blowing, snorting, and coughing. He was waiting for me to speak, but I held my peace. I knew that if I uttered a single word I would be overwhelmed. I also knew that the Professor had expected to see me *before* the mess was cleaned up. As I was leaving the room I turned to the Professor:

"I'm very sorry, sir. This won't happen again."

So surprised was the Professor that he coughed and answered:

"I hope not. Oh, dear me, I hope not." That was all.

During my second term at Aberdeen the city was visited by a religious revival, and one night, out of curiosity, I attended the service. The large hall was packed with people, and on the platform sat the chairman, Mr. Fraser, a rather prosperous-looking middle-aged man, with his leading supporters on either side. Mr. Fraser was a wealthy business man, who, on one of his journeys to Wales, had been "saved" by Evan Roberts, the great evangelist. Rumour had it that Mr. Fraser was undoubtedly a brand plucked from the burning. In gratitude for his salvation he had imported, at his own expense, a band of Welsh revivalists into Aberdeen. Behind the first row on the platform was a choir of two hundred men and women. As I entered the hall a seedy-looking youth was finishing a remarkable sermon based on a text in the book of Daniel.

"What do I see now, my friends? I see four bookmakers playing cards in a first-class railway carriage. They are rich men, far richer than you or I. They are smoking cigars and drinking whisky out of a bottle. They are riding in the chariots of the sun. Suddenly there is a collision on the line; the train is smashed. Where are they now? In hell, my friends, in hell.

"And what do I see now? I see an actress driving in a motor car. She has jewellery and fine clothes, far finer than yours or mine. She gets large sums of money for singing indecent songs in the theatre. She is riding in the chariots of the sun. Suddenly her car crashes into another. And where is she now? In hell, my friends, in hell."

The young man sat down amidst applause. I felt sorry for the actress, but she had no right to sing improper songs in the theatre—the music-hall was the place for that. Now the real business of the evening began. The choir sang a single line: "Bringing in the sheaves."

They sang it over and over again, first very loudly, then softer and softer until the refrain died away into silence. Meanwhile Brothers and Sisters were at work in the audience. As soon as the choir stopped singing there came shouts from various parts of the hall: "Another soul for Jesus." That was the signal for the choir to sing again: "Bringing in the sheaves." The atmosphere was charged with emotion. I noticed that Brothers were converting the women and girls, and Sisters the men and boys. So that was why, after every religious revival in Wales, there was a sharp rise in the illegitimate birth-rate! Beside me sat three girls: two had been saved the night before and had brought the third, who sat between them. A Brother tackled her and soon the girl was sobbing and crying that she was a sinner. The Brother turned to the platform, waved his arms in the air, and shouted: "Another soul for Jesus." The choir answered with "Bringing in the sheaves."

"Let us join hands and pray," said the Brother, and the quartette stood up, holding each other's hands. The girl nearest me indicated to the Brother that I was outside the circle, and each held out a hand for me to take. I shook my head and refused to join the happy band.

The man looked at me. "I'll be with you in a moment, brother."

That was enough. In a moment I was up, out and away. And yet that imported revival left its mark in the civic life of Aberdeen. The revivalists departed, but for weeks the refrain of their mission, "Bringing in the sheaves," was heard in the streets, late at night—sung by drunks going home.

During my last term at Aberdeen my father arrived on a short visit, and on the first afternoon we saw Henry Irving in *The Bells*—a great study of acute mania. After the theatre, we were sitting in the smoking-room of the Station Hotel alone, when two elderly, well-dressed men entered the room. One of them was slightly inebriated, and, to my discomfort, he fixed his attention on myself. So far as I knew I had never seen him before. Was it possible that I had met him on some festive occasion, and was he now going to claim my acquaintance under most unpropitious circumstances? He sat down in the chair nearest to mine, and said:

"You will, sir, I trust, pardon my intrusion on your privacy, but have I the great honour of addressing the conductor of Henry Irving's orchestra?"

It was my father who laughed, and answered: "He has not got a single note of music in his head."

The inebriated one turned to my father with a look of grave disapproval. "You will pardon me. My remark was not addressed to you but to the gentleman on my left, whom you appear to have the honour of knowing."

"Come along," said the other man. "You are only annoying these gentlemen."

"Annoying! That is impossible! The simple remark I vouchsafed will be, I trust, merely the prelude to a most interesting, illuminating and memorable conversation."

Again my father intervened. "You've been seeing Irving?"

"Irving! I have seen Henry Irving every afternoon and evening for the past week."

"Almost a surfeit of Irving!"

"A surfeit! My dear sir, there is no such word as surfeit in the bright lexicon of youth."

At that moment the door opened, and a waiter appeared. "Your tea's ready, and your fish and chips is getting cold."

The disciple of Sir Henry Irving rose to his feet. "Begone, varlet! Horror upon horror overwhelms my soul. Fish and chips in the same breath with Irving! Out, damned spot!"

The waiter bristled. "I'll no' stand that talk from you or any other man. Aye, and I ken fine who you are."

"Rubbish, man," called my father. "You've never been more politely spoken to in your life. You've heard the language of Shakespeare."

"I don't care whose language it is, I dinna like it, and, what's more, I won't have it."

Next day a friend of my father's lunched us both at the club. His name was Mr. Johns. He was a tall, lean, cadaverous-looking man, with brown side-whiskers and fishy eyes. He was a lawyer, an elder of the church, and, so my father said, a most respectable man. To me he seemed a dull fellow with little to say and having no opinions of his own. When he did speak it was only to agree with whatever my father had said. He was a good listener. At lunch we each had a tankard of beer, and at the end of the meal Mr. Johns offered us another. I was the only one who had

47

an extra tankard. The next morning there was a letter from my father written on the eve of his departure. He was glad to know the progress I was making with my studies and that my lodgings were comfortable. But he was perturbed to have seen me drink two pints of beer at lunch without apparently turning a hair. He had never known a beer-drinker who had won success in life. What Mr. Johns would think of me he did not know. Probably Mr. Johns would forget it, or attribute it to the thoughtlessness of youth. Mr. Johns was a most respectable man, whose friendship I should cultivate. He hoped Mr. Johns would invite me again to lunch. . . .

Mr. Johns never again invited me to lunch or to any other meal, and it was many years before he and I met together at lunch for the second and last time.

Before leaving Aberdeen to sit the examination in pathology at Edinburgh, I said good-bye to the Professor, who gave me his blessing.

"And so you are going away! Well, you ought to do very well in the examination. What! But that you have studied under me!" For a moment I thought there was going to be an explosion and that I would depart in the midst of a full gale, but the Professor smiled. "Ah, someone has told you an old story. That cannot happen again—not now. You are capable of passing this examination at Edinburgh or at any other University. Let me know how you get on. And I would be glad to have a telegram with the result."

A week later I was sitting in the examination hall at Edinburgh and smiled when I saw the four questions. I had two hours in which to write the answers, and the only difficulty was—what to leave out. I passed the examination, but the Edinburgh professor detected the stranger within his gates and gave me a gruelling oral examination. This I would not have resented had he given me honours. That

he did not do so left me with a grievance which I explained
to my own Professor.

I was now well on in the curriculum at Edinburgh.
Some of my earlier companions had either left the University
or were a year behind me.

Why do men fail or become "chronics?" It is not always
drink, women, and betting. There was Andrews, a nice
enough lad who had not yet passed his first professional.
He had none of the major vices and was interested in everything except his studies. He was a member of all the literary
and philosophic societies, and went about with a volume of
R.L.S. under his arm. Yet he never wrote well enough
to be published even in the *Students' Magazine*. He was
well versed in Stevensoniana and many other "ianas," which
means that you know more about a writer than he did
himself. Andrews was much sought after by old ladies
for their afternoon teas. He could pass round cups and cakes
without dropping them and could chat easily about Old
and New Edinburgh. Nor would he ever hesitate to miss a
class or leave a textbook for a tea-party.

Another "chronic" was Hunter. He was a quiet, middle-
aged man with a beard. He had a wife, and three children
who went to school. One day he hoped to see his children
as fellow-students at the University. Hunter's father was
a man who, before he died, was determined that his son
should earn his own living. To this end he made a will
whereby his son was to have an allowance of five hundred
pounds a year as long as he was a student at Edinburgh
University. As soon as Hunter graduated, this allowance
was to cease and the capital from which it came was to go
to charities. As soon as this iniquitous will was read Hunter
and his lawyers calculated that there were a sufficient number
of classes at Edinburgh University to enable Hunter to
remain a student for the rest of his life. Thus it was that
every year he matriculated and took out one class, it might be

in the Faculty of Medicine, Arts, Law, Science, Agriculture or Divinity. In fact, thanks to his father's will, he became the ideal student, who realises that there is always something to learn.

There is a social difference between the Scottish and the older English Universities. In Scotland most of the students were educated at day schools, and then, unless their home was in the University city, would go into lodgings. Unless they have friends in the city they may be very lonely, and, when the University gates close at five in the afternoon, the only person who may have any interest in their conduct is the policeman. The Scottish University is therefore an early test of character, and those who come to grief fail in their teens. The undergraduates of Oxford and Cambridge mostly come from public schools, and, when in residence at the University, their lives are still supervised and sheltered. When these men fail it is usually in their twenties, and the wreckage of the English Universities is seen in the remittance men scattered on the shores of the Seven Seas.

At last the day came when I passed the final examination in Medicine. I had also passed other milestones. I had led the Conservatives at a debate in the Cambridge Union on the motion, "That the Labour Party has no place in the House of Commons." I spoke on this topic for sixty-five minutes, which showed some aptitude for politics, because at this time I was also President of the Edinburgh University Liberal Association! The "Final Night" at Edinburgh was a cheerful one. Most of my friends, including "young George," had passed, and we were all to dine together at a restaurant at seven-thirty. He was called "young George" to distinguish him from his father, "old George," the leading consultant in Scotland and a lecturer and examiner at the University. By eight o'clock that night "young George" had not appeared, so I telephoned to his house.

"Is that you, George? You devil, we're all waiting for you. Yes, of course it's Sutherland. What?"

"May I take this earliest opportunity of congratulating you on having passed, and also on your excellent appearance in the clinical examination through which I had the pleasure of conducting you."

"George," I laughed, "don't be an ass! You can mimic your governor as well as I can. What! It is . . . Oh! I beg your pardon, sir, I . . ."

"That's all right. On such a night anything within reason can be excused. I don't mind being called 'Old George,' but to call me a devil and an ass! No, it's all right, and if you should encounter my wandering offspring to-night, tell him that his devoted parent will not sit up for him. Enjoy yourselves. Good night."

Between old George and young George there was mutual confidence and respect. Only once, as George said, had his father ever let him down. That was after a smoking concert which we had attended. These Victorian and barbaric entertainments would be more accurately described as drinking concerts.

This particular concert finished at midnight in an uproarious fashion, when the chairman, who was one of the Advocates-Depute, declared that if we stayed much longer, "the dawn would be rattling in the streets, and the milk-carts breaking overhead."

Two of us saw George home. There was no more reason why we should have seen him home than he should have seen us home, but this was a personal attention which friends were inclined to inflict upon each other.

At the house in Drumsheugh Gardens the latchkey was found and our tall friend passed into the house as silently as a ghost and gently closed the door. For a moment we stood on the doorstep. It was a calm night and there was no moon. Suddenly from within the house there came an appalling crash, enough to awaken the entire neighbourhood, or so it seemed to us. We fled to the end of the square, and, before we parted, I said to my companion:

"That must have been the hat-rack."

"No," he answered solemnly, "it didn't quite sound like a hat-rack."

The next day George told us the story. His father was working late on a clinical lecture, and, when he heard the crash of the bicycle falling in the tiled hall, he came out of his consulting-room and switched on the lights. There he beheld his son entangled with the bicycle.

"Hullo, George," he said. "Had an accident, my boy? Let me help you. No man can talk to his father with a bicycle round his neck." He removed the bicycle, and placed it once more upright against the wall, remarking as he did so: "People shouldn't leave these confounded things in the hall for people to fall into." Then he continued: "I haven't seen much of you lately, George. Come in for a chat before you go to bed." George entered the consulting-room, where his father gave him the easy-chair, and continued what was mostly a monologue. "I hope you are not working too hard, George." George assured his father that he had not been working too hard. "Well, you don't look too fit to-night." And then, as if he had made a great clinical discovery, he exclaimed: "I know what it is, George, I know what you want. You want a whisky and soda and a cigar." These were two of the things which at that moment George did not want, but his father thrust them upon him, and then went on talking in the most natural way about clinical medicine. At last he said good night, and George went to bed, and as he went he rejoiced that, despite the accursed bicycle, everything must be all right. In his room he sought to reassure himself by looking in the glass, and when he did so perceived that round his neck there was hanging, like a halter, the brim of his bowler hat.

On one point George was sensitive, lest any of us should think that he was trading on his father's reputation. Thus, when some of the most distinguished men in medicine were staying as his father's guests, George was inclined to absent himself from meals at home. One morning at breakfast his mother said to him:

"George, to-day Professor von Pappen, the great heart specialist from Vienna, is coming to stay with us. He is to have an honorary degree from the University and will give an address to the Royal College of Physicians. While he is here he will have your room, and you won't mind sleeping in your father's dressing-room."

"That's all right, mother," said George, and left the house.

That night when George returned the household had retired to bed, and he had forgotten all about Professor von Pappen. He went to his own room, undressed, and was about to get into bed when he noticed an unusual appearance on the pillow. It seemed to be a large white mop. The maids had no right to leave a thing like that on his pillow, and he attempted to throw the thing on to the floor. But as he clutched the mop there came from the bed a guttural cry, and from beneath the sheets emerged the pink face of Professor von Pappen. Without a word George seized his clothes and dashed upstairs to the sanctuary of the dressing-room. The Professor was also on foot, and George was followed by a figure in a nightshirt, shouting:

"Stop, who vas you?"

George turned and raised his hand for silence. "I am only one of the family," and the Professor returned to his bed.

The next morning when George entered the dining-room his mother and the Professor were at breakfast, and his mother said:

"Professor von Pappen, I don't think you have met my son."

53

The Professor rose and bowed. "Madame, I have not yet had ze honour of being presented."

Two days later the Professor spoke to George and told him that it was a great honour to receive a degree from Edinburgh University and to be entertained by the Royal College of Physicians, but before he left Edinburgh he would like to meet some of the students. That night there was a function from which he could escape if George would take him elsewhere. Professor von Pappen spent that evening at the Empire music-hall in the company of a few medical students, and we all agreed with George when he said that this Professor was a *rara avis* whose departure from Edinburgh must be marked by something out of the common.

Next forenoon George called upon the station-master at the Caledonian Railway Station. The station-master knew George and was glad to see him.

"You know," said George, "that my father often has very distinguished foreigners staying at the house. I know that the Caledonian Railway Company always likes to show these people a little extra courtesy. Now, von Pappen is staying with us and leaves to-night by the ten o'clock express for London. He has his first-class ticket and sleeping-car berth reserved, but I thought you would like to know who he is. He is the Austrian ambassador."

The station-master rose. "Thank you very much, Mr. Gibson, for telling me. You may leave it to me."

George was quite content to leave it to the station-master, because, after all, it was the station-master's business, and he did his work remarkably well.

That night, when Dr. G. A. Gibson and some of the senior physicians at Edinburgh conducted their distinguished colleague to the train, they were much gratified to note with what respect the Caledonian Railway Company regarded the heart specialist from Vienna. A beautiful coach had been attached to the Scots express, a portion of the platform railed off, and on the platform itself a carpet had been laid down. They may or may not have been surprised to see standing there a small group of medical students, not hitherto distinguished by their interest in cardiology, and that Professor von Pappen greeted these students in the most cordial manner. As the express moved slowly out into the night the Professor stood at the door of his coach. He was hatless, and his great mop of white hair shone under the electric arcs.

"I thank you," he said. "I could not have been sent away with greater honour. No, not even had I been ze Austrian ambassador."

Two days after the Final Examination at Edinburgh there was a kind letter from Aberdeen. The Professor had seen the pass list and had sent his congratulations. If convenient would I come and see him, as he supposed I would be going north for a holiday? The session was over, but he would be working in the laboratory. And there I found him.

"Well, Mr. Sutherland—but it's Dr. Sutherland now—I wondered if you had thought of the future. If you are still interested in pathology I can offer you a small post in this department. The salary would be only one hundred and fifty pounds a year, and it might rise to three hundred pounds. That is not the point. If you take up pathology you must be prepared to dedicate your life to a science without looking for any material reward. You may never be able to marry, or, if you did so, might have to live in penury. You may never become a professor. There are not many Chairs of Pathology, and the competition is keen. Do you care sufficiently for pathology to sacrifice everything? Ah, I see the answer in your face. You prefer the fleshpots of Egypt! Well, I don't blame you. I was one of the fortunate ones. But I hope you will always be as honest with yourself as you have been to-day. . . .

"And how is my colleague in Edinburgh? Yes, I know he has retired. I called on him three months ago when I had a few hours to spare in Edinburgh, waiting for a train. I found he was almost blind. Poor fellow! I read to him for an hour. I think he was glad to see me after all these years. Poor fellow, but he did get us both by the ears, once upon a time, didn't he? Well, God bless you."

That was the last I ever saw of the Professor. In a few years he was dead, and crowned with those leaves that do not thrive on mortal soil. When he died, his teaching lived, because more of his old pupils were Professors of Pathology throughout the Empire than those of any other school. Across the years I see him again as he stood at the end of the rostrum—a sturdy, kindly old man, gazing over his spectacles as he said good-bye to another fleeting generation in a voice that was pleasant to hear:

"And now, young men and women, you will soon be starting out in life for yourselves. You will hear many things that are said of men and of books, but I would only say one thing to you—prove all things, use your sense, and, above all, the common sense that God has given you."

David James Hamilton! You were, and are, the greatest teacher I ever knew.

# CHAPTER V

## NORTHERN SEAS

WHEN I passed in pathology my father sent me on a holiday to the Shetland Isles, where I stayed with a doctor.

"You'll like him," my father had said. "He's rather harum-scarum, and a little careless. Don't take any presents from him; he's a man who'll offer you everything he's got. There is a whaling station five miles from his house. You'll find that interesting. If you go to the whaling station you will probably meet the Planter. He is a recluse—a retired Burma tea-planter, and there are a lot of stories about him because he lives alone. All rubbish. He may ask you to stay with him. He's got a big house at the end of the Voe—that is Norse for an inlet of the sea."

On the steamer, crossing from Thurso, I made friends with two men, older than myself, and at night we drank whisky in the saloon. One was Professor of Anatomy at a Scottish University, and the other invited me to guess his occupation. He was a tall, burly, aggressive-looking fellow, dressed in a loosely fitting lounge suit of Harris tweed.

"A boxer," I hazarded.

"Good enough," he replied, "but when I am not on holiday I am a minister of the Auld Kirk."

The doctor was a happy, boyish, dark-haired man of about thirty, married to a serious, orderly, middle-aged woman, whose wisdom and prudence were in contrast with her husband's freedom from care. There were no children. Their house faced the sea, and there was no other dwelling within sight. They had one other guest, a young tweed manufacturer from Jedburgh, and on rainy days the three of us played cards until the doctor's wife, on finding us sitting down to cards after breakfast, removed both packs and declined to produce them until the evening.

One morning the doctor woke me at seven. "Would you like to shoot a deer?" In a second I was out of bed. "You can see it from the window. Yes, in the middle of that third field. It's a hind, and you'll have to stalk her. No, I shouldn't dress. The grass is wet, so put on a pair of shoes. You'll be going down wind, so you'll have to creep all the way. I've got the rifle loaded downstairs."

I went down in pyjamas, and in the hall he handed me the Martini-Henry rifle. The jute manufacturer, like the doctor, was up and dressed, and I thought it very kind of them to let me have the shot—but they knew I was a good rifle shot.

It was a long stalk across two fields of hay. I moved on both knees and one hand, holding the heavy rifle in the other. The hay was wet and full of thistles, and the ground was stony. I had to wriggle through a hedge, was scratched by brambles and stung by nettles. These discomforts were of no account, provided the deer was not alarmed. After twenty minutes' crawling I reached the hedge of the field in which the deer was grazing. She was within eighty yards, and by good fortune was standing broadside on. It was an easy shot. I raised the rifle, aimed for below her left shoulder, and pressed the trigger. There was a click. A misfire. The hind pricked her ears, stopped grazing, and looked in my direction. Marvellous hearing these animals have! And what good stalking on my part that she did not know I was there! It was the first time I had stalked a deer. She must be a greedy brute! Otherwise why should she come down from the hills and so near a house in summer, when there was plenty of food in the wilds. Very quietly I opened the breech. There was no cartridge in the rifle. Just like the doctor to forget to load it! Careless fellow! But the deer was undisturbed and I could creep back to the house for a cartridge. If I went as carefully as I had come the deer would stay where she was.

Back I crawled through the fields of soaking hay, and did not rise to my feet until within twenty yards of the house. As soon as I stood up the doctor and his friend rushed out shouting with insensate laughter. I was very angry.

"It was your fault, you forgot the cartridge!"

"Forgot the cartridge!" shouted the doctor, behaving like a lunatic. "The cartridge! Do you think I should let you shoot my tame deer?"

"A good thing for you and your deer that I hadn't a cartridge in my pocket."

"A cartridge in your pocket! That's why we sent you off in pyjamas."

"Yes," shrieked the tweed merchant, "and his pyjamas are torn."

"And all he needed," spluttered the doctor, "was a lump of sugar!"

"You're a couple of fools," I shouted. Strange how mistaken we can be in our fellow-men. Up to this time I had liked both of them, but now I realised that each had a streak of low vulgarity!

But the more I cursed the more they laughed. The two of them shouted, rocked, and bent themselves with laughter, until the doctor's wife appeared.

"Have you all taken leave of your senses? And on a Sabbath morning, too! There are servants in this house whose feelings shall be respected, and" (pointing at me, who, with my rifle must have looked like an early edition of Robinson Crusoe) "what is he doing going about in this state? Disgraceful, I call it. Go to your room, sir, and clothe yourself. There are young maids in this house!"

On reaching my room I remembered that I was not on the mainland of Scotland, and that there were no wild deer in the Shetlands. Yes, it was an excellent jest. But curse those brambles, nettles and thistles which had left their marks.

When the wind was in the east the oily smell of the whaling station was carried in the air, and, with a favourable wind, the smell of a whaling station can be smelled ten miles away—like the town of Swansea, where petroleum is refined. At the end of the week the doctor drove me one morning to the whaling station, and waited until we knew if Captain Jensen of the *Sven Foyn* was willing to take me out to see whales caught. He agreed to do so, but would not accept any payment. The doctor had anticipated this, and my luggage consisted of shaving gear, brushes, pyjamas, and three bottles of whisky as a present for Captain Jensen. The *Sven Foyn* was to sail at three in the afternoon, so I had all the forenoon to see the whaling station.

On the beach, above high-water mark, were two large wooden platforms, the flensing stages, raised a foot from the ground. From each platform a broad wooden slipway ran down to the sea, and from the other end of the platform a narrower slipway led to the factory a hundred yards away. On each platform was a whale lying on its belly and with the head towards the sea. One whale was a bull and the other a cow. They were about sixty-five feet in length, and men on ladders were flensing them with knives four feet long. All the employees on the station were Norwegians. A V-shaped flap was cut across the head, and strips of blubber were pulled off on either side from head to tail. These slabs of blubber were dragged up the slipway to the factory, where they were boiled to extract the whale-oil. The first oil to come out is the best, and is sold as Number One grade. The remainder is Number Two grade. The average amount of oil obtained from a whale is twenty-eight tons, and was then worth sixty pounds a ton. The red meat of the whale is desiccated and ground to powder, which is used as a food for cattle. The whole skeleton is also ground down and sold as a fertiliser. Whalebone, so called, is really formed of cartilage hanging from the ridges at the back of the whale's mouth. Strips of whalebone were once used for corsets, but now it is mostly converted into artificial ostrich feathers, and, as early as the fourteenth century, plumes on the helmets of knights were made of whalebone.

The whale is the largest mammal. In its mouth three people could sit around a small table for afternoon tea; but the gullet of the whale is narrow, and no known species of whale could have swallowed Jonah, although the ancient chronicle does not mention the whale, but "a large fish." Yet it is not a physical impossibility for a man to have lived in a whale's mouth for three days. If he stood up against the plates of whalebone he would be knee-deep in water when the whale was on the surface, and, when the whale dived, he would be in a closed cavern of air. As soon as this air became vitiated the whale would rise to the surface to breathe; but a more uncomfortable voyage cannot be conceived!

The whale's main artery as it leaves the heart is so large that I was able to creep into it. The three layers—inner, middle and outer—in the wall of the artery could be seen by the unaided eye, and I cut out a portion of this large tube to send to the Professor in Aberdeen for teaching purposes. I also collected a portion of the tubular kidney, which is the size of a large dining-room table. The whale's stomach contained millions of small sea slugs, on which the whale feeds. In the female whale I found a small embryo, only a foot in length, but already having the form of a whale in miniature. I wondered if this was the smallest embryo ever found, and added it to my collection, which I handed to the foreman, who promised to salt the specimens and pack them in a box; and for his kindness I gave him half a crown.

Usually only one embryo is found in the whale, but twins

61

may occur, and the period of gestation is said to be two years. In all probability that is not an over estimate, because gestation in the elephant is eighteen months. The small fertility of whales shows that they have few enemies, because, as Darwin observed, fertility thoughout the whole animal kingdom is in direct proportion to the chances of death. The conger eel, with many enemies, produces over seven million eggs a year, and the species survives. The fulmar petrel of the South Pacific has no enemies, lays only one egg a year, and continues the existence of its species. Apart from man, the enemies of the whale are unknown. The mate of a tramp steamer once told me of a terrible battle he had witnessed between a whale and a sword-fish; but he had seen more than the seven wonders of the world, including a blazing meteorite falling into the sea beside his ship, which he saved by putting the helm hard-a-port in the nick of time!

The calf of the whale, like all mammals, is fed on the breast, albeit in the sea; but the age to which whales live is unknown. As the elephant may live for sixty years, the life of the whale is probably very much longer. In one of these Greenland whales the head of a *flint* harpoon was found. Either that whale had been alive in the Stone Age, or, as is more probable, there are now tribes in the Arctic regions who use flint weapons. The swimming-range of these whales is the length of the earth. At the end of the northern summer they depart, probably in search of food, for the Antarctic, and, in the month of November, I have seen them crossing the Equator on their way south.

At one o'clock I had a meal with Captain Jensen in his shack. He was a tall, broad-shouldered, sandy-haired man with good features, blue eyes, and was clean shaven when on shore. There was a woman present whom he introduced as his sister-in-law. She had peroxide hair, was powdered, painted, scented, and flashily dressed. She was the only woman on the whaling station, and was Norwegian. After this meal and a glass of Norwegian punch I went back to the flensing stage, where I found the Professor of Anatomy whom I had met on the steamer. He had been trout-fishing that morning, or he would have been at the flensing. The anatomy of whales was of great interest. Some days before he had found a very small embryo about two feet long. If the one I had found was less than a foot it was possibly the smallest ever found. We said good-bye. On my way to the *Sven Foyn*, lying at the jetty, I met a short, stocky man in a knickerbocker suit and a cap. He had white hair, a sharp-pointed beard, small, steel-grey eyes, and carried a walking-stick. Instinct told me that this was the Planter. He stopped in front of me "You are Mr. Sutherland. You are going on the *Sven Foyn*. You will have hard-tack, but youth is the time to enjoy roughing it. I shall see you on your return." And without another word he passed on his way.

The *Sven Foyn* was a wooden, screw steamer, seventy feet long and probably one hundred tons gross. Her funnel was amidships, the single mast was for'ard, and high on the forecastle was the harpoon gun. She had a relatively large rudder which enabled her to turn quickly. In front of the funnel was a small deck-house with the steering-wheel, compass and engine-room telegraph. At full speed she could make twelve knots. On either side of the deck amidships were two wooden improvised bunkers, each containing a ton of extra coal. In the stern was a derrick with the dinghy. The cabin was aft behind the engine-room. There were four bunks, with blankets and pillows, and, on the floor, a collapsible table. Sleeping and living quarters were combined for the captain and engineer. The engineer was of medium height, but his great chest and shoulders reminded me of a gorilla. He had long black hair and a black, square beard, and his features, so far as they were visible, were pleasant. He had kindly eyes, a straight nose, and a pleasant smile. He knew no English, and when he met me he smiled, shook hands, and said "Ja." He and Jensen had the lower bunks, and mine was the one above Jensen's on the port side. I presented Jensen with the three bottles of whisky, and he said he would serve it out every day at noon and at eight in the evening. The whisky was the only luggage I need have taken, for during the cruise none of us ever undressed, neither did we wash or shave. There was fresh water on board, but not for luxuries like washing. The food was the coarsest I have ever eaten. Black Norwegian bread, margarine, salt herrings, salt cod, salt pork, Limberger cheese, coffee with sugar but no milk. Nevertheless I enjoyed it.

Towards evening, as the whaler was passing close to the wild rocky cliffs of the Outer Skerries, I saw the skua, one of the hawks of the sea. This bird is two feet in length, being six inches longer and two pounds heavier than the common gull or sea-mew which it pursues. The hooked beak is dark brown, like the feathers on the back and wings, and the throat and breast are a lighter brown. Between the tips of the extended wings the span is from four to five feet, and the bird has a strong, rapid, dashing flight—in contrast to the easier and slower flight of seagulls. When the gulls are fishing, the sea-hawks are soaring and watching. Having caught and swallowed a fish, the gull takes to flight and is chased by the skua. In this furious chase the neck and feathers of the skua are bristling, until the terrified gull disgorges the recently swallowed fish, and the skua dives to seize with his claws the food falling through the air. The skua has been called the parasitic gull, because it lives by the work of others; but a parasite lives by fawning and by cunning, whereas the skua obtains the property of other birds by bold, open attack; and a better name is the pirate gull, because it will even attack the solan goose, a bird of twice its weight, and also the eagle.

The skua breeds in the Shetlands, mostly on the lonely, outlying island of Foula, on the Hill of Rona on the mainland, and on the northern Isle of Unst. The large nest of grasses, lichens, moss and heath is placed on the tops of cliffs and mountains. There are only two eggs, and, during the breeding season, the skua is ferocious and will attack men, birds or beasts approaching the nest. The skua are popular with fishermen, who think it is a good omen when the birds accompany their boats to the fishing-ground. Farmers on the mountains where the skua nests value the birds because they scare away the eagles that prey on the flocks during the lambing season.

A gale began to blow from the west, and as soon as we were clear of the Shetlands the *Sven Foyn* rolled heavily in the seas. In comparison with the ship the waves looked enormous, especially when the little steamer was at the bottom of one of these swirling valleys of water. But when a wave seemed about to overwhelm us, she rose like a cork up the steep slope and slipped down into the next gulf. Jensen held his course, hoping that the gale would diminish. The deck was so wet and uncomfortable that I went below to my bunk. I am a good sailor, and the only difficulty was to avoid being pitched out of the bunk. At nine o'clock Jensen came down, took off his oilskins, lit the lamp, produced a chart which he laid on the table, and pointed with his finger to a place on the chart. "I think we are here. I do not know. I think we are blown out and back. We are half-way between Shetland and Bergen. If I go to Bergen the gale is behind. If I go to Balta Sound the gale is in front. I go to Balta Sound."

Jensen went on deck, leaving me somewhat apprehensive. The chart, the compass, an old sextant, and a Nautical Almanac five years old were the only instruments of navigation on board. We had altered course, and the *Sven Foyn* was pitching heavily, head to gale. The noise of the sea drowned the noise of the wind. Now and then she shook as water crashed for'ard and rushed aft over the deck. Once an extra heavy shock was followed by a crash and clatter on deck, as the ton of coal on the port side was washed overboard. In the engine-room the telegraph was constantly ringing as Jensen slowed down at the approach of larger waves. After a time the pitching became less as we came under the lee of the Shetlands, and I fell asleep.

When I awoke it was six o'clock, and a bright sunny morning. Jensen and the engineer were sound asleep after their night of work, and the *Sven Foyn* was at anchor. I went on deck and saw Balta Sound, the most northern and natural harbour in the British Isles. There were twenty steamers, mostly foreign, lying there at anchor, waiting for their cargoes of salted herring, and, scattered along either shore, about half a mile away, were the herring-curing sheds and the little shacks where the herring-girls lived. Over a thousand girls were on these shores, and, as the herring moved south so also would they migrate. There was one hotel in Balta Sound, a post office, one policeman, and a few little shops.

About one of these shopkeepers I had heard a curious story. He was a black-bearded man, married for the third time, the two former wives having died in childbed. The Shetlanders expected the third wife to meet a similar fate, having married a man with "a white liver." By "a white liver" they did not mean cowardice or any moral defect, and I never discovered either what the phrase meant or the basis of this local belief.

Two hundred yards from the *Sven Foyn* a black hulk was moored, with the word "Market" painted in large white letters on her sides. This was the herring market, and I decided to get some fresh herrings for breakfast. By means of signs I induced two of the crew to lower the dinghy. I rowed across to the hulk and moored the dinghy at the foot of the companion ladder on the port side. At first glance the hulk seemed deserted. There was nobody on deck, and no sign of fish or anything else for sale, until a young man of about twenty-five appeared from below. He had no hat, but his black hair was well oiled and brushed to withstand the breeze. He had sharp features, was clean shaven, and wore a bright check lounge suit. He blinked a little in the sunlight before coming to greet me.

"Good morning, sir. Alfred Jenkins is my name, and I have the pleasure of meeting Mr. ——? Mr. Sunderland. Glad to meet you, Mr. Sunderland. A good old English name. Blood will tell, sir, as my old dad always used to say. And I'll bet you've come to buy herrings. I knew it as soon as I saw you. Well, you are a buyer and I'm a seller. *Noblesse oblige!* Only a few! No matter, no order is too small or large for Alfred Jenkins, and if you will take my tip, Mr. Sunderland, never apologise for an order. As my old dad used to say, the buyer holds the cash. And before we do business you'll be Alf Jenkins's guest. No, I take no refusal, sir. I'm in the chair, and at your service. My customers are my friends, and one new customer is worth two old ones. For why, because he's a new one. That's logic. To tell you the truth, we had a pretty thick night on board last night, and I came on deck for a whiff of the briny, but a nice bottle of Bass straight off the ice is worth two of that. This way, Mr. Sunderland; no, I won't talk a word of business until we have had our refreshment. After that, as much or as little business as you please. There's plenty of time, it's only half-past six."

He led the way down to the saloon, where a steward was clearing up bottles, glasses, and cards left over from the night before.

"Two nice bottles of Bass," called Mr. Jenkins, and the drinks were set before us on a card table. "Cheerio, and my best respects." Mr. Jenkins took a deep draught, and sighed. "That's better. Before I had that I don't mind telling you that my mouth was like the inside of a gas-pipe."

As I drank my Bass I had two qualms of conscience. Never before had I taken beer so early in the day, and I also reflected that my drink had probably cost Mr. Jenkins more than he would receive from me for the herrings, wherever they were.

He offered me his cigarette-case. "Turks on the right, Virgins on the left." Having lit his cigarette, Mr. Jenkins inhaled deeply, and slowly exhaled the smoke, first through his nostrils and then from his mouth. This done he looked at me steadily. "Mr. Sunderland, who are you buying for? The Spend Von? That's a syndicate! No, don't tell me another word about them. I don't care if they are German, Poles or Russians. Alfred Jenkins is no respecter of persons. It's the same to me who I do business with. No; you let me do the talking. Plenty of time for refs. later on. It's up to Alf to make you a proposition, and before we discuss the price you and me will have a little talk on the strict Q.T. Don't answer in a hurry. Figure it out, and tell me what you want for yourself. Then we'll see what can be done. The figure is all I want to hear."

I did figure it out. What an extraordinary man! Here was the ardent salesman, who could sell harps in heaven and gas-stoves in hell. But what a fuss about nothing! There was the captain, the engineer and myself. Then there were six of the crew. Enough for two breakfasts was wanted, so I answered, "Eighteen."

"Eighteen!" exclaimed Mr. Jenkins, laying down his cigarette. "Almighty God! and I took you for a kid. Eighteen for yourself? No, you have had your say, and I'll have mine. Old man, I admire your nerve. No, not a word. You're the goods all right, and Alf Jenkins is glad to meet you—but the thing's imposs. Imposs., old man, even if I sold

my shirt. What I say is this. Your firm can have ten, and
you can have five for yourself. What about it?" At that
moment a bell rang and Mr. Jenkins rushed on deck.
"Come along, there's a boat coming in. We can finish our
pow-wow at breakfast."

There were now a dozen men on deck, all apparently in
the same business as Mr. Jenkins. They were silently
watching the fishing-boat, as, with lowered mainsail, she
slowly approached. In the bow of the boat a man was
standing up holding a basket of herring, which he flung on
to the fore-deck of the hulk. As the basket fell the herrings
scattered over the deck. And the men rushed to look at the
sample and then rushed back to the side of the hulk. The
fishing-boat was passing slowly, and in the stern an old man
stood up. "Forty," he shouted. The men on our deck held
up their hands and began to signal to him with their fingers.
The old man watched them steadily, and pointed to one of
the bidders, who raised both arms above his head and shouted:
"Smith's jetty." The old man nodded. His catch was sold;
he knew the price and where to unload.

Mr. Jenkins reappeared, and I tried to forestall him.
"Can't I buy some of these herrings on the deck?"

"Of course you can, old man; you can buy anything
you like. You can buy the whole of Balta Sound. But what
about another nice bottle of Bass? No? Well, don't get
shirty! And Alfred Jenkins can tell you one thing. That
last catch was bought by Smiths, but Smiths won't give
you any better terms. What's more, I'll give you six per
cent. for yourself. You don't want it? Of course you want
it. We all want it. Now, now, you are my guest here, so
let me finish. Mistake? No, there's no mistake. Alfred
Jenkins is not the man to make a mistake! You listen to me.
Alf Jenkins will see that everything is O.K. There'll be no
mistake. Not the mistake that sent poor old Higgins to
the workhouse. Big noise he was in the soft goods line.

First buyer for Glover and Lacey—biggest firm in London.
If you had called him Higgins in those days he'd have
said, 'Mr. Higgins, if you please.' Big buy he did in
Switzerland and back he came. The managing-director shook
hands with him. It was a good buy at a good price, and ten
per cent. off to the firm for C.O.D. A month later, for my
dad was there at the time, there came a letter from Switzerland addressed to William Higgins, Esquire, care of Messrs.
Glover and Lacey. O.K. you might think, but it wasn't.
The letter got mixed with the managing-director's letters,
and his secretary opened it. Out there fluttered a cheque
for two hundred and fifty of the best from the Swiss merchant,
and payable to William Higgins. That tore it. When the
managing-director sent for him, Higgins hadn't a word to
say. And his boss told him to keep the cheque because he'd
need it, as it would be the last penny he'd ever earn in the
soft-goods line. A damned shame, I call it! They all know
we do it, but you mustn't get caught. Now, your firm,
Mr. Sunderland——"

"I haven't got a firm," I shouted.

"But you said the Spend Von?"

"That's the whaler over there, the *Sven Foyn*."

"Then what the hell are you doing here? You wanted
to—what! Buy a few herrings for breakfast! And I thought
you might want a thousand barrels." Mr. Jenkins laughed.
"Well, the old dad did say that sherbet was the best tipple
for a growing lad. But you don't look as if you were in the
whaling line! Oh, a medical student. Well, I did hear
that you medical students are always up to larks. But there
are two things you can't do. You can't buy fresh herrings on
this hulk, and you can't tell your pals that Alfred Jenkins
doesn't know what's what. As the dear old dad always said,
*noblesse oblige*. Wait there; I'll be back in a minute." He
returned with two fibre fish-bags, and gave one to me.
"Take as many herrings as you like off the deck. They'll

be swept overboard before the next boat comes in, and the gulls will get them."

I filled one bag, he the other, which he carried down to the dinghy, and when we said good-bye our hands were covered with silver scales.

I rowed back to the *Sven Foyn* and found Jensen on deck. When he saw the fresh herrings he was not annoyed that I had taken the boat away without permission.

"You were lucky that you got them. They do not like people going there."

Outside Balta Sound the gale continued, and we lay at anchor all day. In the afternoon I went ashore with Jensen and the engineer for a walk. The shore was half a mile off, and we left the boat on the beach. A rough road followed the line of the shore, and along this we walked towards the head of the Sound. The road passed numerous sheds, each with a jetty. The sheds were on the grass above the beach, and on the gravel beach were long benches at which hundreds of girls were gutting herring. The girls, in rough blue serge dresses and sea-boots, worked in couples. One gutted the herring, which her companion salted and packed in a barrel. So fast did they work that the barrel filled up like a sand-glass, and, when it was full, a man rolled it away and left another in its place. We watched a red-haired Amazon at work, and she ignored our presence until I remarked in genuine admiration:

"That takes a bit of doing."

Without slackening the speed of her work she replied with a torrent of unprintable abuse. A man, moving a barrel up the beach, turned and grinned. Jensen laughed.

"Ho, she does not like you."

As we walked back to the road I passed the man with the barrel and asked him: "What is the matter with that girl?"

"She took you for a fish salesman."

I learnt that this dislike of fish salesmen was not on grounds of sex but of financial morality. The girls' wages depended on the price of herring, and they believed that salesmen kept the price down, from which our older novelists should learn that sex is not the only ruling passion.

At the end of a two-mile walk we reached the hotel, and I invited my companions to have a drink. Only captains and engineers were allowed into the bar. Sailors had their drinks outside. Asked what he would drink, Jensen answered: "There is only one drink for captains, rum and brandy mixed."

As soon as my glass was empty I knew that if this was the drink for captains it was not the drink for me, and I retired to the hillside, where I slept for some hours. When I awoke it was evening and the Sound was blotted out by a thick sea fog. I sought my companions in the smoke-laden atmosphere of the bar, and found Jensen the centre of attraction. The spectators were standing round in a ring and Jensen, with his coat off, was fighting another giant. Jensen had a red bruise on his right cheek, and his opponent was bleeding at the mouth. It was the end of the fight, for Jensen landed a blow which sent the other man crashing backwards into the onlookers, who stopped the fight. Jensen and the engineer sat down at a little side-table, where I joined them and drank Norwegian punch. I never learnt the cause of the fight, because Jensen would no longer speak English. He was not inclined to return to the ship, even when I suggested this by saying: "*Sven Foyn*," and he resembled the man who told his friends at the end of an evening: "I'll do anything in reason, but I won't go home."

After a few more drinks we set out on our way. At first I walked between the captain and the engineer, but, with a giant on one side and a gorilla on the other, I was now and then crushed, and arranged that Jensen should walk in the middle. This he did, and the trio proceeded arm-in-arm.

Sometimes we lost the road and found ourselves on the shingle of the beach. But the road was easily regained, and I knew the beach was on our right-hand side. At last I recognised the shed below which the girl had cursed me earlier in the day, and we all began to search the beach for the boat we had left. I found it in the fog, and shouted to the others. The tide was out, and we dragged the boat over the beach to the sea, which was as calm as a mill-pond on a still day. I got into the boat and sat in the stern. The engineer followed and sat amidships with his back to me. Jensen, who was wearing sea-boots, pushed the boat into the water with one hand and clambered into the bow. The engineer fixed the rowlocks and began to row. He was rowing the boat stern first, but I made no comment, being afraid that we should be capsized if he attempted to change his position. Thus we paddled into the fog, and every few minutes Jensen shouted like a foghorn: "*Sven Foyn*, ahoy!" and his voice echoed from the banks of fog. We passed many steamers at anchor, most of them twenty times the size of the *Sven Foyn*, but whenever a hull loomed out of the fog, Jensen shouted: "*Sven Foyn*, ahoy!" Once we passed under the counter of a large steamer, so close that I read her name and port of registration, which was Glasgow. Again Jensen shouted, and we were cursed in the accent of the Clyde by a man on watch, who threw a bucket of water, which just missed us. After an hour's rowing and shouting there came a faint answer to Jensen's inquiry. I had no idea from what direction the response had come, but Jensen directed the engineer, and when again he shouted: "*Sven Foyn*, ahoy!" we were almost alongside. The engineer was assisted on board by two of the hands. I went next, and Jensen last.

On reaching the cabin I found the engineer already asleep in his bunk. I took off my boots and clambered into my oily blankets. A strange creature, this engineer, who never said anything except, "Ja." He was said to have a wife and four children in Norway. Did he ever speak to them? And how could anyone ever become an engineer if he only said "Ja"?

Jensen remained on deck and appeared to be arousing the whole crew. Why wouldn't the man come down and let us get to sleep! On deck there was the tramp of feet and the sound of Jensen's voice. Was he going to steam out of Balta Sound in the fog? The snores of the engineer assuaged that fear. Then on deck there was a crash and a heavy fall which loosened some paint from the cabin ceiling. Jensen was getting the dinghy on board. Then he entered the cabin and threw himself on his bunk. As I went to sleep I experienced the joys of an easy conscience—I had taken off my boots, the others had not.

# CHAPTER VI

## WHALES

I AWOKE with a splitting headache. It was seven o'clock in the morning, and the cabin was empty. The other two were up before me, and from the motion I knew that the *Sven Foyn* was at sea. I got up, put on my boots, and went to the bows to get the sea air. We were steaming north, and far behind us the mountains of Shetland were a low, black ridge against the sky. The gale was over, but there was a heavy swell on the sea through which the *Sven Foyn* cut her way like a yacht, and, when she crashed on a wave, threw up fine spray. This cold, grey, northern sea was the cure for a headache.

My reflections were rudely interrupted by the voice of Jensen: "Ho! how is your head to-day?"

"All right," I answered curtly, because it was a rude question. There is only one time when every Christian man resents any inquiry as to his spiritual or bodily well-being, and that is on the morning after the night before. Jensen was obviously in a bad temper. "Ho! when you go back to Balta Sound you will go to prison or pay, I think, ten pounds."

"I shall never go back to Balta Sound. I never want to see the place again."

"Ho! what do you want me to do with that boat you steal?"

"Steal! What boat?"

"You do not like to see the boat that you steal? Come and see. Captain Jensen does not steal boats."

He led me aft, and there I saw the cause of the disturbance on the deck the night before. The stern rail was smashed, one of the derricks was askew, and on the deck lay a boat

75

which was not the dinghy of the *Sven Foyn*. It was a much bigger boat, and therefore had not fitted the derricks. It was also a much better boat, and on it was painted the name and place of the large steamer *from* which a bucket of water had been thrown the night before.

I turned away in disgust. "It's not my boat. Do what you like with it."

"Ho!" shouted Jensen, "it is your boat. You stole it; you are the thief. Captain Jensen does not steal boats. You steal boats at night and I have to get them on deck. The police will find my boat that I left behind."

"There was no name on your boat," I answered, and returned to the bows to commune with the sea. It was rather awkward. I could not be put in prison, and Jensen would find it difficult to explain how he did not know it was not his boat, as he knew or ought to have known his own boat much better than I did. The boat would certainly be missed, and Jensen had given the *Sven Foyn* a free advertisement all round Balta Sound in the fog. Suppose the owners of the boat made inquiries, and sent a claim to the owners of the *Sven Foyn* in Bergen. And if Jensen blamed me! I did not possess ten pounds, and my father would want explanations. Curse all drink! The cook touched me on the arm and pointed aft. Breakfast was served! For breakfast each had two of my herrings, and to make the peace I remarked to Jensen: "Very good herrings."

But he answered: "The thief in prison does not get herrings."

Then he spoke in Norse to the engineer, who smiled at me and answered "Ja."

After breakfast I watched the crew preparing the harpoon-gun for action. This gun was invented by Sven Foyn, after whom the steamer was named, and his invention brought a fortune to the Norwegian whaling industry. The gun was a muzzle loader, swivelled on a gun-mounting in the bows.

The charge was two hundred and twenty grams of black gunpowder to fire the harpoon, four feet long and weighing one hundred pounds. The shaft of the harpoon was inserted into the barrel of the gun, and on the shaft was a groove holding a running ring. To this ring the warp was attached, and, to prevent the rope being burnt by the blast, the ring was drawn to the fore-end of the harpoon outside the muzzle of the gun. Two other portions of the harpoon projected from the muzzle—the four twelve-inch hinged barbs to prevent the harpoon from being withdrawn from the whale, and, in front of the barbs, the sharp-pointed cap containing two pounds of gunpowder, which, on a three-second fuse fired on impact, would explode inside the whale. The effective range of the gun was forty yards, and, on an iron plate on the deck in front of the gun fifty yards of rope were coiled so that the flight of the harpoon would not be deviated by the strain of the rope. This rope was probably the most valuable gear on the *Sven Foyn*, and there was over a mile of it wound on to drums below deck. It was a small three-ply rope of best hemp, and each ply consisted of ninety-two strands. One single strand was so strong that it supported my weight from the rigging. I also watched the crew taking their turn in the crow's nest. This was a barrel fixed high in the mast above the level of the mainstays. At last the man in the crow's nest gave a shout which brought Jensen on deck. The man pointed to starboard. Jensen looked at the horizon to the north, signalled to the man to come down, and altered course. From the deck I could see nothing except sea and sky, but *Sven Foyn* was steaming north and rolling in the swell between the Shetlands and the Faroe Isles.

As I was looking north Jensen pointed to the crow's nest and said: "You would not go up there?" For answer, I mounted the bulwark and began to climb the mainstays. The stays were interlaced with rope to make a ladder, and climbing was easy until I reached the top. The rope ladder ended on a level with the middle of the barrel, which was fastened to the front of the mast. To enter the barrel it was necessary to hold on to the mast and to climb with feet alone on the rope ladder to the end of the mainstays. At this point I looked down and saw the sea on one side, then the deck, and then the sea on the other side. The mast was swaying thirty feet with every roll of the ship. I had climbed from the port side, and, to enter the barrel, had to put my left hand on its rim, my right on the forestay, raise my knees, and swing myself in. This meant maintaining a balance for at least two seconds with two feet and one hand. I waited until the nest was swinging to starboard, got my two new hand-grips and dropped into the barrel. There was a noise on deck, and I looked down from the crow's nest —the crew were giving me a cheer. That would help Jensen! I looked ahead, and, far on the horizon saw small spouts of water rising here and there from the sea. That was the school of whales blowing air as they reached the surface. I fished in my pockets for the last of my cigarettes and began to smoke. The head of Jensen appeared over the edge of the barrel: "Ho, you can get in, but you cannot get out!"

I was tired of Jensen. "I'll get out as soon as I want." And he slipped down the rigging again. I finished the cigarette and looked down. Jensen and the crew were on deck. To get out I had to face the mast, grip the forestay with the left hand, clutch the mast with the right arm, swing out of the barrel and then feel for the rope ladder with my feet. Twice my feet swung outwards in the air before they found the mainstays. The rest was easy, and I jumped from the bulwark to the deck. Jensen held out his hand.

"I forgive the boat that you steal. We will have a drink of your whisky."

On going aft I saw that he had good reason to pardon me. Two of the crew were busy repainting the boat that I had found! It would also be easy to widen the space between the derricks.

Within an hour the *Sven Foyn* was alongside the whales. I asked Jensen if I might fire the gun.

"No. Not unless you pay me two hundred pounds if you miss."

He was right. He and his men worked under hard conditions for small wages, and their only chance of gain was the commission received for each whale killed.

There was a school of about fifty whales swimming westwards in irregular formation, each whale being at least a quarter of a mile away from its nearest neighbour. Jensen was now at the wheel in front of the mast, and the *Sven Foyn* kept parallel with one of the monsters about two hundred yards away. The whale, after blowing out air on the surface and inhaling a new breath, dived on its sinuous course and reappeared again a quarter of a mile farther on. Jensen was judging the distance between each dive, and the speed of the *Sven Foyn*. Again the whale rose and dived, and Jensen altered course. The *Sven Foyn* went at full speed to the place where the whale was likely to reappear on the surface, and the engines were then stopped. Jensen left the wheel and went to the gun. I went to the starboard side and watched the sea. Deep down I saw a great green mass, iridescent with air bubbles, rising to the surface. Any gunnery or torpedo officer in the Royal Navy might have envied the skill and judgment whereby Jensen, without mechanical aids, had brought the *Sven Foyn* to this place in the seas. The whale emerged within ten yards of the ship, and the noise of air blown from the nostrils was that of a boiler letting off steam. As the whale was about to dive, Jensen aimed and fired. The harpoon entered the left shoulder a foot above the water, and the whale submerged.

There was a dull explosion, and in a moment the sea all round the *Sven Foyn* was red with blood. The rope attached to the harpoon was now racing out over a grooved wheel, and a man was pouring salt water on this wheel to prevent singeing of the rope. The whale was diving deep, and Jensen said: "He is dying."

When a whale is dying it makes for the depths, but a wounded whale may swim on the surface, followed by the steamer, for a hundred miles. Once, when following a wounded whale, Jensen had done the thing which had made him the bravest man in the northern seas. Others told me the story. He launched the dinghy, took the harpoon rope in his hands, drew the dinghy alongside the whale, and killed it himself with a great spear.

Over half a mile of rope had run out, and it was now running more slowly. A slight brake was put on the drums below decks from which the rope was uncoiled. Soon all movement ceased, and the rope was slowly wound back until the dead whale, floating belly up, was near the surface. The running noose of a steel chain was passed over the tail and made taut. The chain was dragged for'ard and made fast. A man cut the rope attached to the harpoon, and the *Sven Foyn* steamed slowly ahead, with the whale, tail in front, alongside. The engineer came on deck with a long, sharp-pointed, hollow iron tube, which he thrust into the whale's belly. A strong, flexible hose-pipe connected the iron tube with an air-pump in the engine-room, and the whale was inflated with air until it floated with its belly three feet out of the sea.

The skin on the belly was white and lined with longitudinal grooves about six inches apart. On the distended skin these grooves were about an inch in width and depth, and the whole belly looked like a deck of caulked planks. A man jumped on to the upturned whale, walked along its belly to the iron tube, which he withdrew, and plugged the puncture with a wedge of wood, to prevent escape of air. I also jumped, slipped forwards, and would have slid between the whale and the ship had I not dug my fingers into one of the grooves. The skin was very greasy, and, with fingers and toes in the grooves, I crept to the centre and stood up. It was like standing on an enormous air-cushion, into which my feet sank as I walked.

"Stop in middle. The sea is cold," shouted Jensen, and I was glad to keep on the centre of the upturned whale, as I had no wish to slide into the sea on the other side. A flag attached to a short iron shaft was thrown to the man who was the other passenger on the whale. He drove the shaft into it and the flag, on which was the name *Sven Foyn*, floated in the breeze. He clambered over the whale and regained the deck. I followed him, watching how he balanced himself on that slippery surface, but Jensen threw me the end of a rope lest I should fall.

All the time the *Sven Foyn* was steaming slowly ahead, but now the chain attached to the tail of the whale was loosened, the whale was left floating in the sea, and we set off at full speed—about twelve knots, in pursuit of another. The purpose of the flag was to let any other ship know that the dead whale was our property.

"Whalers are honest," said Jensen; "they do not steal whales." To my relief he made no direct reference to the stealing of boats.

Two hours later another whale was killed, and then a third. As dusk was falling, we recovered our earlier captures, and with a whale on either side drawn by the tail, and another one towed astern, the *Sven Foyn* steamed slowly homewards; and each of the whales she was towing was almost as long as herself.

I told Jensen that my cigarettes were finished, and that the smell of whales and oil was nauseating. He produced a chunk of black tobacco and cut off a generous slice. "Chew."

This I did, and found it an excellent cure. I did not swallow the juice, whereas Jensen swallowed tobacco and all. Late on the following afternoon we were back at the whaling station.

On landing at the jetty I was met by the Planter.

"Mr. Sutherland, you look as though you wanted a wash up and a brush down. You will have dinner and stay the night: you will appreciate a comfortable bed."

On our way to the house I called at the factory to see if the foreman had packed my specimens, and to address the box to the Professor at Aberdeen. The box was closed, and I asked him to open the lid so that I could see if the specimens were all right. This he did grumblingly. The specimens were as I had left them except the embryo. The embryo had grown! It was now over two feet long.

"That is not my embryo!" I declared.

"No," said the man. "The gentleman take your one. He pay me ten shillings for it. He leave you this one. It is a bigger one. No, he is not here any more. He go away to Scotland."

As I addressed the box I wondered if I would ever learn to hold my tongue.

The Planter's house was at the end of the Voe, half a mile from the whaling station. It was a large rectangular building of plain grey stone, and stood alone above the rocks in the centre of an amphitheatre of steep hills of grass. The windows were small, and most of them had no curtains. There were no trees, and the house looked empty and deserted, but in its gaunt, bleak outlines there was strength to withstand the full force of western gales.

The dining-room was large, and on the walls were faded portraits of men and women set in massive frames. Eighteen people could have dined at the long mahogany table, but we sat one at each end, and between us on either side were eight empty chairs. We dined by candle-light, the curtains having been drawn, and during dinner there was no conversation. It would have been difficult to talk without raising one's voice from one end of that table to the other. There was soup, fish, and a very hot curry, followed by fruit. Dinner was served by two boys, aged about twelve and dressed in white jackets. These two boys and a tall, dark, silent Highland woman were the only servants in the house. On the other side of the hall was another large room fitted up as a chapel—with an altar, crucifix and lectern. Here, every morning, the Planter read the lessons of the Church of England, and the two little boys made the responses. They were his only congregation. During dinner we drank water, but there was a wine-glass by my place, and at the end of dinner the tall woman poured out for each of us a glass of port. Then she and the boys retired. I did not touch my glass until my host had taken his, and it was well that I refrained, because suddenly he rose.

"Mr. Sutherland, you will drink our only toast standing up. I give you the toast: 'To His Majesty, the King across the water, Charles Stuart.'" I drank the toast, but did not think the port was very good, and left a few drops in my glass. "Mr. Sutherland, no heel-taps, if you please. Kindly finish your wine."

My host led me upstairs and along a corridor. By the sound of our feet I knew we were passing through a corridor of empty rooms. At the end of the corridor he stopped at a door fitted with a Yale lock on the outside, and took out his keys. "No one is allowed to enter this room. I tidy it myself." As we entered, it was dark, and the door closed behind us with a click. The Planter struck a match and lit a lamp on a round table opposite the empty grate. This curious lamp made a soft whirring noise, and every minute gave a loud click. There was clockwork inside whereby air was propelled towards the flame. The lamp had a green shade, so that although the table was flooded with light, it was difficult to see into the corners of the room. There was a deep, soft carpet on the floor and the windows were covered with heavy curtains which shut out the light of the summer evening. The walls were hung with Eastern tapestries, and decorated with heads, antlers and horns of wild animals. All round the walls were low shelves of books, and on the top of these little book-cases were various curious metal vases, and idols. There was a slight aroma of cedar wood. On the mantelshelf was a large, grinning Buddha, and above the god a solitary picture, its face turned towards the wall. We sat in low arm-chairs with the table between us, and on it my host had placed an ash-tray. "You may smoke." He himself did not smoke.

I told him of my adventures in the *Sven Foyn*, and, as he listened, I realised that he never smiled, and I remembered that his conversation had been didactic and spoken in a monotone. Thinking that he wished to go to bed, I thanked him for his hospitality.

"No, Mr. Sutherland, it is I who should thank you. I have very few visitors. It is a long time since anyone stayed in this house. You may be the last visitor who will ever stay here. The people of the island avoid this house. It would seem as if they had an intuition that it conceals a secret. It does: and a guilty one. I am the secret. I am one of those who have taken human life—who have killed. My revolver is on the mantelshelf beside the Buddha. Outside the arc of light in which we are sitting the room is dim, otherwise you would have seen the revolver when you looked at the Buddha—and the picture. May I fetch you a glass of water? No! I thought you were looking a little white. The movement of the ship, perhaps! Will you not finish smoking your cigarette? I fear the click of the lamp disturbs you? No? That is well, because there is no harm in the lamp. The click occurs every fifty-five seconds and records the flight of time. I have listened to it for many years.

There is no clock in this room, and when I sit here I never look at my watch. You do not carry a revolver? That is wise. It is a dangerous and useless weapon. If you carry a stick you need only use it in cases of necessity. If you draw a revolver you must use it at once, because if you hesitate the other man will kill you. I hope that has been noted.

"The picture with its face to the wall is the portrait of my wife. She was a beautiful woman, and the portrait was painted by a famous artist. No one shall ever see that portrait. When the hour comes I shall burn it in the fireplace. We lived in a bungalow on my plantation in Burma. There were no children. I hope that has been noted. Our nearest neighbour was miles away. O'Brien was his name. He was a tall, handsome fellow with brown hair, brown moustache and blue eyes. Physically he was of the bovine type which appeals to so many women, but mentally he was alert and vivacious. Being an Irishman he had the charm that captivates all women except those of his own race. His personality was more attractive than mine, because then I was no more attractive than I am now. But I loved my wife. He was a good shot, and in the early days he and I often went shooting together. Later on I thought that his visits to my bungalow were becoming too frequent. The native servants were talking, and I told him to stay away for six months. I knew that he was due to go on leave to England, and hoped that he would return with a wife of his own. That would have simplified matters. He had one fault—he lifted his elbow too often. Not that he was a drunkard, but most men who drink, drink too much, and, without knowing, they deteriorate. He did not take his leave, and began to drink more heavily—so my servants were told by his.

"One afternoon I saw him coming across the plantation towards my bungalow with a twelve-bore gun under his arm. My wife at the time was resting in her room. As soon as he was within earshot I called to him that we did not wish to see him. He paid no attention, and stepped on to the verandah. Again I told him to clear off, but he answered: 'I haven't come to see you. I've come to see your wife.' Then I shot him dead through the heart.

"My wife was very upset, but not more so than any woman was likely to be under similar circumstances. She said there was nothing wrong between them, but she had tried to stop his drinking, and that he must have been out of his mind or else he would never have tried to shoot me. She never knew the truth. The Resident Magistrate held an inquiry. My wife was not called as a witness. There was the evidence of O'Brien's servants that, after drinking half a bottle of whisky he had gone out to shoot snipe. There was the evidence of my servants that I had given orders to refuse him entrance to my property. There was my evidence as to what he had said on the verandah, and that he had aimed at me with the twelve-bore. On all that, the magistrate decided it was a case of justifiable homicide. The magistrate never knew the truth. When I shot O'Brien he was carrying the gun under his arm, and that gun was never aimed at me. But I never knew the truth. When he fell on the verandah I found his twelve-bore loaded with buckshot and the hammers at full cock. There is no need for buckshot—to kill snipe, and Mr. O'Brien was, to my knowledge, a very careful shot, a man who always not only put down the hammers but also unloaded when coming to a house. Had he been merely drunk he was all the more likely to carry out an automatic action. A year later my wife died of fever. I sold my plantation and came here, where I remain a prisoner on remand awaiting trial. May I light you to your room? We breakfast at eight. If you care to attend, chapel is at seven-thirty."

"Thank you, sir. But surely—surely, after all these years the case can never be reopened?"

"The case was never really opened, and the trial I await will not be in this world."

# CHAPTER VII

## THE CLINIC

AT the mouth of the Odiel River is the seaport town of Huelva, and after taking my degree at Edinburgh I went there to assist my uncle in his clinic. For nine months of the year the climate was ideal, but during the summer the heat was intense. This he could now escape for grouse-shooting in Scotland, as I would be there to attend to his practice.

In the south of Spain the practice of medicine and surgery was then behind the times, although there were good medical schools in Madrid and Barcelona. Patients from all parts of Andalusia came for treatment to the English clinic. My uncle was a tall, red-haired Scotsman, with blue eyes and a red moustache. He was a good surgeon, a good shot, a good rider and good cricketer. Having pleasant manners, he got on well with the Spaniards, and was shrewd enough to conceal his natural irritation with their foibles in the land of procrastination where he had lived and practised for twenty years. He had been married, but his wife and three children were dead and his eldest sister looked after his house. All his children, on reaching their teens, had died of the same disease—a very rare one.

He lived in a large ground-floor flat in the Hotel Colon. Once this had been a great hotel of four separate buildings surrounding a rectangular garden intersected with paths. It was a garden of palms, pepper, eucalyptus, orange, cherry and apple trees, and the ground was covered with fragrant plants and flowers. In the centre was a fountain. Now the hotel was converted into flats and offices, occupied by the English colony. My uncle's flat was in the front building. The lower floor of the building at the other end of the garden contained a billiard-room and a large ball-room. Beyond this again were four hard tennis courts, stables, and a field. The hotel stood on a small hill above the level of the adjoining streets. All the ground around it was enclosed and at night was patrolled by an armed guard.

The clinic was in a street at the other end of the town. It was an old house with a patio in the centre. The operating-theatre, consulting-room, laboratory and single rooms were on the upper floor. On the ground level was a small ward of six beds for poorer people, and the kitchen. The catering was simple, because every patient had to arrange for a relative, friend, or servant to provide meals. There was an English sister and two Spanish male nurses—father and son—who lived on the premises.

My work at the clinic was both varied and interesting.

One morning we went in a steam launch to a village up the river to see a boy of eight who had dislocated his right elbow in a fall from a donkey. He was lying in bed in a room on the street level, with a crowd of people looking through the window. They blocked out the light and had to be moved away before the patient could be examined. The boy's mother insisted on remaining in the room. Chloroform was needed, and on the way my uncle had told me to let the Spanish doctor give it, but to keep an eye on him, as he had probably never given it before. Consequently there was the following conversation:

*Me:* Señor, as a favour, will you give the chloroform?

*Doctor:* Señor, it will be a pleasure to see you give the chloroform.

*Me:* Señor, I kiss your hand. You give the chloroform.

*Doctor:* Señor, I kiss your feet. You give the chloroform.

*Me:* For the love of God, Señor, you give the chloroform.

The doctor placed the mask over the nose and mouth, removed the stopper from the eight-ounce bottle, and then poured half the contents over the child's face. The child yelled; his mother shrieked, fainted, and fell on the floor; the doctor dropped the bottle and rushed to attend her. As I continued the anæsthesia the doctor was dragging the prostrate mother by the shoulders out of the room. When he returned the manipulation was completed. I asked him for some olive oil, and he helped me to put it into the child's eyes. He was probably quite unaware that anything unusual had happened. Then we went into the dining-room for *desayuno*. There was a *queso* or cheese which was new to me—made from sheep's milk—and I said that I liked it very much. At once the doctor left the table and ran out in the blazing sun to a farm half a mile away to get another cheese. This he gave me as a parting gift. In Andalusia you are always asked if you like your food—and expected to say that you do.

A grand consultation is when the doctor in attendance invites to the house every available doctor who has ever at any time treated the patient or his relatives. In the case of a man with a hernia my uncle advised the doctor and relatives that immediate operation was required. But the relatives wanted a consultation, and at two in the afternoon eight of us were round the patient's dining-room table. The oldest doctor took the chair—he had attended the patient at birth. Being the youngest I was asked to speak first, but had nothing to say except that I agreed with my uncle. It is a wise rule that men should speak in order of juniority, lest the honesty of youth be smothered by the experience of age. Then a young doctor spoke for ten minutes on hernias and their treatment. Upstairs was a man who had needed operation for the last thirty-six hours. When all had spoken, the operation was agreed upon, and three of them waited to see it. Afterwards came much handshaking, many pattings on the back and congratulations. On these occasions a fee is paid, not only to the doctor in attendance, but to all the doctors invited to the house.

Ships of many nations came into the river, and each paid

an inclusive fee for medical services in port. From nine until eleven o'clock sailors who could attend were seen at the clinic, others were visited on board, and serious cases admitted as in-patients. One of these was a young Scottish engineer, brought in badly burnt. A paraffin lamp had exploded at the end of a gangway alongside the engine-room and the passage was set ablaze. Beyond the flames was the chief engineer's cabin, cut off by the fire. Thinking his chief was asleep, the young assistant went through the flames to rouse him, found the man was not in his cabin, and came back through the fire. More than a third of his body was burnt and death was almost certain. One morning he had been visited by the chaplain attached to the English colony in the town, and that afternoon, as I was dressing his burns, he said: "I know I'm going to die, and I'm wondering if there's anything to be frightened about afterwards. D'ye think I'll be punished for my sins?"

"Were you talking to the parson this morning?"

"Aye, but I did not understand what he was saying. Maybe I was sleepy."

"There's nothing to be frightened about. Whatever happens to the rest of us you'll never be punished. Men have got the V.C. for less than you did."

"Eh?"

"You've done the greatest thing a man can do—you've given your life for your friend; and you know what the Bible says: 'Greater love hath no man than this that he lay down his life for his friend.'"

"I never thought of that."

"Think of it now."

"Aye."

Next day he was dead, and at this time I who reassured him was an agnostic.

> Parson and doctor!—don't they love rarely
> Fighting the devil in other men's fields.

Fear is a painful state of consciousness. In moments of danger it arises from the sudden perception of anything immediately antagonistic to the will to live. But the fear of death, known to all mankind, comes to young and healthy people far removed from natural death. They wake at night and think of the time when they will cease to be, and of their bodies, now warm and comfortable, as a mass of cold, putrid corruption from which even those who love them would recoil. It is no consolation, whatever poets may say, to know that eventually the ashes of our bodies may nourish a rose, or blades of grass. "Man does not fear death," says Renan, "he fears annihilation." That is only a half-truth, because it is possible to fear what survival after death may bring. To banish the fear of death it is necessary to think : "I shall not be there; the dead body I have pictured is not me." The truth of that thought is universally accepted, because it is self-evident. The materialist says: "That corpse is not me because it is dead, and when I am dead I cease to be." He may be left with the fear of annihilation, and to banish that fear it is necessary to think: "That dead body is not me, because at the moment of death my spirit left it." That is part of the Faith. But if a man shall say: "I don't care two hoots what happens to my body; you may drag it by the hind leg and bury it in a hole in the garden," then he is a heretic, because the body was the temple of a spirit, and deserves the respect that is due to an ancient ruin.

The fear of death arising from anticipation appears to be more painful and disagreeable than the act of dying. A most acute and distressing fear sometimes overcomes those who are ill, but there is seldom any sign of fear in those who are dying, even for days. Priests of the Roman Church, who see more of death than doctors, are of the same opinion. When a sick person is afraid, their death is not imminent, and when death is overtaking them there is no fear. A few have no fear at any time and welcome death with a smile.

I have twice seen that smile, once on the face of an old Highland woman waiting, as she said, "for the call," and again on the face of a nun dying at the age of twenty-five. A vision of Paradise had lit that smile. The unbeliever may welcome death as a relief from the pain of life, but he does not greet it with a smile. Nor does any suicide, nor even those who go to war with the hope to die—with honour.

Only once have I seen a deathbed where some who attended were shocked. That was in a sanatorium. The dying man had been a gold-miner in South Africa, but from scraps of conversation he had probably known other callings. He was a taciturn man, breaking off in the middle of any talk that might give an inkling into his past, and at times his face wore a mask-like expression that is often seen on the faces of those who have been in prison for a long time. He had no visitors, and only once received a letter. This he handed unopened to the nurse, and asked her to burn it in the ward fire. In doing so she noticed that the envelope had an Australian stamp, and that the handwriting was that of a woman. One day he spoke to me more than usual.

"I'm very uncomfortable. It's the weakness. I can only last a day or two longer, and then I'll be dead. The world's all right, but I made a hellish mess of it. I'll be glad to be dead. There's nothing after, and I'll be dead as a stone. All I want you to do is to give me an overdose of morphia. Will you?"

I told him he could have all the morphia he wanted to make him comfortable, but not an overdose. He became silent. Here was a man who did not fear annihilation. A few mornings later he was sinking, and in the afternoon they sent for me. He was very weak, and matron and nurse were beside the bed. His voice was a hoarse whisper, and I had to lean over to hear what he said.

"Will you do me a favour?"

"Anything I can."

"Will you give me a cigarette and a whisky and soda?"

I fetched a cigarette, a three-finger glass of whisky, and the siphon. When the mixture was the right colour he nodded, and nurse propped up his shoulders a little. He got the cigarette to his parched blue lips and I lit it, but after a puff he dropped it and shook his head. An emaciated arm reached for the whisky, and I helped him to get the glass to his mouth. He sipped it and nodded. Then he took a gulp, stared round for a moment, slipped sideways, and was dead. The sudden stimulus of the whisky on an empty stomach had stopped the exhausted heart.

The matron and nurse were very distressed. They seemed to think that the cigarette and whisky had jeopardised this man's immortal soul. "What a terrible death! To die with a cigarette and whisky!" said the matron, and shed a few tears. The man had carried his secrets to the grave. Whatever his life may have been, his dying thoughts would have been bitter had his last request been refused.

Sailors of many nationalities came to the clinic, and I thought that those from Northern Europe bore pain more stoically than those from the Mediterranean. Most of their illness was venereal, contracted in ports. The men land after a voyage, fit and with money. They go to a low *posada* near the quay to have a drink, which consists of bar leavings —all the liquor left in the glasses emptied into a barrel, from which sailors are supplied. One or two glasses, and they have lost control. When venereal disease is. contracted from another race its virulence is intensified, and the disease becomes as severe as it was in England at the time when Fielding described it in *Tom Jones*. Much has been done by seamen's institutes to allay the sailor's temptations ashore, but the difficulty is to find the right type of paid worker to run these places. If the wrong man is appointed, very soon he becomes a *souteneur*.

Pity the bird that has wandered!
Pity the sailor ashore!
Hurry him home to the ocean,
Let him come here no more!

There was one German captain who arrived holding his hand to his jaw. He had a bad tooth which he wanted me to extract. I gave him the name and address of a good Spanish dentist. "No," he said. "I prefer the doctor. I like the doctor to take out my tooth." I told him that dentists were much better at this than doctors. "No, I like the doctor best."

It was a shocking fang—large, firm, decayed, and so inflamed that the local anæsthetic had little effect. I put on the forceps and began. He gave a yell and rose from the chair. The forceps slipped, and round the room he went, holding his jaw. In a minute he was back, and sat down. "I am sorry, I will do better next time, doctor."

Again there was a yell, a breakaway, and round the room he went bellowing, with the tooth as firm as ever. Back he came to the chair. "Doctor, I will do better."

But I put the forceps aside and sent him off to the dentist.

Next morning he returned smiling and laid three dollars on the table. "I thank you, doctor, very much."

I told him there was nothing for which to thank me, still less for which to pay a fee.

"Oh, no," said he, "if I pay the dentist I pay the doctor. The dentist get the tooth out, but the doctor make it loose." And off he went, leaving the fee on the table.

This German captain was not unique. Even in England three people at different times have told me they prefer a doctor to extract their teeth, and there must be others. Noble people! I admire you. You have the faith that moves mountains, even if it fails to move teeth, and so I shall tell you something to your advantage. There are qualified dentists who are also qualified doctors. Go to one and you will find a doctor who can and will extract your teeth. And do not tell me that if a doctor is also a qualified dentist he is *ipso facto* less capable of extracting your teeth, or I shall cease to admire you and may even begin to think you are foolish.

Next day the German captain called again and asked me to go to his ship to see the cook who was ill. "He say he have the dropsy—the water round the stomach. He cannot work, and will stay in the bunk until he get to Hamburg."

I sterilised a large trocar—a metal tube containing a circular stiletto—put dressings in my bag, and off we went. The cook was one of the fattest men I have ever seen. He lay on his back and groaned gently. By reason of the fat it was difficult to know whether or not there was fluid inside. I was in doubt, but then cook had told the captain that fluid had been there before. One could but try. Having disinfected the skin I held the trocar like a dagger two feet above his abdomen and stabbed hard. But I had under-estimated the depth of fat. The cook, with a yell, sat up and dragged the implement out of himself and out of my hands. Clad in his shirt he was out of his bunk and out of the cabin before I had time to pick up the trocar. On deck above me there arose a hullabaloo, in which sounds of scuffling could be distinguished, and much shouting in the languages of Germany and of Spain. Then cook returned to his cabin, escorted by two *carabineros* with slung rifles, and followed by the captain. The *carabineros* had been on guard on the quay to stop any smuggling from the ship. One of them had once been a patient in the clinic, and both offered to hold cook down on the floor if I wanted to do anything to him. "This most wicked and ungrateful one," they called him. Meanwhile cook was telling captain in German that now all was well and that cooking would be resumed at once. So eager was he to return to duty that the *carabineros* had some difficulty in persuading him to allow me even to dress the stab-wound made by the trocar. Once again the captain thanked me. "You are very good, doctor," he said, and as I left the ship the *carabineros* never even asked me to open my bag.

There are good and bad cooks in every country, and at nine o'clock one morning an English cook was brought to the clinic by his captain. At first glance I thought the captain was the patient. He looked pale and shaken. That morning when he and the two mates were sitting at table waiting for breakfast the cook had rushed in with a blood-stained handkerchief over his mouth, and had coughed blood all over the white tablecloth. Apart from the shock, the captain was concerned that a consumptive cook should proceed in the ship on a long voyage to South America. It would be better to have him sent home to England. On examining the man I found nothing to account for hæmorrhage. I asked questions, and his answers aroused my suspicions. Then from his pocket he produced the handkerchief drenched with blood. That hanged him. Squeezing out a drop on to a glass slide I put it under the microscope, and saw the blood of a bird. Taking the cook into the next room I told him that unless he admitted his deception and told me from what bird he had got the blood I would order him a mixture to be taken under the captain's supervision every two hours, and so potent that it would cure any tendency to consumption, or indeed to any other illness except sea-sickness. It turned out he had decapitated one of the fowls carried on board! What the captain said when he heard this cannot be printed, and later on the two mates were probably equally voluble. *Moral*: Test your own evidence before you produce it.

On a German cargo-boat I found three sailors with typhoid fever. All the water-tanks were infected, and, from the captain's account, nearly every one on board must have had the disease. Two he had buried at sea. The three sailors were removed to the *lazaretto*, a small fever hospital two miles outside the town, and twice daily I rode out to see them. They were the only patients there. I knew no German and the sailors no English or Spanish. To explain why they were being starved, I showed them two words in an English-German dictionary—bread and death. Each man nodded his head and said "Ja."

The next day I found that the Spanish male nurse in charge of the *lazaretto* had given my patients old English magazines which had been left there three months before by English sailors who had smallpox. On the third day I looked at the male nurse and said: "Señor, do you know what is the matter with you?"

"Si, señor, *viruelas* (smallpox), and my wife and two children are also ill. I think the youngest is going to die." She was, for she had black smallpox.

Then I turned to the man. "And you are nursing these German sailors with typhoid fever!"

"Si, señor, I do my duty."

"Your duty!" I shouted. "In England you would be in jail."

Late that afternoon he walked into the town, saw the civil governor, and complained of my having said that a poor man with smallpox ought to be in jail. The next day I re-vaccinated myself with Spanish lymph, and when that did not take, telegraphed to Paris and London for other supplies. The German consul told me that the three sailors had been re-vaccinated a year ago.

The *lazaretto* was not the only evidence of a local lack of interest in public health. Every street in the town had its own peculiar smell, so peculiar that a blind man could have passed down them without a stick. Their odours became so great that reform could no longer be delayed, and a local contractor suggested to the municipal council a Simple Plan whereby all malodorous vapours could be subdued, namely, that he should be given a contract to cover the gratings of all the street drains with cement. This was done, and all went well for a couple of months. Then in the middle of the night came a tropical storm. I was wakened by the noise of thunder and torrents of rain. The Hotel Colon stood on a hill, and, on opening the inner shutters of my window, I saw a fearful sight. The sky was one blaze of lightning, and below, in what had been a street, I saw a roaring torrent of water, on which flotsam and jetsam, some of it supporting human beings, was being swept towards the river, and on the bank of this torrent houses were collapsing. At dawn, instead of a street, there was a ravine thirty feet deep. That day the inventor of anti-smell concrete covering for street drains was lodged in jail, and there also should have been the municipal council.

Once a week, at night, lepers came to the clinic. They could not be seen during the day, as the other patients would have objected to their presence. Five of them had nodules on the fingers and toes, but one girl of twenty-three had these swellings on her lower jaw and nose. This gave her the *facies leontasis* (the face of the lion). As a child of six she had lived in the same house as an old leper, and ten years later the disease had appeared. Most of them knew when, in the past, they had come into contact with leprosy, and there was usually an interval of seven to ten years before it appeared. I removed pus from the nodules, sterilised it, and once a week injected it into a goat. At the end of two months, blood was taken from a vein in the goat's neck, and the serum injected into the lepers. The idea was to make the goat immune to leprosy bacilli, and then transfer this immunity to the patients. It was a failure, and the serum had no effect on the disease. Once a test-tube of leprous pus broke and the glass cut the back of my little finger. I treated the cut, but for many years took a great interest in the scar that was left.

The goat was a nanny-goat, and at six every evening I milked her in a shed at the foot of the garden. After a week or two I found little milk to remove, and thought the inoculations were stopping its production. But one afternoon on going to the milking an hour earlier than usual I discovered the true cause.

*Me:* You! What do you want?

*Man:* Señor, I am a very poor man, and I was only taking a little of the milk from Your Excellency's goat.

*Me:* Your can is nearly full.

*Man:* Never, señor, it is only half-full.

*Me:* You may have all the milk. You may milk that goat every night.

*Man:* Señor, I kiss your hands and your feet. Many, many, many thanks.

*Me:* Do you know what is the matter with that goat?

*Man:* No, señor, the goat looks well. It is a fine goat. It is the best goat in the town. The milk from Your Excellency's goat is very rich.

*Me:* Into that goat I have put "el mal de San Lazaro."

*Man (dropping can and bolting from shed):* Muerte de Dios! Muerte de Dios! (Death of God!)

How wonderful if I had found a cure for leprosy! And how lucrative! A Russian prince with his retinue, on arriving in Seville had gone to the best hotel. In the hall he was met by the manager. "Your Highness, I am most sorry, but you cannot stay here. My other guests would leave instantly."

"Let them leave," said the prince. "I take the whole hotel."

What would not such a man give to be cured of leprosy? All, all that a man hath will he give for his life. And had that story and text kindled my interest in the poor lepers of Huelva? God only knows.

99

I made another experiment. Leprosy occurs in Spain and in Norway, countries in which dried fish is a staple food, and some had suggested that it was a fish-borne disease. I inoculated six Spanish trout with living leprosy bacilli from the lepers. On leaving Spain I brought the trout back to Scotland, where my mother looked after them. As each one died it was sent to the Professor at Aberdeen for examination. In none of them were any leprosy bacilli detected, and one had lived for two years after being inoculated.

In Huelva I wished to start a voluntary Tuberculosis Dispensary on the lines of that founded by Professor Calmette at Lille. One of the doctors in the town had received a legacy of four hundred pounds to be given to a medical charity of his choice, and he was very willing that the money should go towards the dispensary. Other people also promised money, and we formed a small committee. One day there was a letter from the civil governor to say that he warmly approved of our project, and so great was his interest in the fight against tuberculosis that he wished to be president of the committee. All my little committee and their promises of money silently faded away.

Open corruption ran throughout the underpaid public services of Spain, with one exception—the civil guards, who were unbribable. There was my friend, Señor M——, a merry little man with twinkling brown eyes and grey hair. He was a collector of taxes with a salary of two hundred pounds a year, yet his carriage was drawn by two Arab stallions, and whenever I wanted to borrow a horse he had always one to lend. That was a great token of friendship, because there is a Spanish saying: "Lend everything to your friend except your horse, your gun or your wife."

But all things, good and bad, must come to an end, and one evening the military governor called on Señor M——.

"You and I, M——, are old friends, but I have in my

pocket a warrant for your arrest. I will show it to you. It is not issued by the Provincial Government, but from Madrid, and must be executed. It says that you have taken twenty thousand pounds in ten years."

"Never, never! Twenty thousand pounds! No. It might have been ten thousand pounds, but twenty! Never! I speak the truth."

"My friend, I believe you. But this warrant is from Madrid, and I must do something. The best I can do is to give you forty-eight hours' start. In that time you can put two Provinces between you and me, and if you tell me where you are going I shall be searching for you elsewhere."

"Señor, you are my very good friend, but if you think I am going to run you are mistaken. The judge is also my very good friend, and I stay here."

He stayed, was tried, and acquitted.

There are degrees of infamy, and corruption in Spain was open and taken for granted. The only man who tempted me there was an Englishman, the travelling representative of a large firm of London contractors. He came to Huelva after having contracted a contagious disease in Seville. This malady annoyed him very much, because he had paid ten pounds in the hope of avoiding it. I treated him at his hotel for a fortnight, and before leaving he called at the clinic to settle his account. I told him it was twenty-five pounds, and he produced his wallet. As I was making out a receipt, he said: "Make the receipt for forty pounds and I'll give you thirty."

Being unused to the ways of high finance I asked: "But why? The account is twenty-five pounds."

"A matter of business," he replied. "You are running this practice for your uncle who is away. You account to him for twenty-five pounds. If I give you thirty pounds that is five pounds for yourself. On your receipt the firm pays me forty pounds, and that's ten pounds for me."

I told him all fees went into the practice, and that my receipt would be for what he paid.

"All right, have it your own way. Make it out for twenty-five pounds. You'll never make money. And what are you smiling at?"

So I told him. "You're the first man I've met who's tried to make money out of this disease." That news annoyed him, and, having paid his bill, he left the room without saying good-bye.

All national corruption eventually oppresses the poor, and in Huelva some of the local taxes were farmed out to syndicates, as in the time of Herod. One syndicate paid a lump sum for the right to collect the tax on market produce entering the town. To recover their capital, with interest at from fifteen to twenty per cent., they increased the amount of the tax. An old countrywoman bringing her basket of eggs to market had to hand over two out of every fifteen eggs to the syndicate's collector. As the previous syndicate had taken one egg out of ten, the old woman grumbled, and there was a rise in the price of eggs in the market. Under greyer, colder skies these eggs might have hatched out a revolution, but in that warm, amiable climate, very few people were interested in how they were governed.

Among the few who worked for a reformation was the editor of *El Mundo*, an anti-clerical and a republican. On Sunday afternoons he addressed small meetings, which had to be held in the *campo* outside the town. At these meetings the red flag was flown and the "Marseillaise" sung, but one night over a cup of coffee in the Cercle he imparted startling information.

"Señor, your uncle has been twenty years in this town. What is going to happen to-morrow will not affect him. To-morrow there will be a rising throughout Spain and Portugal, and by evening the Iberian Republic will be proclaimed. The signal for the people to rise will be the assassination of the King of Portugal on the Spanish frontier. He knows he is in danger in Lisbon, and to-morrow will seek safety in Spain. He will set out for the Villa Viciosa, near Seville, the home of his mother-in-law, the Countess of Paris. He will never get there. He will be killed at the frontier and so will the Crown Prince. The Queen will be spared and the younger son. The other two deserve death. The King of Spain! No, he will not be assassinated, but deposed. To-morrow will bring the Republic."

All this was news that thrilled. I had always longed to be in Ruritania, and the next best thing to assisting in the restoration of a monarchy was to take part in deposing one. Next day nothing happened, but a week later, at night, a fleet of motor cars passed through Huelva on their way to Seville. That morning the King and Crown Prince had been assassinated in Lisbon, and the Queen with her family fled to the protection of the Spanish Court, then at Seville.

The popularity of the King of Spain was a barrier against revolution. It was an absolute monarchy, in the sense that the King could veto any act of his parliament, but the monarch himself was the most democratic in Europe. Every subject had the right of access to the Throne, if he desired to petition the King, who was generally spoken of as Don Alfonso. All this was in harmony with the old Spanish saying: "The beggar has the right to ask the King for a light." The courage of their King was also beyond dispute. When dynamiters were busy in Barcelona, the Prime Minister begged the King to cancel a visit to that city, where the Premier was not popular.

"No," said Don Alfonso. "I am going to Barcelona. I shall drive through the streets in an open carriage, and you, my Prime Minister, shall sit beside me."

At this time the city of Barcelona was in a state of nervous tension. The object of the dynamiters was unknown, and if people saw a leather bag on the pavement they became panic-stricken lest it contained a bomb. Whenever a motor car back-fired, passengers in tram cars would jump to their feet. One bomb had exploded at the door of a little sweet-shop kept by an old woman, and the victims were usually simple, harmless folk whose presence in the world could not have interested anyone outside their own circle. There were many opinions as to who was responsible. Some said the Government of Catalonia had arranged these outrages in order to force the Cabinet in Madrid to grant self-government to the most progressive province of Spain. Others said the Cabinet in Madrid were the guilty party, the bombs being intended to make the world think that Catalonia was not fit for self-government. International anarchists were also suspected, likewise the Pretender, Don Jaime, and some maintained that the whole affair was the work of Jesuits.

The Provincial Government was making every effort to detect the criminals. Large numbers of the civil guard had been drafted into the city. These troops in some ways resembled the old Royal Irish Constabulary. All the men were of good physique, and no man served in the Province where he had been born. On their loyalty the Crown could rely, and their vigilance, as I discovered, had now been increased by the most extraordinary measures. I had travelled from Madrid and reached Barcelona at eleven-thirty one night. On the platform was a civil guard, a magnificent figure in his dark blue uniform with red facings, and three-cornered hat also faced with red. He was armed with a sword and revolver. Wishing to find a cab, I went up to him and said: "Señor, el favor, donde está un coche?"

To which he answered: "Cab, sir? The rank's first on the left outside the station."

"Good heavens," I exclaimed, "but you're from London!

Bow Bells! What on earth are you doing in the civil guard?"

"Well, sir, you see we're just keeping an eye on you even out here!"

"Yes, but what's the real idea?"

"Dynamite."

# CHAPTER VIII

## SEÑORITAS

ON most mornings I was awakened by the pawing of a horse on the gravel path below my window, and went for a ride in the cool, brilliant early sunshine into the *campo*, along roads that were cart-tracks between low cactus hedges, through groves of olive and orange trees, and past fields where oxen were dragging the wooden plough as in the time of Christ. Then back, to call for hot water (*agua caliente*), a bath and breakfast. The Spanish saddle with its lining of sheepskin and broad stirrups is very comfortable. In front is a high pommel, and the cantle is also high. This protects the rider if the horse falls and rolls over, whereas, with an English hunting-saddle the rider is more likely to be thrown clear of the horse. My horse, a hired one, was brought round by an evil-looking ruffian, who during the season was a *picador* in the bull-ring. He was a little man with a most disagreeable countenance, and we referred to him as "Little Pic." One morning he produced a horse which I soon discovered had the habit of bringing down the off-hind hoof out of step at all paces. This constant jolting of the spine brought me back with a headache, and I told *picador* that the horse was no good. At this he spat on his hands, clapped them together, and swore by most of the hierarchy of heaven that it was the best horse in the town. Then I called him a shameless liar, and when I said "Mentiroso sin verguenza," he scowled and led the horse away. My uncle said it was unwise to have used the words "sin verguenza," and that if I had added one phrase—the Spanish equivalent of the English "You have no guts"—Little Pic would probably have drawn his knife. That night at eleven o'clock I was walking in the Calle Concepcion, a paved street for pedestrians only, and among the people coming along I saw Little Pic. Yes, it was a pity about the words "sin verguenza," but perhaps *picador* would pass without seeing me. No; *picador* had seen me and was rapidly approaching. It was really a great pity about those words. . . . Then he rushed and struck me across the chest with his open hand. I gave a shout and landed a blow with my right fist on *picador's* left shoulder. He stepped back, apparently surprised, and now there were people standing round us. "Señor!" he exclaimed, then darted at me again and pulled out of my breast pocket a smouldering handkerchief, which ash from my badly-made cigarette had set on fire. I thanked Little Pic most cordially, apologised for hitting him, then we took off our hats and shook hands. The next morning he produced a good horse.

Near the clinic was a convent, a plain building with vertical iron bars across the windows and a massive door studded with iron nails. On one side of the door was an iron grid, closed by a shutter on the inside. The shutter was drawn aside when anyone knocked, and the caller was recognised before the door was opened. It looked like the entrance to a prison, and as unfriendly.

Our neighbours were Little Sisters of the Poor, one of the humblest and noblest communities in the Church. They shelter the aged who are destitute and visit the sick who are poor. In Huelva there were a number of poor families, some so poor that they lived in caves hewn out of the face of a large hill on the outskirts of the town. The Sisters who help them are also poor and must beg for their friends. In all large towns in Europe you may see them, sometimes standing for alms at the doors of Catholic churches, or carrying away leavings of food from the large hotels and restaurants. The Mother Superior brought Sister Teresa to see me. She had pain in her right knee. It was swollen and hurt her when she walked, especially on the cobbles. At night there was pain when she went to bed. She had a tuberculous joint, which meant months in bed and weekly inoculations. At these visits she was always cheerful and working, either sewing or doing drawn thread work—in which threads are drawn out of a sheet of linen until it has a beautiful open pattern like heavy lace.

She it was who told me the story of Don Pedro's dream. Don Pedro, a rich old man, was a benefactor much eulogised by the Mother Superior, and at one of his visits he said: "Mother, I dreamed of you last night."

"Yes," said she, "and what was your dream?"

"I dreamed that you and I were walking along a narrow path with a ditch on either side. On my side the ditch was full of mud, but the one on your side was full of honey."

"Yes," smiled the Mother Superior.

"It was the path to Heaven, and we were warned not to fall into the ditch on either side. But I fell into the mud and you into the honey. We scrambled out and went on until we reached the Gates of Heaven. When Peter came out, he said: 'How dare you two present yourselves in this disgraceful state, one covered with mud, the other with honey!' We told him what had happened, and then he said we might come in, but only on one condition."

"Which was?" she cried eagerly.

"That first we licked each other clean."

When the time came for me to leave Spain, the nuns gave me presents—coloured pictures of saints on little thin cards—and hoped I would always keep them because they had been blessed by the Pope. Was this superstition? Did they really believe that a Pope's blessing gave to a scrap of paper something that was not there before? I never asked them. The little cards were soon mislaid and it was many years before I learnt that the blessing of a thing is the prayer of the Church that good may come to its owner. We value a book in which a friend has written, "With best wishes," although the wishes are not in the book but in the mind of our friend. Sister Teresa gave me a silk handkerchief with a floral design and the word "Hilario" in one corner; so fine was the design that it might have been imprinted, but it was sewn by hand and the thread was a girl's hair—not Sister Teresa's, for hers was cropped. She must have sewn for many hours. By the nuns I was called Don Hilario, by others Don Enrique, for nobody could translate my most unchristian Christian name.

I had arrived in Spain during Carnival, and one night there was a Ball at the Cercle to which some of the English colony were asked. The ballroom was lit by Chinese lanterns and round the room were seats for the mothers and duennas, to whom the girls returned after every dance. It was here that again I met Inés, the child who had ridden behind me on a donkey five years before, and was now a woman. Her beauty was of a type rare in Southern Spain. She was a pale beauty, that is, her hair, which curled in rich waves, her eyebrows and eyelashes were a chestnut brown, but her eyes were blue, and in complexion she was pale, except for the rose colour of her cheeks and the deeper crimson of her lips. The chin may have been a trifle full and her mouth a little wide, but behind the lips were perfect teeth. She was of medium height, her figure had grown in symmetry, and in her walk and carriage was the grace of a queen. She walked well, and, like all Spanish girls, danced the Sevillana, which is the most graceful dance after the minuet. The new American dances she despised.

"Why should we of the white race take our music or our dances from the negro?"

In the course of the evening the room became very warm, and so I said: "Es usted caliente?" meaning to ask if she felt the heat. In an instant she left me and returned to her mother, whose face rapidly assumed the forbidding expression of a disinheriting aunt. The British vice-consul had seen the incident and asked me what I had said.

"Good heavens!" he said, "you used the wrong word. You ought to have said 'Tiene usted calor?' 'Caliente' is never used with the verb *ser*—in polite society. I'll go and tell them you don't know the language."

This he did, and Inés returned to dance. But he was not so noble as I thought him. In a few days I realised only too well that his entire lack of discretion made him totally unfit to hold any position whatever in His Britannic Majesty's Consular Service. People would stop me in the street and ask: "How's your Spanish getting on?" and, on getting a civil answer, would add, "Can you yet ask for hot water in the morning?"

Later that evening I danced with a sportive young Irishwoman, Mrs. O'Grady, who told me that Mrs. Portman, with whom I had not danced, thought I was dancing a lot with Inés. Mrs. Portman was a stout and kindly soul of over fifty and lived for her "At Home" day. Life was kindest to her when those of the English colony who came to her afternoon teas were above the average, either in numbers or in social status. Each lady in the English colony had her "At Home" day, in which she took a just and honest pride. I say a just and honest pride, and let no highbrow, icy smile or lowbrow coarse guffaw mar these simple pleasures. We are all the same. You, madam, preened your feathers when the Duchess of Haltingtowers arrived at last, and you, sir, when the Cabinet Minister came to dine. Yes, I know all about it, for if you've told me once you've told me a hundred times. But Mrs. Portman had her faults. She had lived fifteen years in Spain without learning the language. At times she seemed to be under the impression that Spain was a British colony, and had said that I went about too much with the "natives," including Inés' family, who held, as an heirloom, the signet and poison ring of that Duke of Medina who sailed with the Armada.

After the ball I escorted seven ladies back to the English quarter. It was a dark night, all the street lamps were out, and we drove in a ramshackle closed *coche*—a bus seating four on either side. My aunt and I were the last to get in, and sat facing each other on either side of the door at the back. My aunt was an elderly lady who, in appearance, dress, and, some said, manner, resembled Queen Victoria. Inside the coach it was too dark to see anyone, but when I was tickled lightly in the ribs I guessed that the sportive Mrs. O'Grady was beside me. I tickled her in return, and received a rather strenuous nudge from her elbow. Evidently the lady was in a playful mood. Then she tickled me in earnest, and I retaliated with zest, selecting a point below the arm and above what felt like a pair of whalebone stays—only to receive from her elbow a most severe blow which struck me over the heart. The woman must have been out of her senses. The whole business had ceased to be a jest, if indeed it ever was one, and I pitied her husband. As a boy at school I had learnt:

O, Woman! In our hours of ease,
Uncertain, coy, and hard to please,

but the fool beside me had as much idea of coyness as the clown in a harlequinade. It was a most severe blow, and the next morning there was a bruise. I leaned forward, looked out of the window, and the woman, being ignored, ceased from her folly. When the coach stopped at the gates of the Hotel Colon I got out and assisted my aunt to descend. Mrs. Portman followed, and as I held out my hand to help her, she raised her umbrella and struck me across the forearm.

"Don't dare to touch me, you are no gentleman. Mr. Portman shall hear of this to-night."

Then came the ringing voice of my aunt. "Mrs. Portman, you forget yourself. *My* nephew could *never* behave otherwise than as a gentleman."

And again the accusing voice of Mrs. Portman, now almost in tears. "He insulted me in that coach. See if he denies it. Ask him."

But no opportunity for anybody to ask him anything could be granted. The present situation was untenable and unexplainable. It was now long past midnight, and Don Hilario, the friend of nuns, turned and fled. And as he went there came from inside that Cimmerian, hearse-like coach the ghastly sound of Irish laughter from she who had been sitting on the other side of Mrs. Portman!

As I ran up the avenue towards the main entrance of the hotel I remembered that my aunt had the key. No matter; that morning I had seen a small ladder lying beside a flower-bed in the garden. With the ladder on my shoulder I ran round the corner of the building and tried to enter by my bedroom window. The window, a French one, was locked on the inside, so I left the ladder there, returned to the main entrance and awaited my aunt at the door of the flat. I ran all the way because the night was very cold. When my aunt appeared she handed me the key in silence, and I opened the door. In the hall, before marching to her room, she spoke. "I have told Mrs. Portman that anything she *thought* might have happened in the coach was owing to the jolting. I also reminded her of the text, 'Judge not, that ye be not judged.'" Safe in bed, I laughed. Poor Mrs. Portman! The world must have seemed very upside down to her that night.

Before falling asleep I heard the cry of the *sereno*, or night-watchman, in the street. "Ave Maria Purissima! Es la una media, y sereno" ("Hail, Mary most pure! It is half-past one in the morning, and the night is serene"). With that cry the watchman counted the hours and quarters through the night, and, as the weather was nearly always fine, the word *sereno* came to be identified with the man, and he was called *El Sereno*.

At breakfast next morning I had no reason to laugh when my uncle said: "Someone was very nearly shot dead last night. Did you try to get in by your window? Quite so, and this morning the guard has reported an attempted robbery, He saw a man running in the garden with a ladder. He called to him to stop. He aimed his rifle, but before he could fire the man disappeared round a corner. The guard ran to the other corner to intercept him, but the man escaped. When it was daylight the guard found the man's ladder outside your window. I shall not explain it, because the guard was doing his duty. It is sheer folly to be running about with ladders in the middle of the night, and whenever you hear that word, 'Alta,' it's advisable to stop and stand quite still. It's the only warning you get from any of the armed guards in this country."

That morning the local newspaper, *El Mundo*, had an account of the dance, each girl being described according to her looks in the following scale of beauty: (1) "muy afamada"; (2) "muy brillante"; (3) "muy preciosa"; (4) "muy bonita"; (5) "muy simpatica."

Inés was described as "Muy afamada y brillante," and these personal descriptions must have pleased all the señoritas, except those described as "muy simpatica." Other adjectives were applied to the men, and I was not displeased to read that amongst those present was "el muy ilustre y distinguido medico, Señor Don Enrique."

One evening, a week later, I met Inés, her mother, and the duenna walking in the *plaza*. We spoke, and then walked together, with her mother and the duenna in the rear. She took trouble to improve my Spanish, making me repeat sentences over and over again, and never laughed at my mistakes. She also told me many things that are not in guide-books. Why did well-dressed young men play guitars and sing in the street at night? There was a señorita on a balcony. The young man had never spoken to her, but he admired her. If she liked his looks she would stay on the balcony, but if she did not, then she would go indoors, and then, after a few nights, the young man would come no more. If she liked him she might even come downstairs and speak to him through the iron bars of a window on the ground floor. That explained the Spanish proverb: "The lover lives on iron." Then her father would find out about the young man, and might invite him to coffee at the club. If that interview was satisfactory the young man would be invited to the house. As soon as he crossed the threshold the young man and the señorita were virtually engaged. She had a *novio* and he a *novia*. Surely of all the words in all languages these are the most beautiful in which to designate sweethearts, for in their very sound there is at once novelty and admiration.

Once the two are thus engaged they may go for walks, but always with the mother and duenna behind, and it may be that the man has no opportunity of kissing the girl until they are married. I once asked Inés' mother the reason for this supervision.

"Do you not trust your girls, señora?"

And the answer was: "Señor, we do not trust our men."

Inés thought that English girls had a better life both before and after marriage.

"They play games. I play tennis because my father permits it, but I have aunts who do not approve of a girl playing tennis."

There were other things I wanted to know. Suppose the young man neither played the guitar nor sang, how could he show his admiration for a señorita?

Inés said that was a simple matter. "There are always dances. He can speak to her when dancing, and, if the girl wants to know, there is the language of the fan. There is always a way."

At a dance the girl drops her fan and the young man

picks it up. There are three ways in which he may return it, and each has a meaning. If he returns the fan closed, he does not like her and she is sorry that she ever dropped it. To return the fan half-opened means: "Let us go on as we are, friends for the present." A fan returned full opened is a declaration of love. And the girl gives her answer in the same language. If she uses the fan full open as received she also has declared her love. Otherwise she will just half-close it, or close it altogether. When she receives a half-opened fan she may use it as received, or close it, or even open it herself. One of Inés' friends had opened the fan and the young man had ceased to admire her. It was very stupid of the girl. When a girl had a *novio* she embroidered a handkerchief with her hair. That was hard work, needed good eyesight, and took her many weeks to do. The girl would not grudge the time, because she would be thinking of her *novio*. All these things I learnt from Inés, but she never dropped her fan to me, nor was I ever invited to her house.

Was I in love with Inés? By the canon law of love I was not. I admired her grace and beauty, which differed from that of other Spanish girls. I was always glad to see her, but never counted the days between our meetings. She was attractive, but never once did I dream of her. Neither did I ever sense the fragrance of her hair, and the fragrance of a girl's hair is also the fragrance of her kiss. Nor was there the true basis of love—the desire to know and to be known. Wherein love differs from infatuation.

Among the señoritas was a wind-swept woman: the tall, plain, elderly French governess, Miss Duprez. She was one of those brave, lonely women who earn their living in foreign lands. Once she had been a governess in England and in France; now she taught a few children of the English colony, and also had a finishing class for the señoritas. Her features were plain, her greying hair was brushed straight back, and her usual expression was one of alert anxiety.

She always dressed in black, but at dinner-parties the black of her dress was relieved by a lace scarf covering her thin shoulders. It was at my uncle's parties that I met her, because I, being the youngest and least distinguished male, took her in to dinner. Yet I sent the British vice-consul about his business one night when he remarked to me before dinner: "Hard luck, you've got Miss Duprez." Little did he know that Miss Duprez was more entertaining than any of the pretty and well-dressed women who were there. As soon as she began to enjoy her dinner and to forget the worries of the day, Miss Duprez sparkled. She had the knowledge, wit and gaiety of the educated Frenchwoman. It was she who told me all about the señoritas whom she tried to teach.

"Bah! they are little sillies. I try to teach them English and French and geography, because they know nothing. Do they want to learn? No; they will not attend. All the time they chatter about *novios* and *novias*. It gives me a headache, but I listen, and even then they will not take my advice. There is Carmen; she weeps when she speaks of Gonzales. He will not look at her. She thinks it is because she opened her fan to him at a dance. I tell her she is a little fool. Would any man, worth calling a man, be interested in this silly language of fans? No, he would not. He would despise it. He wants a girl who is intelligent and could be a companion. Do they believe me? No, they do not. They do not care whether the capital of Germany is Berlin or Vienna. I tell them that no Englishman would ever marry any of them unless they learn. How they chatter, chatter, when I say that! Oh, yes, they are pretty; they are beautiful little animals. But when they are thirty where is their grace and beauty? They take no exercise and get fat. If they are married they do not mind. They have that proverb which so pleased your aunt. Hush! She cannot hear me, so I will tell you. She went to be photographed, and asked the man if her cap was straight. The man knew she was a widow with two sons. So he bowed to make her a compliment, and said: 'Señora, in Spain it is enough to be a mother.' No, your aunt was not pleased; she was very indignant. But yes, all Spanish girls are not the same, that is true. If you go to Madrid you will meet Spanish girls who have been educated in Paris or in London. That is another thing. I have been speaking of the girls you know in this town—but you will never tell them what I said. I have told you the truth." Dear Miss Duprez! You were my first and only duenna.

One night the Amateur Dramatic Society produced a play in the local theatre. The performance was in aid of the Jesuit schools, and Inés had a small speaking part. Afterwards I was invited to have supper with the players in a hotel near the theatre, and the civil governor presided over a gay table. All the players were in their stage costumes. After supper every girl was given a large box of chocolates, and every man a box of cigars. Everybody looked very happy except the Father Superior of the Jesuits. He was probably the only person there who had the slightest interest in education. He was a little man with large spectacles, his face that of a scholar; and all the evening his countenance was overshadowed with the pale cast of thought. Nor did he look much happier when the civil governor made a most eloquent and impassioned speech on education, on schools, and on Jesuit schools in particular. Why did the Jesuit look so unhappy?

"Oh," said Inés, "he is thinking of the money. Yes, yes, the theatre was full, and there was a lot of money, but—look at this supper, and there is also the civil governor."

Inés was right, and Father Superior was even sadder next day when he called on the civil governor to ask how much money had been collected.

"Money?" said the governor. "That is the very sad

news I have to tell you. There is no money: the expenses were so great. I myself am out of pocket."

On the eve of my leaving Spain there was a dance in the Casa Colon, and, as I was dressing, my uncle entered my room and addressed me as "Sir." Whenever he did so I knew that there was trouble brewing.

"Look here, sir, I suppose you know that Inés and her people are coming to the dance to-night? Very good! All I have got to say is that I hope you intend to dance as much with that girl to-night as you have done in the past. It would be a pretty poor show if you slighted her. People have been talking. You are going away, but I have got to live here, and that girl's family are as proud as Lucifer. That's all."

My aunt received the guests in an ante-room, where a Spanish maid announced their names. Two German ladies arrived together, as their husbands were coming on later. These Germans had made money, the one by making scent and the other by making artificial manure. Their factories were on adjoining properties in the *campo*; and each on his property had built a beautiful villa. The scent manufacturer called his house the "Villa Fragancia," which the Spaniards accepted as a most appropriate name. The manure manufacturer named his house the "Villa Lohengrin," but the people rejected the name. To them Lohengrin meant nothing, and whatever the German called his house, they called it the "Villa Guano." Amongst peasants and those accustomed to the possession of land, the man who owns the land is often not known by his surname, but by the name of his property. This is common in the Highlands of Scotland. When the two ladies arrived, the maid was unable to pronounce their German names, but she knew who they were, and announced the first as "La Señora de la Fragancia," and the second as "La Señora del Guano"!

In the ballroom I noticed a young Spaniard with a ham-coloured rash on his wrists. There was a similar rash on his forehead, where it is named *corona veneris* (the crown of Venus). Only once before had I seen this rash at a dance, and that was in London. It was impracticable to speak to him, as I was not his doctor, or to suggest to his host that he be asked to leave. I was left with three hopes: that he would not kiss anyone, that no one would drink out of a glass after him, and that he would not dance with Inés. He did not dance with her, and the other hopes also were probably realised, because soon afterwards he went away.

Inés danced with me, and towards the end of the evening she said: "This is an English dance. Let us go and walk in the garden." We went down the marble steps and along the path under the palm trees. This led to a fountain in the middle of the garden, and around the fountain were garden seats, set against a background of eucalyptus trees, with ragged, untidy bark and broad, glossy leaves, and pepper trees with narrow leaves and long, straggling bunches of pale pink berries. We walked in silence, but on the way my mentor and I were having an unpleasant conference.

We sat by the fountain and she spoke in quiet tones, never raising her voice to that high falsetto in which most women express annoyance.

*Inés:* So you are going away?

*Me:* Yes, señorita, I leave to-morrow, and I am sorry to go.

*Inés:* The Spanish girls have taught you Spanish, but you never asked any of them to marry you?

*Me:* I have no money.

*Inés:* Your uncle has money.

*Me:* My uncle will never give me his money. He offered me a share in the practice, but not enough. I can make more money in England.

*Inés (after a pause):* My father has plenty of money.

*Me:* Señorita, I will come back to Spain.

*Inés:* No, you will never come back. And if you do you will bring one of those skinny Englishwomen, all bones and skin, like the wife of Don Charles. My God, do you think she was worth her fare on the steamer? (*A long pause.*) Come, let us go back. You may dance the next two dances with me. Then I, my sister and mother will go home."

We walked back as silent as we had come, and she held her head erect. Although we were of the same height I felt small by her side. As soon as we entered the room we began to waltz. It was a famous waltz, and whenever I hear it now I remember Inés.

# CHAPTER IX

## THE GATE OF THE SUN

ONE of my Spanish patients was a cork merchant from Alicante, a middle-aged widower with two children. He was reputed to be wealthy, his expression was habitually sad, and he took me to Seville as his guest. This was my second visit to Seville, as I had been there during my first visit to Spain.

We arrived in the evening, and at the railway station the head porter, who knew my friend, carried our luggage to the *coche*. This porter was a very tall old man, with white hair and a large moustache. He towered head and shoulders above the others, and walked the length of the platform to select his "clients," as he called them. For forty years he had met the trains, and his "clients," many of whom he knew by name, were from every country in Europe. Some would write in advance to ensure that the old man was there to see them safely out of the station. He carried a lot of money, and gave honest change for foreign currencies. If he saw more than one "client" on the platform, his selection was made according to rank. "A thousand pardons, señor, but at present I attend the Marquesa." Once past the ticket barrier the old man earned his money by forcing a path for his clients through a howling mob of loiterers, beggars and unofficial porters, all clamouring for custom. Beyond this crowd was a line of hotel buses, each with its shouting, grabbing conductor, and many a timid traveller may have been seized, thrown bag and baggage into a bus and driven off to a hotel where he or she had never intended to stay. A carriage-drive through Seville was always exciting, as some of the streets through which the electric tramway runs are so narrow that two *coches* cannot pass.

When walking in Seville and other southern Spanish

towns I was often followed by beggars, who saw I was a foreigner and pestered me until I gave them money—or had learned the password of escape. The beggar begins by a volley of blessings, and, if these are not effective, ends with curses. Yet to escape one had only to say: "Pardon me, for God's sake," and the beggar went away quietly. Some of them sat around the doors of churches, exposing their deformities, cancers, and open sores so that people should be moved to give them alms. In England we give most of our alms through the compulsory Poor Rate, which is fairer to all, but impersonal. Every beggar in Spain has his principal patron, and a man even moderately well-to-do would be ashamed if he did not sustain at least one beggar. The beggar knows this, and when one patron had refused to increase the weekly alms, the beggar replied with dignity: "Very well, señor, I can easily find another patron, and then you will not have a beggar."

We dined that night between the fountain and the palm trees in the patio of the Hotel Madrid. The floor of this open court is of white marble tiles, and all around its white walls are growing orange trees of green and gold. After dinner I met a young Englishman of about my own age, who, being abroad, recognised me as a member of the island race. He had pleasant manners and the banjo voice, whereby, in addition to the vocabulary of the fifth form, it was once possible to recognise all over the world the English public-school boy—who had not been to Oxford or Cambridge. These universities have been bitterly criticised, especially by those who have failed in "Greats," but they certainly altered the banjo voice and vocabulary. Alas and alack! these social barriers have now broken down, and the banjo voice, which once inspired one of Kipling's noblest rhymes about those who linger on the outposts of Empire, may now be heard on the lips of young gentlemen who have adopted the profession of merchandising in London emporiums.

My new acquaintance was enthusiastic about all things English: "Jolly good"; "useful chap"; "topping girl"; "wonderful show"; "a ripping time." He had learnt Spanish in London, had been a month in Spain, and was there to do business for his firm with the Spaniards. He would probably have done a lot of business but for five things: (1) he "loathed the country"; (2) the Spaniards were "a lot of dagoes"; (3) their food was "poisonous"; (4) their customs were "absolute rot"; (5) their religion was "all bunk." He described the bull-fight, which he had never seen, as "utterly brutal and cowardly," and began to suspect me when I agreed that it was utterly brutal but not cowardly, because in the arena men risked their lives.

Next day my Spanish friend showed me the sights of Seville, and of these the greatest is the cathedral. Visual memory is often deceptive, as every one who has revisited the scenes of childhood knows. My visual memory of Notre Dame is that of a little cathedral, probably because I saw it first from the heights of Paris, but the memory of Seville Cathedral is one of immensity, as was the intention of the builders. When the Great Mosque of Seville became too small for Christian worship the Chapter decided in 1401 to rebuild it alongside the Giralda Tower, and to rebuild it on so vast a scale that posterity would think it was the work of madmen: "A church, such and so good that it should never have its equal." The building, 380 feet by 250 feet, roofed by seventy pointed vaults supported on thirty-two columns, was finished in 1506. The exterior roof is decorated with hundreds of flutings, volutes, friezes and buttresses, so perfect in proportion that they resemble the model of a city of bridges, buildings, churches, spires, steeples and minarets, laid out on the top of the cathedral. Behind the high altar is the Chapel of Our Lady of the Kings, and over its iron gates is the text, in letters of gold: "Per me Reges Regnant." Above the altar in this chapel is the statue of

"La Vergen de los Reyes," made of ivory, with hair of spun gold, and shoes embroidered in gold with the lilies of France, and the word "amor." My friend said that the hair of the statue grew, and that anyone who touched it would be struck blind. When I asked him if he really believed this, he replied: "I do believe it."

Superstition is misdirected reverence whereby supernatural power is attributed to material things, and this primitive instinct is so deep in our minds that we only laugh at those superstitions in which we have no belief. My friend believed in the growing hair of Our Lady of the Kings, but he laughed at the idea of the number thirteen having a malign influence on human destiny; and yet the one belief is as incredible as the other, although the story of the statue may at least have served a useful purpose. It was reputed to have had a miraculous origin, was always carried in battle on the saddle-bow of that King Ferdinand who defeated the Moors and was canonised. After a siege of fifteen months he took Seville on 23rd November 1248, and rode into the city with this statue on his saddle. He presented the statue to the cathedral, and it may be that his son, Philip, who became Archbishop of Seville, sought to deter collectors of souvenirs and relics by announcing that anyone touching the statue would be struck blind. If so, he was a wise man.

During Carnival and on the Fiesta de la Concepcion there is the unique ceremonial of "The dance of the six boys" in the cathedral. The "Seises" dance with castanets in the sanctuary before the high altar, and represent the Israelites dancing before the Ark. Their costumes are those of the fifteenth century, in order that the dance may survive a Papal decision. One of the Popes was petitioned to abolish this local custom as irreverent, and he ordered that the dance should cease as soon as the dresses were worn out. Immediately a Guild of Ladies was formed for the purpose of keeping the original costumes in repair. New pieces of cloth have been added from time to time, and the costumes have lasted for over five hundred years.

In the belfry of the Giralda Tower I saw the leap to the bells, now forbidden. The tower, on which a thirteen-foot figure of Faith gyrates as a wind-vane, was once the Tower of the Great Mosque, and was designed by Geber, the Moor who invented algebra. In 1568 the belfry was added. The way up the tower is a series of inclined planes, and the platform of the belfry is surrounded by a low parapet between the great arches, in which the bells are suspended thirty feet above. In each arch a bell is fixed to the centre of an iron axle, the ends of which are inserted into sockets in the masonry. The upper part of the bell-rope is wound round the axle on one side of the bell. Above each bell is a superstructure of alternate planks of wood and slats of iron, bound together, and to the bell and its axle by iron bands. This superstructure resembles a target four feet wide and from six to eight feet high, and its purpose is almost to balance the weight of each bell—the largest bell weighing eighteen tons. When the rope is pulled, the bell begins to swing and then revolves outwards or inwards, according to the winding of the rope on the axle. When the rope is unwound the bell continues to revolve by its momentum and the rope is rewound on the axle.

At two minutes to eleven the rope of each bell is held by a boy. He begins to pull and the great bell moves gently to and fro. With each pull on the rope the bell swings more and more. The boy stands on the parapet and throws his weight on the rope. Again he does this, and the bell and superstructure begin to revolve, and with each revolution the tongue strikes with a deafening clang. The boy continues, dragging on the rope, and the bell revolves faster and faster, until the rope is unwound. Then the boy ceases to pull and the rope is wound up again on the axle. The bell I watched was revolving outwards, that is to say, the upward sweep of the bell and the superstructure were outside the tower. When enough rope had been wound up on the axle the boy stopped the bell. Twisting the rope round his wrists he jerked it towards the centre of the arch. There it was caught by the edge of the superstructure moving outwards and upwards, and the boy was swung clear out of the belfry. This flight through the air at the end of the rope towards the revolving mass thirty feet above resembled part of a parabola, and he landed with his feet on the upper surface of the superstructure in its next revolution. His weight and the leverage act as a check, and the bell swings horizontally in the arch. Inside the tower is the bell; outside is the platform of wood and iron on which the boy is standing; and the whole is moving gently as a see-saw three hundred feet above the city.

Two coils of the rope are now round the superstructure. The boy moves to its farthest edge and leans back; his end of the see-saw goes down; the bell swings upwards; the rope unwinds; and the boy at the end of the rope is swung back into the belfry. The other bells are ringing, and amid noise that shakes the tower the rest of the boys are leaping like demons, some inside and some outside the belfry, to and from these clanging monsters. When the ringing ceased, the boy spoke:

"The señores saw the bells? Many people run away when they see the leap. No, I am not afraid. I had great fear at first; that was two years ago. I was fourteen then. It does not make me giddy, even at night, but the lights seem a long way below. Once a man was killed. No one saw, but they found him on the stones—down there. Some said he was drunk. There is now an old man in charge of the bells. He is sixty and blind, but he can do the leap to the bells. In an hour, if the señores will give him ten pesetas? No? Many, many thanks, señores, you are very kind. May you walk with God."

126

From the tower is a view over the undulating Andalusian
plain, bounded on the north by the Sierra Morena and on
the south-east by the mountains of Granada, whose lower
slopes grow palms and orange trees and whose peaks are
hidden by perpetual snow. Here and there on the plain are
small towns and villages built on little hills and so far away
that only the spires of their churches can be seen as land-
marks. The Guadalquivir crosses this plain from north to
west, and far down its course is the Isla, a great island on
which the bravest bulls are bred and tried. On the right bank
of the river is the oldest part of Seville, chosen by Cæsar as
capital of a Roman province, and where Gerontius preached
in the time of the Apostles. From the Romans Seville passed
to the Vandals and the Visigoths, and was their capital until
the Moors built their palace, the Alcazar, on the ruins of that
of the Cæsars and made Seville the capital of a kingdom.
Under the Christian kings of Spain Seville became capital
of an empire; but it was the river that made her great, and
on the quay there is a square building called the "Tower of
Gold," where once the looted wealth of the Occident was
stored. Even now for one week in April Seville is the Queen
of Europe, and during the fair the long white Seville road
becomes a busy street of chalets, bungalows, tents and
pavilions. On a rainy day in Paris I have seen on the
boulevards the gay placards of the south telling the fortunate
few how, by Sud-Express, they may go to this carnival of
wealth and beauty, the scene of Mozart's *Don Juan*, of
Bizet's *Carmen*, and of Sheridan's *Duenna*.

Men have praised Seville as they praise a woman. One has
called her "The Gate of the Sun (La Puerta del Sol)," and
another has written, "Quien no ha visto Sevilla, no ha visto
la maravilla (Who has not seen Seville has not seen the
wonderful)." In the revolution of the "Communeros," when
Madrid was against the central authority of the Throne,
Seville remained loyal and was rewarded by Charles V with

the motto: "Ab Hercule et Cæsare nobilitas, a se ipsa
fidelitas." And the motto of the city was now: "Very noble,
very loyal, very brave and invincible."

Seville is the city of Europe on which Africa has left
her mark. From this tower, on which the *muezzin* once called
"Great is Allah," the city, with its Moorish walls, white
houses, shadowy, winding streets, immense bull-ring, and
gardens of orange trees, looks as if it were in Morocco.
The Moors have long since gone, but Seville remains their
city. On the left bank of the river is a suburb mostly occupied
by the gypsies, the greatest and wealthiest horse-dealers in
Europe. The largest factory is the tobacco factory where
girls make cigarettes. On the wind-vane of the building is
a cock, and the image of the bird is said to be miraculous,
because it will crow so loudly as to arouse the whole city—
whenever a virgin enters the factory. Up to now the miracle
has not happened.

The newer houses in Seville are in the modern French
style, but the older houses are Spanish, and their charm lies
in the central patio. It was the patio, with its fountain,
orange trees and flowers, lit in the evening by coloured
lights, that made a German say: "Wen Gott lieb hat, dem
gibt Er ein Haus in Sevilla (He whom God loves has a
house in Seville)." But the kindly German should have
added—in the winter. In summer the heat is tropical, and
there is typhoid and malarial fever.

Walking that night in the Calle Sierpes—a long, winding
pavement with shops and cafés illuminated on either side—I
met the Litri (the bull-fighter who lived in Huelva) and
invited him to a café where we drank coffee. Many people
looked at him, knowing by his short pigtail that he was a
matador, and in Spain it was as great an honour to be seen
in the company of a matador as in England it would be to
walk down Bond Street with a Cabinet Minister. Amongst
those who saw me in the café was the young Englishman

from the Hotel Madrid. The Litri refused a liqueur. "No, many thanks. No, it is true, in the season no torero touches wine or women. Why? You are a doctor and must know. To face a bull needs all a man's strength, nerve and courage." The Litri was stout, rather short, over forty, with Roman features and clean shaven almost to the level of the upper ear—as are all toreros. He could have cut his pigtail and retired, had he saved the money he made—but in the winter he spent it. The critics said that in the arena he knew neither art nor fear. He taught me what little I know about the "running of bulls." The Mr. Finck, quoted by Baedeker, saw one bull-fight. Had he known anything about it he could have written much to its discredit, but he could never have written what he did write, namely, that apart from the cruelty it was the "most unsportsmanlike and cowardly spectacle I have ever witnessed." To understand the bull-ring it is necessary to know at least something about the art of playing a bull.

All matadors, or "killers of bulls," fight under a *nom de guerre*, and each has a *cuadrilla* of four assistants, or *chulos*. If the matador be injured, his chief assistant, the *sobresoliente*, takes his place. The English word, "bull-fight," is not a good equivalent to the Spanish *corrida de toros*—a running of bulls. The word *toreros* is generic, including the matador and the *chulos*, who act as *capeadores* and *banderilleros*, and there is no reason why, for *matador*, we should use the Italian word, *toreador*, as there are no bull-fights in Italy. The fights are on Sunday afternoons from Easter to October. During the winter there are no *corridas*, but amateurs or *chulos* sometimes fight *novillos* (three-year-old bulls) at *novilladas*, in which few are interested.

The average matador, in proportion to his skill, earned from twenty pounds to fifty pounds an afternoon, and his income ranged from five hundred pounds to one thousand pounds a year. The outstanding matadors made more, and in the season of 1894 Guerra received fifteen thousand pounds, which meant a fee of six hundred pounds for every fight.

When a bull has selected what he is going to toss, he makes a blind rush, which gives safety to a man in the arena provided he can do two things. First, when the bull is approaching, he must stand with one foot in front, keeping his legs, spine and head rigid. The cloak is held out towards the bull with both hands, at arm's length, and a gentle swinging of the *capa* should be the only visible movement. When the bull is almost on him he swings the *capa* outwards to one side. The bull follows the *capa*, and, when the horns are tossed, they are behind the man's outside arm. The bull rushes on, then turns and makes another charge, but the position of the man's feet enables him to face round more quickly than the animal. Secondly, the man must judge the exact moment for making "the pass"—swinging the *capa* outwards. That moment depends on the speed of the animal, and on the expression in its eyes. From the eyes the man can tell when the bull is about to toss the *capa*, and only then can he swing it in safety. If the *capa* be swung too soon or too late the horns get the man. A *torero* is often unconscious of the spectators; the eyes of the bull are all that he sees; and from those eyes his gaze never wanders as long as the animal is near.

When a bull stops near the man, say at three yards, and begins to charge, a different pass is used. With his feet together and holding out the *capa* at arm's length but motionless, he faces the bull. Then, at the right moment, keeping the *capa* in position, he moves to one side, and, when the horns rise in the *capa*, the man is running towards the animal's tail in order to gain distance. In this pass it is the man and not the *capa* that moves, and in a good pass the *capa* is swept over the animal's back. There are many other passes. And there is the story of the blind bull. A

130

*torero* was receiving the rush of a bull and swung his *capa* to the left. It was a perfect pass, but the bull never swerved, and the man was gored through the chest. The bull had a cataract in the right eye.

Matadors often visit the *ganaderias* (stud farms) to see the bulls they will fight. The bulls, aged from four to five years, are bought by an *impresario*, and may cost from forty pounds to sixty pounds each, but all he has bought is the right to have them killed, and after the fight their flesh is given to the poor. By contract, any animal not killed in the ring is returned to the *ganaderia*, and from the famous *ganaderias* bulls are never sold to breeders.

In the course of our talk the Litri offered me a cigar from his case, on which was inscribed in letters of gold: "Litri, from Alfonso XIII."

"It was nothing, señor. At Cadiz I killed three bulls. The people were very kind. They carried me on their shoulders to the royal box, and afterwards Don Alfonso sent me this."

Then the Litri told the story of the bull Paeguero:

"This bull, Paeguero, señor, lived near here on the plains of the Isla. The matador and his friends had gone out to the *ganaderia* to see the bulls he was to fight in two weeks' time—here, in the Seville ring. They found the little daughter of the breeder petting the bull, which used to come around the house. She was a child of eight, and was stroking the bull's face and saying: 'Bueno, Paeguero, bueno,' as you would speak to a horse or a dog. Most of them said: 'Bah! he is tame and will never fight. He should be killed for meat.' But the matador said: 'No, in his veins is the best strain in all Spain. The gentler the bull on the *campo* the braver he will be in the ring.' So they disputed, and the dispute became the talk of Seville. There were letters in the newspapers, and one letter said the little girl was broken-hearted because the pet bull was being sent to the ring. Señor, had I been rich and a breeder of bulls, I think I would have given Paeguero to the little girl. Ah, the children!

"The day came, the swing-doors opened, and Paeguero was in the ring, looking about him. Thousands shouted: 'He is tame and afraid,' but thousands more cried: 'Wait!' A picador rode up to him with lance across his saddle and shouted and laughed at Paeguero. Señor, in a moment that picador and horse were thrown clean over the six-foot barricade, the horse being killed instantly. Now there were no two opinions. All shouted for Paeguero. What horses he killed, what thrusts he took, I do not know, but when at the end the matador came into the ring a great cry went up, 'Pardon his life! Pardon his life!' The matador looked to the President of the fight, and he from his box said: 'His life is pardoned.' The matador looked round, and in the middle of the ring was Paeguero raging and charging at the *chulos*, who held him in play with their *capas*. Naturally, the matador did not wish that the bull should have all the glory. He called to his men: 'Fuera gente (Let the people go),' and they went behind the barricade. The matador threw away his sword and flag and walked unarmed across the arena to Paeguero, saying all the time what the little girl had said: 'Bueno, Paeguero, bueno.' The gates leading to the bull's den had been opened. The matador walked there, and behind him—Paeguero the bull, as quiet as a lamb. The ring was as silent as a church, because the people thought they had seen a miracle; but when the matador returned alone the cheering was so great that it deafened the angels of God in heaven. The story was told all over Spain and Portugal. The King of Portugal heard of it, and Paeguero went through a Portuguese fight with his horns padded, as is the custom there, lest any horses or men be killed. The King saw the fight, and afterwards at a royal garden-party Paeguero was led round and was made much of by great personages. Ah! there will never be another bull like Paeguero! What happened to him after that? Nothing. He was the pet of the little girl until he died."

On the opposite side of the café I had noticed a young Spaniard sitting with a tall, deep-breasted woman, who every now and then stared boldly around. As the couple rose and passed out I saw that the man was wearing a pigtail, and I asked the Litri if he knew him.

"Yes, that is Navada, the matador."

"But he was drinking *crème de menthe*, and you said . . ."

"Señor, I spoke the truth, and that man is a lunatic. Last Saturday, for a large bet, he killed six bulls in the Seville ring—without horses or men. They were young bulls, and not very brave. Next Sunday he has to fight in the Huelva ring, and the bulls there will be from the Herd of Death. This morning I asked him to come with me to the *ganaderia* to see the bulls they are sending. But no, he was to spend the day with that woman, and he will be with her all night. The man is mad."

"And her name is Delilah," I said.

"No, señor," he answered gravely, "her name is Maria Teresa, and she is a rich widow."

That night in the hotel I again met the young Englishman, who asked me with whom I had been sitting in the café.

"Why do you ask?"

"Well, of course he was a Spaniard, but I have never seen a man who looked more physically fit."

"He is the Litri—a matador."

# CHAPTER X

# BLOOD AND SAND

She loved the games men played with death,
Where Death must win.

FOR a week the town had been placarded with bright-
coloured posters of a bull's head, and the notice:
"Festival of St. Michael. Grand Bull Fight at four in the
afternoon. Six magnificent, full-grown bulls: from the most
famous *ganaderia* of His Excellency Señor Don Miura.
Matadors: The Litri, Bombita III, Navada."

Each of these matadors had to kill two bulls.

On that Sunday afternoon clouds of white dust rose from
the sun-baked road leading to La Plaza de Toros (the place
of Bulls) to which thousands on foot and many in carriages
were making their way. Those who went in carriages had
someone to watch their horses, because a contractor who
supplied horses for the bull-ring once obtained a pair from
one of the waiting carriages when his own supply gave out.

The bull-ring is a large open circular building of red
brick, in design roughly resembling the Coliseum in
miniature, with many entrances admitting to seats at various
prices. Inside, the surrounding wall throws a shadow over
part of the enclosure. The cheap seats are in the sun, the
more expensive in the shade. The *redondel*, or arena, is
eighty yards wide, around it a five-foot wooden barricade, and
behind this a narrow space for those awaiting their turn in
the arena. From the level of the barricade the seats (*asientas
de barrera, de contra-barrera, de tendido,* and *de grada*) rise
tier upon tier up to the wall, and highest up in the shade
are the *palcos,* or boxes, where the *ricos* sit. Adjoining the
larger bull-rings is a small hospital ward and chapel. Around

the Plaza de Toros were the mounted *guardia civil* in their dark blue uniforms with red facings and three-cornered hats, shouting vendors, and wizened old women with fruit and sweets on barrows. At one entrance a man offered tracts to passers-by: "The Church has condemned the *Corridas de Toros*."

As people stream in the band is playing, and boys, selling water from earthenware beakers are calling, "Water, water, fresh and cold as the snow." In the arena the attendants spray the sand, and three men in long black cloaks call them hither and thither. One place is too wet, another too dry. These are the matadors. A bull-fight is one of the few punctual functions in Spain, and by four o'clock the ring is full, the white dresses and gaily flowered hair of women sparkling in a setting of black-coated men. There is applause for the president of the fight—the governor of the province—as he enters a box draped with flags. The band begins the "Matadors' March," swing-gates open in the arena, and to a roar of welcome the *toreros* enter—*El Paso de la Cuadrilla*.

The three matadors are in front, four yards abreast. Their costume, of rich satin embroidered with gold thread, is the short Andalusian coat and vest, tight knee-breeches, silk sash, white stockings and flat shoes. The shoulders are protected against a fall by decorated pads, and over the left shoulder each carried a short, richly embroidered cloak. Under a low, black velvet padded cap, with a tassel on either side, hangs the short, ribboned pigtail. Behind are the *cuadrillas*, less richly dressed, and four mounted picadors, on seedy, worn-out horses. The man's right leg is protected by an iron casing (the *espinillero*) and he carries a fourteen-foot *garrocha*, or lance.

The *toreros* go behind the barricade, and the picadors take their positions at four equidistant points at the side of the arena. A fanfare of trumpets and a well-mounted cavalier (the *torelero*) rides in. From the president's box a key with streaming ribbons is thrown down, and this the *torelero* catches in his hat. It is the key of the bull's den (the *toril*) and a bugle calls for the first matador and *cuadrilla*. Then a whitewashed tub is placed upside down in the centre of the arena, and a man, dressed in white fleshings and covered with whitewash from head to foot, stands on the top of it. He is there to amuse the people, and all who play this part are called "Don Tancredo."

In the arena swing-doors open on a dark tunnel, and something is moving in the tunnel, something with large eyes that shine green in the dark. As the bull enters there is a shout, and the doors of the tunnel close. He is a coal-black bull with a long tail, clean horns, and holding his head like a stag. The muscles of his neck are like a buffalo's and he comes of a famous herd. From their home in the well-watered meadowland that stretches from the Guadalquivir to the Sierra Morena, they have carried the fame of their breed through Spain, and are now called the "Herd of Death."

The bull's first run is to Don Tancredo, but the whitewashed man has become a living statue and the bull stops within a few feet and sniffs suspiciously. There were white stone pillars in the sheds at home, and these hurt the horns of young bulls who butted into them. He is not interested in Don Tancredo, but there are Don Tancredos who cannot stand as motionless as marble, and to the people's amusement, they must run for their lives. The bull looks round and charges one of the *cuadrilla*. The *chulos* are ready to play the bull with their red *capas*, and Don Tancredo, much applauded, walks out.

The *capeadores* attract the bull towards one of the horses— a poor, starved beast, with the right eye bandaged. This bandaged eye the picador kept towards the bull, but the ears are twitching, the nostrils distended, and now and then the horse shivers, although the air is very warm. Poor beast! There was an hour when, well-groomed and accoutred, you awaited your master in the cobbled street that rang to your impatient pawing, and from some flowered balcony bright eyes admired you. The picador levels his lance at the bull, and sometimes rides to meet him. The brute charges, receiving the *garrocha* (the thrust of the lance) in the left shoulder, the horse is gored, and horse and man thrown over the bull's head. Picador is on the ground, lying quiet for safety beside the struggling horse. The bull is on them again, but a *chulo* with his *capa* draws him off. Now, wild with blood, the bull is charging the men at full speed. "Ollé!" shout the people. And picador is on his feet, lashing the horse across the face. It may be his mount is fit to meet the bull again, and money saved for the contractor. The animal staggers to its feet, blood pouring from its wounds, and then falls dead. Picador drags off the shoddy harness. It is wanted for one of the spare horses waiting outside. On goes the carnage, the trembling horses sniffing the air, mad with fear. Down goes another, gored through the heart. One is ripped open and totters about, trailing its entrails on the blood-stained sand. "Ollé!" is the cry, until above the shouting the bugle sounds. The bull has received the three regulation thrusts, and the first part of the fight is over. The uninjured and wounded horses that can walk are led out. They will have a little rest, and some will be patched up until they are wanted for the second bull.

It is time for *banderillos*. These are thirty-inch darts with barbed points, the shafts decorated with ribbons and paper flowers. A *chulo* with a dart in each hand approaches the bull. Down go the horns as the bull charges, and the man runs to meet him. When the two have almost met, the man springs aside, and, a second later, as the bull is passing, plunges a *banderillo* into each shoulder. A roar of applause is the reward of darts well placed, for this is more dangerous than playing a bull with a *capa*. As the bull tries to shake them off, the darts flap about his neck and a little blood trickles down his forelegs. When three pairs are inserted, the bugle sounds and the second part of the fight is over. This bull was brave, and his *banderillos* were gaily coloured. But if a bull has refused to face the picador's lance, then the cry of "Fuego" (fire) goes up, and a red handkerchief is waved from the president's box. This means blazing darts of squibs and crackers (*banderillos de fuego*), and the maddened beast dances round with a halo of fire and smoke. That is the only time a bull-breeder has been known to leave the ring in tears—his herd was disgraced.

The breathing of the bull is now like the tearing of cotton, and his head is lower. *Garrochas*, horses, and *banderillos* have weakened the neck muscles. That was their use—to lower the head; and the bull's den is pitch-dark lest for five hours before the fight the animal should be looking upwards. When the head is down there is an unprotected place of three inches on the back between the shoulder blade and the first rib. Beneath that space on the right lies the largest artery, and this the matador's sword must sever. If the sword strikes bone the man is on the bull's horns.

There is silence when the bugle calls for the matador, and the Litri faces the president's box, where his embroidered cloak is displayed on the balcony.

"I dedicate the life of this bull to the people of my town. I will kill it in a manner that will do honour to them or remain in the arena."

For a present of ten pounds any well-known person may have the honour of the cloak and dedication. He throws his hat to the crowd, and, with a small red flag (the *muleta*) in his left hand, and a short sword (the *espada*) in his right, approaches the bull. With the flag he plays the bull into position, until it is standing a yard in front of him with its forefeet together. He slowly lowers the flag until it is across his thighs, and the bull's head follows this movement. Simultaneously his sword-arm is raised above the shoulder, and all the time he is watching the animal's eyes. Rising on his toes he aims the sword for the three-inch space, and moves the flag beyond his right thigh. Man and bull rush together; as the horns toss for the last time they are beyond the sword-arm, and the dull thud of a dead bull falling on the sand is drowned in thunderous applause. When a fallen bull is not dead, a *puntillero* with a dagger piths him in the neck. A more difficult method of killing is the *descabellar*, when the matador pierces the spinal cord in the neck with the sword.

A team of six mules, bedecked with silver bells and streamers gallop in to drag out the carcass, and return to pull out the dead horses.

When the tunnel opened for the second bull, no bull appeared. A hitch somewhere, and a lazy-looking ring attendant, hands in pockets and cigarette in mouth, strolls along and wanders into the darkness. Nothing happens, a little *guardia municipal*, holding his baton, marches boldly in and disappears. From the cheapest seats an urchin of twelve or so drops over the barricade, and, with his ragged coat thrown over his shoulder like the *toreros*, he swaggers into the tunnel. But nothing happens. Then from the tunnel comes a fearful yell and the trio emerge racing across the arena minus coat, cigarette and baton, with the bull a yard behind. The bull stopped, as do all bulls on entering sunlight out of darkness, but the speed of the race for the barricade was accelerated by shouts from the people: "Look out, he's got you."

At the time for *banderillos*, the matador, Bombita III (incidentally a Master of Arts of Seville University) faces the president, and, holding up a pair of darts, dedicates the thing he is about to do. A wave of excitement seethes round and people are standing on their seats. They are about to see the most dangerous thing ever done in the arena—not seen once in a hundred fights since the great Guerra died. It is called "El Quiebro" (the Twist) and it has been done seated in a chair. Bombita lays his handkerchief in the centre of the arena, and stands on the little patch of white. He is opposite the bull, now goring a dead horse at the barricade, and is alone in the ring. His arms are extended towards the bull, and in each hand is a dart. He shouts; the bull turns and charges at full speed across the arena. The matador stands motionless. When the bull is three yards away the man sways his arms and chest to the right, and the horns follow the movement. Then he sways his chest to the left, and the bull passes by his side and underneath his outstretched arms, which plunge a *banderillo* into each shoulder. He has done it, and picks up the handkerchief from which his feet had never moved. And then ten thousand people stand shouting: "El mejor in España (the best in Spain, the best in Spain)." His *cuadrilla* rush in to hold the bull in play; Bombita walks round the arena, gravely acknowledging the ovation, and, as he passes by each sector, the air is black with hats, presents, and dollars thrown at his feet. But the great artists of the ring never smile in their moment of triumph.

The people are murmuring when the third matador, Navada, is about to kill. As he raises his sword, a cry of astonishment comes from the front benches, for the bull's head is high and his feet wide apart. The bull charges, the man makes a lunge but jumps aside and misses the animal by a foot. Shouts of laughter! He curses the bull, tries again, misses, and above a pandemonium of laughter, jeers and abuse, the bugle sounds the first warning. Howls of derision greet the next attempt, and a horn has ripped his jacket. A second warning from the bugle. He has one more chance to kill, and, if he fails, the next call of the bugle will be for the civil guard to enter the ring, shoot the bull and arrest the matador. That was the law of Spain. He will also be expelled from the Association of Matadors. His *cuadrilla* are holding the bull in play, but the man is listless and his face is as white as a sheet. He has played with Death, now Death is playing with him. Turn to the bull, matador! There is life in his eyes—death is ringing in their laughter. Now, forgetting all rules of the ring, he has taken his eyes off the bull, and stares at the howling mob in the amphitheatre. In the arena is a brute beast, and all around is *la bête humaine*. Why do you stare, matador? In that sea of faces what face, by a miracle, do you expect to see? The face of Delilah? And if you found it now, what message would she send?

> If one should love you with real love,
> Such things have been,
>       .       .       .       .
> You'd give him poison, shall we say?
> Or what, Faustine?

Suddenly the tumult ceases. The Litri and his men are in the arena. His men play the bull to the centre, and the Litri speaks to the matador. Only those very near heard what he said: "Less hurry and more courage, señor." It was enough. He and his men left the arena, and within five minutes the bull was dead. He is a rough man, this Litri, and a man against whom the knife has been drawn more than once. But beside me was a woman, who, when the carnage of horses had reached its limit, turned and said: "Which is the more cruel, señor, a bull or a man?" Even in the bright light the pupils of her eyes were dilated, and I knew the blood lust, twin of sex lust, possessed her:

> She drank the steaming drift and dust,
> Blown off the scene;
> Blood could not ease the bitter lust
> That galled Faustine.

In England, when a Roman province, soldiers of the legions fought bulls single-handed, and in Spain, after the disruption of the Empire, mounted Arab-Spanish knights speared bulls as a warlike pastime in times of peace. This was the *corrida caballeresca*. At first none but the aristocracy witnessed the fights, but in 1100 the public were admitted as spectators, and, in 1418, the first *plaza de toros* was built. In the year 1750 professional matadors fought bulls on foot (the *corrida gladiatorias*), and this was the beginning of the modern bull-fight. The source may have been the Coliseum or a sport of the ancient Celt-Iberians in the time when Spain was infested with wild bulls. Of this sport, the *corridas populares*, in which the bull is not killed, may be a relic. On festivals in the villages of Valencia and Andalusia an enclosure is made of wagons and planks, and in this a less-fierce bull is provoked by those who care to take the risk. The spectators sit on the wagons or on the roofs of houses and enjoy the sight of their friends playing the bull or running out of his way. When the *corrida* is held in the street the bull is usually tethered by a long rope. Afterwards a tame cow is let loose and the bull follows her quietly back to the pen, or to the slaughter-house if the meat is to be eaten at a public feast.

To the northern races of Europe the Spanish bull-fight is an example of sickening cruelty, an offence against the moral and æsthetic sense, and many Spaniards endorse this condemnation of their national sport. In any matter where powerful emotions are aroused it is well to define the words of criticism. Cruelty means indifference to the pain of others or a delight in their sufferings, and the giving of pain does not of necessity imply cruelty. In the bull-ring the vast majority of spectators are indifferent to the suffering of the horses, although their suffering so moved a Frenchman at Bordeaux that he drew a revolver and opened fire on the *toreros*. The degree of cruelty is the indifference of the men and spectators to the suffering of the horses, and the cruelty is sickening because the mutilation of a large animal is an outrage against the æsthetic sense, whereby we appreciate what is beautiful. To arrive at a just conclusion it is essential to make that distinction. Fox-hunting is cruel because the hunt is indifferent to the suffering of the fox, but the cruelty is not sickening because the animal is small, and the æsthetic sense is not outraged when the fox is torn to bits by hounds. All blood sports are not cruel. Shooting is not cruel. Good shooting means instant death to the animal—an easier death than Nature has in store for her wild creatures, and moreover very few men who shoot are indifferent to the suffering of a bird or animal they have wounded. The man who takes long shots, more likely to wound than to kill, will soon hear adverse comments from his friends.

There are two degrees of cruelty, and it is more cruel to find pleasure in the sufferings of others than to be indifferent to their pain. The spectators in the bull-ring are indifferent to the suffering of the horses, but occasionally they delight in the pain inflicted on the bull. That only happens when the bull refuses to fight and is "fired." I saw that once in the bull-ring at Tarragona. I was in the cheapest seats, "in the sun," and the bull was a tame animal which would have bolted out of the ring had he been allowed to do so. He was "fired." All around, the crowd were shouting and jeering at the bull, and I so far forgot where I was as to begin shouting at the matador, who was no braver than the bull: "A la carcel, carnicero, a la carcel (to the prison, butcher, to the prison)." A most evil-looking ruffian beside me told me with oaths, and his hand on his pocket, that the matador was a friend of his and the best matador in Spain. I readily agreed with him, and held my peace. With a brave bull there is no cruelty, because the people admire him, and, very occasionally, when the bull is very brave, may demand of the president that the bull's life should be pardoned. It is in the bull's nature to fight with his horns, and most animals enjoy fighting. Dogs, whom we know best, often thoroughly enjoy it.

Any defence of the bull-ring that I have ever read is based on the assumption that all critics are ignorant of its technique, and are no more capable of appreciating the skill and courage of the *toreros* than is a Hottentot of appraising a game of cricket. There is some truth in that assumption. Foreigners have declared that people go to bull-fights on the chance of seeing the shedding of human blood, and others, equally ignorant, have stated that the men are never in danger. Thus, an Edinburgh professor, having seen one bull-fight in Madrid, wrote in the *Scotsman* that "There is no more danger in crossing the bull-ring of Spain than in passing through an English park full of sheep." That is the kind of comment which is naturally welcomed by any apologist of the bull-fight because it is so easily refuted. Every year at least a dozen matadors are killed in the ring, and, when Guerra died in his bed, the scars of over two hundred previous wounds from horns were found on his body. But no Spanish apologist has ever attempted to answer the main foreign criticism, not always unenlightened, concerning the cruelty to horses. They rely on the *tu quoque* answer, which proves nothing, and of all sports usually select boxing as a cruel English custom, although in the case of our heavyweights, the vanquished one, five minutes after having been knocked out, is generally explaining to a group of reporters exactly how he lost the fight and why it only lasted for one minute. A more effective *tu quoque* answer would be to point out to English critics that there is no society in Spain for the prevention of cruelty to children, and that a society for this purpose is not required. Although foreign criticism was ignored by apologists, one of the first acts of Primo de Rivera, when he became Dictator, was to make it illegal for any horse to be used in the ring unless the whole of its body on the side exposed to the bull was protected by a thick leather shield to prevent the animal being gored. He also declared it illegal to "fire" any bull, but this law raised such an outcry amongst the enthusiasts of the bull-ring that it was cancelled, although those who know most about the ring are, I think, agreed that the "firing" of a bull has never yet improved a bull-fight.

The greatest objection to the bull-fight is its effect on the spectators—the danger of the mind becoming insensitive to cruelty. In 1883, when twenty thousand people had seen a Spanish bull-fight in the city of Nîmes, Bishop Besson issued a pastoral letter forbidding this amusement to his flock—"as if it were a *lawful* pleasure to see six bulls killed, sixteen horses gasping under their feet, and, in the midst of this butchery, the first swordsman in Spain exposing his life in such a sea of blood; that is the glorious spectacle offered to a great city."

As far back as 1567 Pius V issued the following general prohibition:

"We, considering these spectacles, where bulls and wild beasts are baited in a circus or amphitheatre, as contrary to Christian mercy and charity, and wishing to abolish these cruel and wicked shows, suitable to demons rather than to men, and to do all that we can, with God's help, for the salvation of souls, forbid all Christian princes, secular or ecclesiastical, imperial, royal, or of any other dignity, under pain of incurring excommunication and anathema, to allow this kind of spectacle, where bulls or other beasts are baited, to take place in their provinces, towns, estates, or territories. We forbid soldiers and all other persons to fight in these shows, either on foot or on horseback. And if they die in such combats, they are to be refused Christian burial. We also forbid all clerics, regular and secular, to be present, under pain of excommunication—and we command our venerable brethren, Patriarchs, Primates, Archbishops,

Bishops, and other local ordinaries throughout the world, in virtue of holy obedience, and remembering the judgments of God, and threat of everlasting malediction, to cause these our present letters to be published in their cities and dioceses" (1st November 1567, Const. *De Salute*).

It is doubtful if this prohibition was respected in Spain, because in 1575 Gregory XIII excepted laymen from the foregoing penalties. In 1597 Clement VIII forbade bull-fighting on holidays of obligation—the solemn festivals of the Church—and prohibited the clergy from attending. These last prohibitions have been and are obeyed, but it should be noted that all three papal pronouncements referred to the older forms of bull-fighting. The modern bull-fight did not begin until the middle of the eighteenth century, when Francisco Romero, a native of Ronda, invented the *muleta*, and was the first on foot to kill a bull. He published the first book on the art of bull-fighting, *De Arte Taurino*, and his son, Juan, was the first to organise a *cuadrilla de toreros*.

All moral theologians are agreed that to risk life without reasonable cause is an offence against the natural law—the law whereby the will of the Creator is expressed throughout creation, but two moralists, Vromant and Gury-Ferreres, are of opinion that the Spanish bull-fight is not forbidden by the natural law, because the skill and dexterity of the *toreros* precludes immediate danger of death or of serious injury. This is not a very happy argument. If the men ran no risk of death or injury, the bull-fight would be what it is not—a cowardly spectacle. And if the men run no risk, why should the Church permit a chapel to be attached to the bull-ring? The chapel is there in order that men seriously injured in the arena may receive the Last Sacraments.

# CHAPTER XI

## THE TRIAL

THERE were over two hundred and fifty bull-rings in Spain, and although a bull-fight did not happen every Sunday, there were at least four fights in every arena during the season. In each fight six bulls were killed, and therefore over five thousand bulls were killed every year. To supply these bulls for the ring a great animal industry existed— mostly on the plains of Andalusia—and in relation to that industry there is a magnificent sport. Between the ages of two and three the young bulls (*becerros*) are tried for the ring at the *tienta* or *tentadero*, and a three-year-old bull may be so large and fierce as to be almost ready for the ring, where he will fight between the ages of four and five. At a *tentadero* the young bulls are segregated in a corral alongside the *ganaderia*, and the rest of the herd, amongst which are tame oxen (the *cabestros*), are driven two miles across the plain.

A young bull is released from the corral, and immediately makes off to join the herd. He is chased by two men on horseback, who ride about fifty yards behind and twenty-five yards on either side of the bull. The man riding to the right of the bull carries a *garrocha* (a fourteen-foot ash lance). This is the same as is used in the ring, but now the point is protected by layers of string, so that only a quarter of an inch of steel projects—enough to prick the hide but not to pierce the muscles. When the bull breaks into a trot, the man riding on the left gallops ahead so that the bull alters course and is running across the path of the horseman on his right. The man on the right carries the *garrocha* and charges the bull so that the point of the *garrocha* strikes him on the upper part of the haunch, and the bull is thrown over. The horses used in the *tentadero* are trained to make the charge, and the *garrocha* must strike the bull on the haunch. If it strikes the bull on the flank it is likely to pierce the body. A valuable animal will be injured, and the rider will not be invited to ride in another *tentadero*. Once the bull is thrown the two men ride back to the corral. The bull rises and continues on his way to join the herd, but half a mile farther on he meets a mounted picador armed with a *garrocha*. The bull now recognises the man, the horse and the *garrocha*. as his enemies, and if he be brave he will charge the picador, who protects himself and his horse with the *garrocha*. If the bull charges three times and takes three pricks of the lance the picador gallops off and the bull returns to the herd, with which he will live for another year before going to the ring. The bull that fails to charge the picador will never go to the ring. He will be fattened and slaughtered for food.

When bulls are going to the ring they are either sent by train, or, if the distance be short, by road. It is a wonderful ride by night. The six bulls, with six tame oxen, walk by night accompanied by horsemen. On this journey, which leads through sleeping villages and towns, you may neither speak nor smoke. Nothing may be done which might excite the bulls, and the only sounds are the tinkling of the cow-bells around the necks of the oxen and the metallic clink of the horses' hoofs striking the hard road. Two men ride a quarter of a mile ahead of the bulls to warn approaching traffic on the road to draw aside and remain stationary until the bulls have passed.

A *tentadero* is the opportunity for those who desire a career in the bull-ring. Once a bull is thrown any member of the party may go out and play it with the *capa*. One or more matadors are usually present, and if they see a young man who shows skill with the *capa* he may be remembered for the next vacancy in the *cuadrilla*. Even the children of the south play at bull-fights in the streets. One child has bull's horns strapped to his head, and charges the others, who use their jackets as *capas*.

The heifers from which bulls will be bred are also tried and tested for courage. They are taken one at a time into a corral, where they must charge a picador three times, and receive three pricks of the *garrocha*. At one of these trials the breeder's son, a boy of sixteen, jumped into the corral to prove his skill with the *capa* for the benefit of his *novia*, who was also present. Now a cow does not charge straight, like a bull, but gives side-jabs with her horns. The boy was gored through the arm and thrown. The agonised father turned to the Litri. "Señor, for God's sake save my son." But the matador remained seated and answered calmly: "Señor, I am a killer of bulls, not of cows." Others rescued the boy. This was not an example of cowardice but of a strange convention. Had the Litri even been scratched by a cow he would have been jeered at on his next appearance in the ring.

For two weeks before my first *tentadero* I practised with the *garrocha* every night in my bedroom, and every morning I galloped my horse at cactus bushes on the *campo*, aiming the heavy lance for a particular lead. At last the great day came. A bull was out of the corral and we were after him. My companion raised his hand and galloped ahead. I paid out the *garrocha* over my rein-arm, until I saw the ribbon which told that enough of the shaft was left to go under my armpit. I swung the weapon over the horse's head, and leaned forward to the right of the saddle. Next, I gave the signal to the horse to charge—running the knuckles of the left hand up the mane. We charged, and as we neared the bull my thought was—now for the bump. There was no bump. The tip of the lance struck the bull on the haunch, and so great was the combined momentum that he went down like a piece of paper.

I rode back to the party in front of the corral, placed my

*garrocha* against a tree, and watched others "trying" the bulls. At the back of the group I spoke to the Litri's son, Juan Miguel, who was carrying a *capa*.

"Señor, will you do me the favour of lending me your *capa*?"

"With pleasure, señor, but—does your uncle know?"

"That is my affair."

"It is as you wish, señor." And he handed me the *capa*, which I strapped to my saddle-bow.

The Litri had shown me some of the passes, and, at a dinner-party in my uncle's house I had said that if one knew the passes it was not so difficult to play a bull, and that I would like to do it myself. My uncle had looked at me, and I knew he thought I was boasting. Well, now he would see his mistake. I handed my *sombrero* to Juan Miguel.

When the next couple started I rode fifty yards behind them. They threw their bull and returned. I went on, dismounted twenty yards away from the animal lying on the ground, unstrapped the *capa*, and left the horse, which trotted back to the corral, a quarter of a mile away. I had not bargained for that nor for the size of the bull when he rose to his feet. He looked bigger than I had anticipated. He had no doubts in his mind, either, and came straight for me. Putting my left foot forward, I held the *capa* in front and stood steady, waiting and watching those eyes. The Litri was right. It was the eyes, the eyes, and nothing but the eyes. I must remember about the eyes . . . and to stand steady . . . only the *capa* to be moved. The rush of the bull could only have taken a few seconds, but they felt like hours. Now! And I swung the *capa* to the right. The eyes and horns followed the movement, and the animal charged blindly past me, only the *capa* being touched by those cruel horns. "Ollé!" I shouted. That was one moment in life that I would like to recapture, when fear, anxiety, and doubt were replaced in an instant by triumph. The glory of achievement was in my soul as never it has since been—not even when five thousand people gave their applause at the end of an hour's oration. I wheeled round. The triumph was not complete. Again the bull was at me, and there was less time to think. I swung the *capa* to my left, and again he charged. Not so good this time! His shoulder nearly pushed me over as he passed. He was getting nearer and nearer. I must do the third pass and gain distance.

Standing square to the bull with the *capa* before me I waited again, watching the eyes. When I thought he had fixed on the *capa* I moved to my right, and in an instant the eyes of the bull told me the game was lost. I had moved too soon. He had them fixed on me. Flight was impossible; it was a matter of seconds. I dropped the useless *capa*. Instinctively I put out my hands to save myself. In those few seconds I spoke aloud in an ordinary voice four words: "My God, I'm finished." The base of the horns struck me under the wrists, and, my arms being held stiffly downwards, I was thrown backwards six feet through the air into a cactus bush, where I fell on my back, and watched him charging again. I knew that I should feel no pain. I hoped that he would not gore me in the kidney, because that would be difficult to repair. And I watched his eyes. They were brown eyes and they were business-like eyes. What yellow eyelashes he had! That was my last thought at the moment when I expected the horns in my body.

My attention was distracted from the bull's eyes by what seemed to be a shadow above me. I looked up and saw the Litri standing astride me, and heard his shout of "Ollé!" as he played the bull away from my body, first one side, then on the other without moving his own feet. One of the bull's hoofs trod on and bruised my thigh. Now other people were shouting "Ollé!" and when the Litri helped me to rise I saw that two of his men were enticing the bull away from us. The three of them had galloped out as soon as the performance began. I had not seen them, and it seemed a long time since I had seen anything except the eyes of the bull. I should not easily forget them. Nor had I felt the cactus spikes, although now my back was smarting and bleeding from them. The bull was on his way across the plain. The horses of the Litri and his men had, like mine, departed when left alone, and we all walked back to rejoin the party.

As we approached them I saw that my uncle was standing apart from the others. The courteous Spaniards had probably withdrawn lest their presence should mar the affectionate reunion of nephew and uncle. I found my uncle in a temper that did not suit me at that moment, but which was doubtless well deserved.

"A poor show, sir. What the devil would your father have said to me had you been killed? You have no regard for other people. You think only of yourself."

To which I replied: "*You* think only of yourself. Talk of family feeling! I leave for Madrid to-night."

Our reunion, or parting, was interrupted by the approach of the Litri, followed by all the Spaniards.

"I'm off," I said. "I don't want any of their palaver. I know that I played the bull badly, and so do they."

"Don't be an ass," said my uncle, "and don't let us row in front of the Spaniards. After all, the man saved your life. The least you can do is to stay and shake hands with him."

The Litri came up, solemnly held out his hand and took off his hat, as did all the others. We shook hands, and I again thanked him. From the serious faces of the others we might have been holding a religious service in the open air.

The Litri spoke: "Señores, I am a *matador de toros*, and I cannot congratulate Don Enrique on the manner in which he played the bull. Never in my life, señores, have I seen a man who played the bull more on to his own body and less on to the *capa*. That is not why I congratulate him. I congratulate him because he is the first Englishman I have known who tried to play a fighting bull. Ollé!"

Next Sunday I went for a long ride with the British vice-consul, and we stopped at a village five miles from the *ganaderia*. There was a *posada* with a rustic fence round a little garden. We fixed our reins to this fence on either side of the gate and went in to drink beer in a cool room with white-topped tables and sawdust on the floor. Four other customers, villagers, were refreshing themselves, and a billy-goat went from table to table begging scraps. The Spanish beer tastes cool, and that is the best I can say of it, because it is as sweet as glycerine. As we drank I noticed that the other people in the room were looking at us with interest, and when I called for the reckoning, the landlord said: "Is your honour the English señor who played a bull last Sunday? Señor, there is nothing to pay. You have done my poor *posada* a great honour, and you are always welcome as my guest."

The vice-consul was as surprised as myself. "What the deuce is all this about?" I had said nothing to anyone about the adventure, because it was neither a feather in my cap nor a bee in my bonnet. The landlord told him, and the story had grown. A bull, so fierce that it might have come from the Herd of Death, had been played by the señor for twenty minutes alone. The señor was thrown. This narrative was interrupted by a disturbance outside the *posada*, and we all went out. My horse had knocked down a portion of the rustic fence, and was dragging it at the end of the reins across the road. I offered to pay for the damage, but the landlord declined. "It is nothing. I can repair it in a minute."

We said good-bye to him and rode homewards. After a time the vice-consul remarked: "I think you will become a legend in this place." He was right. Years later, in London, an English girl told me how she had heard around Huelva the story of the English doctor who wished to be a matador, but was prevented by an uncle from adopting this promising career!

That evening my uncle announced: "There is to be another *tentadero* next week. I don't know what you think now about the *capa*, but I think you owe it to yourself to play another bull. People have been talking, and what you did has naturally been exaggerated; if you go to the *ganaderia* and don't play a bull they will say you have lost your nerve. And you know what the Spaniards think about that. . . . Very good, but I will see that you have three *chulos* with you."

When the time came the *chulos* stood on the plain thirty yards in front of the corral. The bull came out and they held him in play with their *capas*. As I walked across to join them I felt irritated. The bull was small; he had not been upset and therefore was not roused. He was making short rushes at the men and wheeling round three yards behind them. At last the bull saw me and rushed. I swung my *capa* to the right, and as he passed I felt a burning pain in my right hand. The back of one horn had razed the skin on the edge of my hand. Honour was satisfied!

After a big *tentadero* the breeder entertains his friends to supper, and for their entertainment during supper a bull is driven into the room. This ensures that everybody rises from table. Some take off their coats and play the bull, while others seek safety under the table or on the top of it. On one occasion, when the bull had departed, and the guests were again seated, it was discovered that the local priest was missing. He was presumed to have escaped from the house during the uproar, and, being elderly and stout, no one blamed him. After a time strange noises came from the large open fireplace, and the unhappy man was pulled down by the legs out of the chimney, in which he had become stuck.

In Spanish country-houses the usual after-supper enter-

tainment is dancing, and at a house in the Province of
Estremadura my uncle had a curious experience. His host
told him that he would see a wonderful dance, which was
very old and peculiar to that district. A girl rose, and, to
the music of a guitar, began to dance. My uncle said he
would like to dance with her. "Impossible, señor," said his
host, "you cannot know this dance. It is known to none
except those who have lived here. But, if you wish to try,
well, do as you please." He did try, and, to the amazement of
the Spaniards, he and the girl were dancing the same
dance—the Highland Fling. The Highland soldiers who
were there during the Peninsular War were forgotten, but
their dance remained.

The vice-consul and I were in a café one night when
two young Englishmen entered whom we knew, and sought
his assistance on behalf of a young friend of theirs. The lad
had arrived from England that morning, and they had been
showing him the night-life of Huelva, including a disreputable *posada*, where they had sat watching girls dancing
the *fandango*. There had entered an apparition in shirt and
trousers, with bare feet, long golden hair like a girl's and a
painted face. This apparition so surprised their friend that
he pulled out a revolver, fired, and missed. The apparition
fled into a garden at the back of the *posada* and climbed
an iron ladder to the roof. The lad fired a couple of shots
in the garden but missed the target on the ladder. Two
civil guards entered the garden, raised their rifles, and said:
"Alta." All three Englishmen held up their hands. One
civil guard passed his hand swiftly over their clothes, and
took the revolver from their friend, who was then marched
off to jail between the two guards. The lad was due to
report for duty at the Rio Tinto mines the next day, and
unless something could be done he might as well have
returned to England by the next steamer.

The obvious thing to do was to get him out of jail, and

having counted our money, and finding a little over ten pounds between the four of us, we set off to the prison. After much knocking on the iron gate we aroused a sleepy jailer, who grumbled when the vice-consul asked if a young Englishman had arrived. "Yes, señor, he is here. The civil guards brought him. It is very late now for visitors, nearly midnight, but if the señores wish to see him you may come in. What! Let him out! Absolutely impossible!" So surprised was the jailer that he stepped out of the prison to join us in the street. "He tried to kill a man. No, I do not know how it happened. . . . Ah! that was it. Good! It was natural for the young man to shoot just to frighten the shameless one. No, no, señor, I cannot let him out. What! Two pounds! This is a jest, señor. I have a wife and children. Ah! the young man has a mother. His poor mother!" It was dark, but I could almost see the tears in the honest fellow's eyes. "Four pounds! No, señor, I cannot do it. This is the young man's first night in Spain! It is very sad, señor, for the young man to sleep his first night in prison. Eight pounds! And you have no more! Very well, señor. For the sake of the young man's mother. If you will come in, señores, there is a light in the arch of the prison, and in a moment I will bring the young man to you." We entered, counted our money under the flickering oil lamp, and in a couple of minutes the young Englishman was with us. As we left the prison the jailer shook hands with the five of us, wished us good night, and hoped that we might walk with God.

The open sesame of this escape was money. The civil guards of Spain, being a military force under the administration of the Crown, were independent of the municipal police, who looked after the prison. In all probability no one ever checked, except in cases of serious crime, the names of those arrested by the civil guard with the names in the prison book, showing those who had been lodged there either by the civil guard or by the municipal police. The two civil guards who had arrested the young Englishman would have no further interest in their prisoner unless they were called as witnesses at his trial. If not so called, they would know that for some reason or another their prisoner was not being prosecuted; and people cannot be prosecuted if the pro-curator-fiscal is unaware of their existence, as he would be if their names were not entered in the prison book.

The vice-consul had assisted other young Englishmen whose troubles were outside the scope of the Foreign Office regulations. Young Tom was earning sixteen pounds a month and lived with his widowed mother. His weakness was a belief that he could win money at roulette, and from time to time the widow had to draw on her savings to make up what her son lost in play. One day he told her that he would risk his month's salary in a last flutter at the Cercle. In her distress she went to the vice-consul. He had no power to prevent the boy from entering the Cercle, but devised a plan whereby the young man was saved money and taught a lesson.

The widow handed sixteen pounds to the vice-consul, and that night he went to the Cercle and played against the son. When the young man backed red, the vice-consul placed an equal amount on black. Whatever the boy did the vice-consul did the reverse. When the widow's son left the table without a penny the vice-consul rose from the table with thirty pounds, representing the original sixteen pounds, plus fourteen pounds winnings. After a night's play the widow and her son had lost two pounds to the bank, and a loss was inevitable whenever zero appeared. Had the son won he would have won from his mother, and the vice-consul threatened to repeat this performance if necessary. It was not necessary.

A similar plan was once adopted by a wealthy Liverpool shipowner, whose sons had taken to backing horses. The father said he had no objection to their betting, provided they placed their bets with him, and he gave them the same terms and facilities as the bookmaker. In place of telephoning to the "bookie," they telephoned to father, and soon lost their interest in betting. I also knew a doctor who in this way weakened his wife's interest in racing. There is a curious taint in human nature whereby some of us would prefer to lose money to a total stranger than to those to whom we may owe what money can never repay.

Every year the vice-consul bought a ticket for himself and his friends in the Christmas lottery. A whole ticket cost forty pounds, and consisted of a square, perforated sheet, containing four hundred vouchers worth half a dollar, so that it was possible to buy anything from one four-hundredth share in a ticket. The first prize was a quarter of a million pounds, and people said the lottery was the only fair thing in Spain, just as the bull-fight was the only thing that was punctual. The numbers and prizes were drawn by two orphans. There were two great revolving cylinders in the Hall of Justice in Madrid, and the winner of the first prize was supposed to provide for the two orphans for the rest of their lives—a task which anyone would willingly undertake.

This lottery taught me a lesson. I told the vice-consul I wished for eight shares in his ticket, and these he promised to keep for me. I said I would give him one pound the next day and take my vouchers. I forgot about the one pound and the vouchers. The lottery was drawn two days later, and the vice-consul's ticket did not win. Next week I handed him one pound, which he refused to accept. "Had the ticket won you would not have won anything. You paid nothing, and for all I knew you might have changed your mind. There is a rule about these transactions, and it must be kept. Otherwise people might put their friends in a very awkward dilemma." He was right. Straight gambling all over the world is governed by three rules: pay and play; where you cannot win you cannot lose; where you cannot lose you cannot win. As for the ethics of gambling, I think those moral theologians are right who maintain that in this instinct of the human mind there is no essential evil, provided firstly that a man does not risk more than he would be entitled to spend on any legitimate amusement, according to his position and duties in life; and secondly, that all parties to the transaction have a fair chance of winning. Thus it would be wrong to bet on what we knew to be a certainty; but that is a sin which few of us are ever likely to be able to commit on the racecourse.

This was not my first visit to the prison. If my horse failed to arrive in the morning, one of my first inquiries would be whether Little Pic, the man who brought him, was in jail, and when he was there I went to see him. When visiting a friend in jail it was customary to bring a present of wine, fruit, provisions or cigarettes, because the prison fare was very meagre. You find your friend sitting at one of the plain deal tables in the open courtyard, probably playing cards with some of the other prisoners, and when he has borrowed a few glasses from the jailer, you open your bottle of wine. For those who are friendless the hardships of prison can only be relieved by the charity of more fortunate fellow-prisoners. It was also possible for English sailors to remain in Spanish prisons for weeks or even months without trial, if their captains had failed to report them as missing to the British consul.

One morning a sailor, released from the prison, arrived at the clinic with a six-inch open wound on his scalp. He was from Glasgow, and his ship had sailed without him. "I'm feared the captain will be awfu' angry, Doctor. But it wasna ma fault. Ye ken I'm a jokey sort o' chap, and I was walkin' back to the ship at night when I sees on yon pier yin o' they sodjers. He was sittin' on a barrel and looked half asleep. Weel, I'm a jokey sort o' chap, an' I'd had a drink, so I pulls out ma pipe an' holds it like a pistol. Then I sticks it in his face an' says: 'Your money or your life!' An' d'ye ken, that sodjer got up an' struck me on the heid wi' his sword. Aye, I'm tellin' you."

I looked at the cut. "A good thing for you he used the back of the blade."

"Weel, doctor, the very next thing I kent was the next day, and I was in jail. They'd put a hanky round ma heid. I was in that place for four days. The food was awfu'. Dry breid, and a queer, cold, watery kind o' soup. Some o' they Spaniards had better food, and yin o' them gi'es me an orange an' anither a bit o' sausage. But I didna ken their lingo. To-day a Spanish gentleman came in and spoke to me, but I didna ken a word of what he said. Then they turned me oot, an' I found the institute an' they sent a boy wi' me here. Ye ken, Doctor, I'm a jokey sort o' chap, but no' a bad chap, an' if you could put in a word for me wi' the consul, I'd be greatly obleeged. I'd like fine to get anither ship, and get oot o' this country. It's an awfu' place. D'ye ken Glesgy? Noo, that's a fine place."

## CHAPTER XII

## A CASTLE IN SPAIN

DURING my last week in Spain I went hunting with the Litri and his friends. The meet was at a farm on the *campo*, to which the horses and hounds had been sent on the previous day, as the place was fifteen miles from Huelva. We went part of the way by train, starting in the darkness at five in the morning. I was half-asleep in the carriage when I noticed a figure moving along the footboard, and a white face peered through the window. The door swung open and the guard asked for tickets, the speed of the train being about fifteen miles an hour. At a wayside station we got out in the darkness and waited for the mail-coach that would take us the last five miles. The few people on the platform knew very little about the coach. One said: "The coach? Ah, señores, there will be no mail-coach this morning. It is too dark."

Another said: "The coach? The coach left an hour ago."

At last there came the beat of hoofs on the hard road, the jingle of bells and the crack of a whip, and the coach with its mule-team and outrunner appeared in the darkness. Inside the air reeked of cigars and garlic. Dawn came rapidly in the south. A grey light spread across the sky, and soon the first blinding rays of the sun struck the coach and threw long shadows on the plain.

At the farm there was *desayuno* of coffee, rolls and butter, and the cavalcade of a dozen riders set out across the plain, the horses walking in line behind the hounds, who were running hither and thither looking for scent. I have written "hounds" out of respect for those who live in English shires, but in truth they were mongrel dogs. Twenty years before my uncle had imported a couple of English fox-hounds, and now any dog whose appearance suggested some far-off link with these aristocrats was called a hound. The hounds with which we were hunting belonged to different members of the party, and there was some fighting amongst the pack. The air was chilly, but the sunlight was warm, and from the *campo* came the fragrances of spring in Spain.

The thin grass of the *campo* grows on a pale yellow soil, but the ploughed earth around the farms is a rich chocolate colour streaked with reddish shades. The plain on which we rode was alongside the low Sierra Hills. On some of these hills are woods of dwarfed pines, cork trees and the encina, an evergreen oak. Other hills are overgrown with wild rosemary and the jara, a large green bush, very sticky with gum, and having a white flower the size of a dog rose, but with dark red spots on white, silky petals.

The dogs started a hare and ran for the high ground covered with brushwood, followed by the horses crashing between bushes that reached the saddle and over ground full of rocks and rabbit-holes. These Spanish horses are sure-footed, and have a good deal of Arab strain. After a time the scent was lost and we returned to the open plain. Many hares were raised and a few were caught. The hunt led through orchards of lemon and orange trees, and no one really knows the orange unless he has plucked it from the tree. Long natural avenues led through plantations of olive trees laden with fruit and grey-green shimmering leaves. Interplanted between the olives were fig trees, whose branches looked withered because their season had not yet come. Soon after midday we met the pack-horses and ate a meal on the *campo*. There were fat capons, pigeons, partridges, hams and sausages, rolls of bread and a small cask of olives. The wine, Rioja and Malaga, was out of round leather bottles made of goatskin attached to a neck and cork of hard wood. There were neither plates nor forks, but from his hip-pocket each man produced a large and useful clasp knife.

The Spanish are a very temperate people in their use of wine. A man may become *alegre* or even *muy alegre* without offence, but drunkenness is despised. The drunkard in Spain drinks *aguardiente*, which is usually a raw spirit made from potatoes, but in all my time there I only saw two Spaniards drunk. In Spain it is regarded not so much as a moral as an æsthetic offence against the dignity of man. Two circumstances tend to make them temperate. The moods of the mind are powerfully influenced by environment, and the blue sky and sunshine engenders a natural happiness that does not need the aid of alcohol. They have also a deep belief in the dignity of mankind, which is part of the Faith.

At the end of the hunt I rode back to Huelva with the Litri. In crossing the plain to reach the road we passed through a great herd of wild bulls. We walked the horses and did not speak. When passing close to a bull, he would stop grazing, raise his head, and gaze with large brown eyes. The rider must ignore him, look straight ahead, and pretend that he has not seen the bull—and to do this for the first time needs more resolution than to cut your worst enemy in the street. Once on the road the horses went at the easy Castilian pace (the *paseo*) at which a man may almost go to sleep in the saddle. In England this pace is called the run.

Soon the sun was setting over the Atlantic, and the western sky became a blaze of dazzling light. In the south the sun sets quickly, falling inch by inch behind the ocean, and for a few moments after it has gone a green light lingers on the horizon—then it is dark; a thin vapour comes in from the sea, and the air is chilly. Far down in the northern sky is the Bear, and ahead, flashing like a diamond by candle-light, is the South Star.

The road passes a *fonda*, and from its open door, throwing out a river of light, comes the music of a guitar, the clash of castanets, and a glimpse of dancing-girls in gaily coloured dresses. Now the road leads through palm trees that rustle in the slight wind, by wayside ponds where bull-frogs are croaking, and by brushwood alive with the myriad sounds of insects which are awake at night. Beside a lonely cluster of trees is a statue of Our Lady, the Star of the Sea, who watches over sailors, and on the steps of her statue a girl is praying. Overhead is the cloudless pageantry of the stars, and behind a silver haze in the east the moon is rising on the cold Sierras, where the wolves will now be howling. For the Litri and for me the sun has set on a Castle in Spain.

The Litri was not a talkative man, except when he was telling a story, and for the most part we rode in silence. In the starlight he looked like a Roman emperor, and I wondered if Severus had looked like that when he led the legions over a roadless country from York to Inverness. On the outskirts of Huelva we came to the parting of our ways and said good-bye, wishing each other health, wealth, and all the other things; and that we might walk with God—he in South America and I in England. He was sailing soon for a season in Brazil, where matadors are well paid.

There he made money and returned to Spain. On his return the Litri gave his son, Juan Miguel, a place in the *cuadrilla*, and within five years the young man had become his father's *sobresoliente*. His name was then approved by the Society of Matadors, and the day came when he qualified as a matador by killing a full-grown bull in public. This took place in the Huelva ring. The Litri killed the first bull, and, when the second was ready to be killed, made a speech to the president, kissed his son on both cheeks, handed him the sword and *muleta*, and, in the presence of ten thousand people, named him Manuelito.

Within five years Manuelito had surpassed his father and was acclaimed "the best in Spain." His timing with the *capa* or the sword was perfect, and he had done the "twist" sitting on a chair in the centre of the ring. It is true of many other games, such as tennis and cricket, that the timing of the stroke proclaims the champion. Manuelito made money, and had a *novia*. She was of the people, but very beautiful, modest and loyal. They were to be married after his last fight of that season. This fight was in Malaga, and in the presence of King Alfonso, Queen Ena, and twenty thousand people. The Litri was one of the other matadors in the ring.

When the bull was released for Manuelito, experts in the audience became apprehensive. The bull was not charging straight, but often jabbed to one or other side. Had the bull defective vision? No one knew, but when Manuelito went to kill the bull he was caught, gored through the muscles of the right thigh, and thrown. It was then that the Litri entered the ring and killed his last bull. They carried Manuelito to the clinic of a Spanish surgeon in Malaga. He was an able surgeon, had been educated in Germany, and his treatment was orthodox. Yet the wound went badly for Manuelito, and on the fourth day the Litri telegraphed to Huelva.

My uncle had died, and the clinic had passed to my cousin, Ian Macdonald, the pioneer of abdominal surgery in Southern Spain. He left Huelva for Malaga in his car at eleven p.m., and a large crowd had assembled outside his house to see him go. Such was the popularity of Manuelito.

As Macdonald drove through the night to Malaga he remembered a professional secret, a thing that Manuelito had revealed to him alone. Occasionally the matador suffered from a slight twitching of the left eye. This only lasted for a few minutes, but while it did last the man saw double.

Macdonald had warned him that no man with such a defect should risk his life in the ring, but Manuelito had only laughed. "It never comes on in the arena." Did it come on in the Malaga ring, and was 'the vision of both man and beast distorted on that Sunday afternoon? Who can say?

In the morning Macdonald found that the case was hopeless. Gas gangrene had supervened, and Manuelito died.

Then the two surgeons had a strange talk. The Spaniard said: "I must send his body to-night to a private mortuary. My other patients would not like the idea of it remaining here." He had been educated in Germany, and in sentiment had lost touch with his own race.

"Good heavens!" exclaimed Macdonald, "you can't do that. What harm can his body do your other patients? There are walls between his room and theirs. Don't you realise that this man was the idol of Spain, and that these people hate the idea of anyone being placed in a mortuary? If you send the body out of your place before the funeral, it is not what the people will say but what they will do. They might burn the clinic to the ground. Let us go for a drive in the open air and discuss this matter quietly."

The two surgeons went driving for an hour and continued the argument. On their return to the clinic they saw four silent men standing on the pavement. Three were dressed as *toreros* and the fourth was in mufti. Macdonald recognised them as Manuelito's *cuadrilla,* and the tall, good-looking young man in mufti was the *sobresoliente.* As the surgeons alighted, the *sobresoliente* stood in front of the Spaniard, looked him straight in the face, and spoke three words in a low voice: "He stays here."

It was a command, and the surgeon agreed.

In Malaga they still talk of the funeral of Manuelito, when the streets were lined by several hundred thousand people, and all traffic in the city was suspended.

After the funeral the Litri cut his pigtail and left the ring for ever, and when he died there were scarcely a hundred people at his funeral. It was not that the people had forgotten the famous matador, but that they remembered one other thing. The Litri was a widower, and when Manuelito died he invited the son's *novia* to his house. A year later he married the girl. And the people did not approve.

# CHAPTER XIII

## THE ASYLUM

THERE was a dance at the asylum on the first Saturday night after my arrival. On returning to Scotland I had taken a post as clinical assistant at Craig House, Edinburgh. This was my father's advice, he having himself specialised in that branch of medicine. These institutions were once called mad-houses, then asylums, and are now known as mental hospitals. There has been more than a change of name. It is a far cry from the good old days, beloved by unhistorical idealists, when lunatics were chained, starved, beaten and soused with water, to the humane, reasonable and often scientific treatment of modern times. Indeed, some believe that the name mental hospital will even remove the stigma attached to insanity, but these optimists forget that in every healthy community a social stigma is attached to all inheritable diseases, and that a change of name is often merely a modern short cut out of difficulties. If the middle-classes are suffering from a scarcity of servants, all we have to do is to drop the word servant and say "domestic help," and then thousands of people will offer their services. One of the titles of the Roman pontiff is "the Servant of the Servants of God," but so far no one has proposed an alteration to "the Domestic Help of the Domestic Helps of God."

At the asylum dance, the patients, who were all of the richer classes, wore evening-dress, as also did the doctors. There were male attendants in dark lounge suits and female nurses in uniform. A few visitors were present and gave the dance a semblance of reality.

The first patient with whom I danced was a fair-haired, blue-eyed girl of twenty-three. She had been brought by train from London in the charge of two nurses, and I had received her on admission earlier in the week. The reception-room, with oak-panelled walls, table and chairs, was on the left of the outer hall next to the main entrance, and I was seated at the table when her car rolled up the drive. On entering the room she freed herself from the nurses and stood facing me across the table. She was very agitated, and was obviously struggling to pull herself together and to escape the inevitable. I rose to shake hands, but this she scorned. "It is not usual to shake hands with hotel-managers. I insist on knowing the name of this hotel. You look honest. Is this the North British Hotel, and are you the manager?" I told her I was a doctor and that she had come to a hospital for those who were very tired and needed a rest. She sank into a chair and sobbed, with her head on the table. "The liars, the liars; they told me I was going to the North British Hotel! I know what this place is—it's an asylum. Oh, my God, my God!"

One of the nurses who had brought her, handed me the order for her reception. I nodded to the nurses and they left the room, their place being taken by two of our nurses, who stood one on either side of the patient. Again I spoke to her: "You must be very tired and need a good sleep. The nurses will show you your room. When you are in bed I will come and see you."

"You'll drug me," she cried.

"No, I won't," was my answer, "and I will never give you anything without telling you what it is."

The nurses touched her on the arm and she left the reception-room quietly. The next day one of my colleagues told me that this was not the best way to receive a patient, and that for the time being I should have become the manager of the North British Hotel. This I disputed on the ground that if the girl had any sense at all she would know the place was not an hotel, and that this knowledge would only add to her fear and confusion.

M

A doctor attached to an asylum cannot certify any of his patients insane. The order whereby a patient may be confined in an asylum is issued by a magistrate in consequence of a petition and statement, usually made by the patient's nearest relative, supported by two independent medical certificates. The doctor signing a certificate must state the facts indicating insanity, observed by himself at the time of examination, and also the facts communicated to him by other people. These certificates are scrutinised by the Board of Control and if the evidence is insufficient or out of order the certificate is returned to the doctor for amendment. As a fact indicating insanity, one doctor wrote: "He called me a damned fool."

My father returned the certificate with a marginal note in red ink: "The remark quoted is not necessarily evidence of an unsound mind."

There is another case where a patient was alleged to be a lunatic because "he revoked at whist!" The evidence of insanity must be definite, and no wise doctor ever lightly signs a lunacy certificate.

The asylum dance was in the large central hall, oak-panelled and with a good polished floor. On the walls were a few pictures in oils, the work of former patients. These pictures interested visitors who sought thrills in the work of insane artists, but there was little distinction in the paintings, except that they were crude in form and indifferently painted. The insane, in their calm intervals, can paint, write, play or sing according to their natural ability in these arts. From his paintings in the Tate Gallery, it is clear that Blake, who had genius as a painter and a poet, transferred to canvas in his sane intervals some of the horrors of the mind which in moments of madness he had known. During actual attacks of insanity, there is not only confusion of mind but also grave interference with the higher co-ordinated movements, such as writing or painting, and therefore no creative work can be produced. When patients try to express themselves during an attack, their work is always confused, obscene, or imitative. Thus, at Christmas, one lady patient wrote a poem, of which I can only recall the first two lines:

> The screams of a thousand children
> Burnt on a Christmas tree.

I do not think that is great verse, but upon my soul I should not be surprised if some people did not hail it as immortal. When I am told that the beautiful fantasies of J. M. Barrie are psychologically obscene, and that books banned by the police are in reality highly moral, I conclude that in the world of to-day there is only one standard of comparison left—the gold standard—and even that has been abandoned in England.

At the far end of the hall was the stage, occasionally used for amateur theatricals, and now occupied by a string quartet. The blue-eyed girl with whom I danced dragged her steps behind the music, so that it was I who had to suit my step to hers, and when I spoke to her she never answered. She was a slow, lifeless automaton. I wondered in what ballroom her last dance had been and what had really brought her here, and when I looked at her in the middle of our dance her eyes were full of tears, so I said: "You would like to stop now, wouldn't you?"

And she spoke for the first time: "I wish I were dead."

I led her back to the nurse by whose side she sat down. The nurse smiled, patted her hand, hoped she had enjoyed her dance, and led her off to bed. Enjoyed her dance! Almighty God, can such things be? To a young healthy girl every dance is a gay adventure in which she is happy and excited. When the dance is over she goes home tired and looks in her mirror. If she be a sensible girl she looks at herself as critically as she has looked at all the other girls she saw that night, but the night may come when she will

forget to look into the mirror and will go straight to bed
—to sleep, perchance to dream. That is the night when
She has found Him and He has found Her out of all the
world.

Love laughs at locks and bars, but only once have I known
romance come to a girl when certified insane. She was a
poor girl and a patient in one of the large London asylums,
and the man who brought her romance was proprietor of
the oldest theatre in Europe—a Punch-and-Judy show. One
afternoon this entertainment was provided for the female
patients, and the Punch-and-Judy man saw the girl through
a peep-hole in the curtain round his show. In one of the
intervals in the drama of Punch the man handed the girl a
note which the nurses read, allowed the girl to read, and
to write an answer on the back of the paper. To the nurses
this was better fun than the Punch-and-Judy show, and what
a sport the Punch-and-Judy man must be! The jest was
even better when the Punch-and-Judy man called to see
the girl next visiting day, and the girl was teased about her
young man. Next visiting day the two sisters of the man
called on the girl and brought her little presents and notes
from the man. There came a visiting day when the two
sisters came for the last time. They saw the girl in the large
day-room, where many of the patients were receiving their
friends. At one end of the room was a cupboard in which
brushes and dusters were kept. Some careless nurse had
left the cupboard unlocked, and into it slipped the girl and
one of the sisters of the Punch-and-Judy man. The girl
took off her uniform of coarse grey calico, and the man's
sister took off her outer dress, for on this afternoon she
wore two dresses, one over the other. The girl put on the
dress, also a little hat, and the two women came out of the
cupboard. The two sisters and the girl walked quietly out
of the asylum. When the escape was discovered there was
great excitement, the police were informed, and the asylum

authorities appointed a special committee of inquiry. All in vain. Somewhere in London the girl was hidden for fourteen days, and once an escaped lunatic has been at liberty for fourteen days he or she cannot be taken back to the asylum without being re-certified as insane.

When the girl was eventually traced, the authorities could do nothing, because she had then become the wife of the Punch-and-Judy man. It was no doubt a very quiet wedding, and whoever gave the bride away, I am certain that it was not the President of the Eugenics Society.

Having danced with the blue-eyed girl, I watched the others dancing. It was good for the patients to have exercise, and those who were recovering enjoyed these dances. To those who were ill the dance must have seemed a mockery, and yet we who danced with them were pretending that all was well. Everything was done to conceal the fact that between two classes of people at the dance there was the bar sinister of insanity, which makes the poorest sane peasant greater than the maddest king. It was the same throughout the institution. When visitors were shown round, there was no unlocking and locking of doors. The doctor merely turned the handles and led the way from room to room. Visitors were impressed by the apparent absence of restraint. And yet there was restraint. The handles of the doors of public rooms worked on the outside but the handle on the inside was a dummy, and to pass out required a key. The absence of restraint was as unreal as the delusions of the patients. As I watched the dance I knew that the asylum was finding my weakness, and that I lacked the calm self-sufficiency of the bovine, without which no man or woman can, with impunity, associate for a prolonged period with the insane. Insanity was unreality.

These reflections were interrupted by a tall man, who remarked that there was something pathetic about an asylum dance. The stranger looked like a lawyer, and I answered that it was very kind of visitors to come and brighten the evening.

"Most kind," he agreed, "but personally I wouldn't come unless I was forced. You didn't know that I was a patient, Doctor?"

"No," I laughed, "and you'll soon be going out."

"I hope not, Doctor, because I'll never go out until I die. That is inevitable, because I happen to be the only sane man in the world. In a mad world there is no place for a sane man. Therefore they put me in here. It is quite reasonable when you come to think of it, and if you ever should discover what I have discovered—well, they'll put you in here. What have I discovered? The greatest thing of all—what life is. You don't know what life is, but I do. *Life is very nearly an Almost.* The discovery is easily proved. Let me ask you a simple question. When you last saw the Scotch express entering the station did you throw yourself under the engine? You say 'No.' But you are wrong, because 'No' is a negation, and there is no such thing as a negation in the universe. The correct answer is 'Almost.' Let us try again. To-night at dinner did you swallow your knife? Again you say 'No,' when you should say 'Almost.' It is as I feared. You cannot see the truth. Well, I suppose now we should both do our duty and find ourselves partners for the next dance."

My new friend had not been incarcerated on account of his beliefs. No one ever is. But he had an occasional tendency to put his philosophy into practice, to the danger of himself and others. Had he been content with the preaching without the practice he might have made a fortune by founding a new cult or religion.

*Life is very nearly an Almost.* More fantastic statements have drawn crowds of adherents, but the prophet should have silvery hair with a flowing beard, and must always wear a white nightshirt.

When Herr von Recklinghauser visited the asylum my
colleagues began to suspect me of delusions. I was on duty
the day the Herr arrived, and he brought a card of introduction from a well-known Edinburgh doctor. The Herr
spoke excellent English, and as I showed him round the
wards I realised that he was not a doctor and had little
interest in the treatment of insanity. It was only when we
reached the kitchens that his interest was really awakened.
How much porridge could be cooked in the cauldrons?
Did we bake our own bread? What was the capacity of the
ovens? What was the maximum number of people for whom
the kitchen could cater? What foods were kept in the store-
rooms? Our visitor was apparently a hotel proprietor, or
was interested in catering for institutions. Before he left
I gave him afternoon tea, and inquired when he thought
war would be declared between Germany and England.
This tactless question annoyed him, and he declared there
would never be war between two great and friendly nations.
This was in 1908, and I was a reader of L. J. Maxse in the
*National Review*, so I asked the Herr why Germany was
building a fleet. "To protect her colonies. It is not aimed
against England, and I who say that should know, because
I am a German naval architect." He went away, and that
night my colleagues laughed me to scorn when I suggested
that our visitor knew how many troops could be billeted in
our institution. I myself never believed the stories of German
officers in mufti drawing maps of England. They could
buy our Ordnance Survey maps, on which every pond is
marked, in Berlin! But this interest in kitchens? Maybe
I was wrong. In 1920 Mr. Winston Churchill said that a
small number of very stupid people happened to be right
in their foreknowledge of the Great War, and that a large
number of very clever people happened to be wrong. A
comforting doctrine!

At the asylum I made a few friends and a few enemies.

One of the patients who disliked me at first sight was Mr. A——. In their likes and dislikes the insane are as instinctive and unreasonable as the rest of us, but have less control over their feelings.

To each of us the majority of other people are neutral, but now and then we encounter someone whom we immediately appraise as a potential friend or foe. Sometimes we are wrong, but often we are right, and in the main these instinctive likes and dislikes are protective. In dogs this instinct is highly developed, and they instantly recognise potential antagonism. Mr. A—— was not a certified patient, but a voluntary boarder, with a suite of rooms in one of the villas in the asylum grounds. He lived there of his free will to escape a certain annoyance which he might have encountered in the outside world, and it was I who unwittingly brought this annoyance into his cloister. He was an author, and, under another name, contributed articles on history, politics and economics to one of the leading English reviews. One morning, when going round the villas, I knocked at his sitting-room door. "Good morning, Mr. A——, I called on you when passing."

The old gentleman laid down his pen and looked at me from his writing-table, on which many books of reference were piled. "How long have you been here? A week! No honest man would answer in that way. He would say 'One week,' or he might say seven days, but not 'A week.' By God, you are not the first of your breed to sneak in here, and you can't deceive me; I knew you at a glance. You're a Jesuit. Get out, you scoundrel, before I do you an injury. Report to those who sent you that I can detect a Jesuit at sight, howsoever disguised."

I withdrew and thereafter another doctor visited that villa. I never saw Mr. A—— again, but remembered, on reading his essays, that this violent antipathy to Jesuits is shared by many who have never sought the shelter of an asylum, and that many Roman Catholics have similar delusions about English Freemasons.

These voluntary patients found the asylum a haven of peace where they escaped from the worries of life. In an age of incessant mechanism this yearning for peace leads men and women to the solitude of mountains or to retreats in convents or monasteries, where the mind is calmed and refreshed. Some of our patients returned to the world for months or even years, but nearly always they came back to their refuge—the asylum.

Mr. X was a voluntary patient who liked me. The name under which he was known in the asylum was not his real name, which I never knew. He was a tall, broad, elderly man with grey hair and beard, and lived in his own suite, where I saw him daily and tested his blood pressure. Occasionally he went out for the day in a carriage and pair. On his return from these excursions there was sometimes trouble. He was expected to be back by nine o'clock, but was often a little late. One night I was sent for at ten-thirty. Two attendants were in the corridor outside his bedroom, in which he was making an uproar. Through the open door various articles of bedroom furniture were being hurled into the corridor. I stood beside the door; a chair hurtled through the air and I entered the bedroom. There was not the slightest risk. As soon as I entered the room Mr. X dropped the wash-basin stand and shook hands, much too firmly. "Glad to see you, Doctor! Come to take my blood pressure? That's right. I'll lie on the bed. One hundred and ninety! Put it up to three hundred! What, three hundred would burst my arteries! Put it down to one hundred and seventy. Thank you. That's much better."

It was my turn to speak. "Mr. X, your conduct is disgraceful. Yes, I know you've had a day out. That is no reason why you should disturb the whole place. Disgraceful! This must be the last time. If ever this happens again you'll have to clear out. We can't allow you to stay in the asylum if you behave like this."

That threat was the one hold I had over Mr. X. He was well aware that if we refused to keep him as a voluntary patient and sent him out, he would very soon be sent back as a certified patient. Mr. X valued his liberty to drive unattended in a carriage and pair, and to dine now and then extremely well at the most exclusive club in Scotland.

"I'm sorry, Doctor. This shall be the last occasion. I shall go to bed. Kindly close the door as you go out, and tell those fellows outside to come in in five minutes' time and put the furniture straight." A week later I found him in the avenue driving out in his carriage and pair, and as he acknowledged my salutation by raising his white top-hat with a lavender-gloved hand, I noted his strong resemblance to one of the reigning monarchs of Europe.

Mr. W——, a large landowner, was a certified patient, and one of the most cultured Scotsmen I have ever known. He was a good talker, and I regretted the fact of his epilepsy because it precluded him from inviting me to shoot over his moors. Once I saw him standing on the top of a mound in the grounds feeding the birds he loved. They were strutting about on the grass around his feet. An attack came on, the birds flew away, and he danced on the mound, shouting out in lalling speech which resembled no language I had ever heard. The attack passed off, the birds returned, and he resumed feeding them.

"What did *he* say, Mr. W——?" I asked; because it was the patient's conviction that in these attacks he was possessed by the devil, and nothing more symbolic of a devil dancing and speaking have I ever seen or heard.

"This time the message was too terrible to tell you, Doctor."

"Tell me, I don't mind."

"Well, *he* said this: 'The Cross is closed to the world.'"

Could the devil himself have said more!

Another epileptic was the Duke of ——, now dead. Once a week it was my duty to go to his villa in the evening, and play whist with him and his two attendants. He taught me little at cards, but he did give me a lesson in etiquette. "Please don't say 'Your Grace.' I prefer that you call me 'Duke.'"

One of the happiest patients was "The Baron," so named because he believed that he was a mediæval baron, and the asylum his castle. This tall man with his black moustache did resemble "the Wicked Uncle" in the pantomimes of my youth. I was walking one forenoon through the grounds with the medical superintendent, when we met "The Baron." He ignored the medical superintendent and addressed me: "Ha, varlet! And how many knaves hast thou hanged on the battlements this day?"

"None, Baron," I replied.

"None! Then dost merit a sound whipping for thy sloth. In thy company I behold a sorry caitiff who shall surely die. He is short, stout, and rosy in the cheeks. Is it not written in the Book of Life that the rubicund in face shall not inherit the earth? The sun is not yet high. See to it that he be hanged from the battlements at noon, and peradventure I may behold him dancing at the end of a halter."

"The Baron" passed on, and although I had not smiled, the medical superintendent looked at me sharply. "You know 'The Baron' is not half as mad as he pretends to be. All that impertinence was for my benefit."

Mrs. B—— was a woman who suffered the tortures of the damned. She was a widow, aged thirty-three, whose only child was dead, and, when I first knew her, she had acute melancholia, her nights being passed in hell. In her bedroom were one hundred telephones, and every night they rang, all except one, which was painted white. When she answered these calls it was always someone to whom she had once told a lie, and they were telephoning to ask if what she had said was true. One night the white telephone rang. "Is that you, Mother?" It was the voice of her little girl, who had died at the age of eleven.

"Yes, Helen, it's the voice of your mother."

There was silence for some minutes before her child spoke again. "Was it true what you told me about Father?"

"No, it was a lie. But why do you take so long to answer?"

Again there was a long silence before the voice replied. "Because I'm a long way off, Mother. . . ." When the nurses came to her she was unconscious on the floor.

Under treatment she recovered, and was a fascinating brunette. She taught me one thing I did not know—that patients, when they recover, have a distinct memory of kindness or unkindness shown to them in moments when anyone might think them incapable of appreciating anything. Mrs. B—— left the asylum, and two months later I was invited—to her wedding!

The only people who labour under the delusion that all lunatics are always irresponsible in their conduct are those who have never lived in an asylum. In ninety per cent. of the ordinary affairs of life a lunatic will act as anticipated— otherwise it would be an impossibility for anyone to manage an asylum. In the main, lunatics also know the difference between right and wrong, although, by reason of their infirmity, they may be incapable of acting on that knowledge.

Mrs. H—— was a stout, elderly, white-haired lady with the staring eyes of mania, and she disliked me. Every morning I saw her in the acute female day ward, and had noticed for about a week that she was always standing nearer the door by which I entered than any of the other patients. Thinking she wished to speak to me alone, I asked her one morning if she did.

"No. You find the conversation of others, sir, more entertaining than mine." And she bowed stiffly. The nurses told me her grievance—that I had favourites—which was true.

When I entered that ward I always closed the door behind my back, so that I was facing the inmates all the time. Lion-tamers never turn their backs on the animals in the cage, and the wisdom of this I learnt after having been assaulted by an erotic young woman. One morning on entering I moved my head just in time, and the blow from Mrs. H——'s weapon caught me on the top of the left shoulder. I seized the weapon, and in a moment two nurses were holding Mrs. H—— by the arms. In a crowd of normal people the incident would have caused some excitement, but none of the other inmates were in any way interested. It was a curious weapon. It was one of Mrs. H——'s stockings. The foot of the stocking was full of earth and stones, held in place by a string tied round the ankle of the stocking. From this mass of earth and stones old rusty nails projected, so that the foot of the stocking looked like the head of a spiked club. My shoulder was bruised and I was angry. "Mrs. H——, you are a disgrace to the ward." Mrs. H—— wept, and I think she wept for two reasons, because her carefully planned plot had failed, and because she knew that she had done wrong. From the laundry list it was probable that Mrs. H—— had concealed that stocking under her dress for at least two weeks. It had been attached to her underskirt by a safety-pin. When out in the enclosed garden she had gone behind bushes in flower-beds and there patiently collected the string, earth, stones and nails. In her action there was malice, intention, patience and resource.

After six months' asylum experience I lunched with my father at his club in Edinburgh, and told him that I was unsuited for this branch of medicine. Mr. Johns of Aberdeen also lunched with us that day. I had forgotten all about him until I remembered our last meeting at Aberdeen when

I had taken two pints of beer. Mr. Johns looked more cadaverous than before and had little to say. My father was going to Aberdeen the next day and Mr. Johns did say: "Give them my love. I was called away in a hurry, on business. I'm going to London and will be back in a week."

After he left us I said to my father: "That man is ill."

"Rubbish," replied my father, "he is always like that. A very quiet, respectable man."

My father was wrong. Mr. Johns was a very sick man, but the sickness was in his mind. He was on his way to Liverpool, not to London. He was going on a sea-voyage in a small steamer to South America. A liner would have been more comfortable, but liners carried wireless and Mr. Johns did not wish to be disturbed. For twenty-five years he had been a trusted lawyer and a most respected elder of the kirk, and was now going on holiday. Nor was he going empty-handed. We had lunched with a man in possession of fifteen thousand pounds. Of this money ten thousand pounds belonged to his Church and five thousand to his sisters. The police never found him, so he must have been miserable. Mr. Cairns, the London magistrate, sometimes asks his friends: "Would you rather be guilty and acquitted or be innocent and found guilty?"

Most people answer: "Guilty and acquitted."

Whereupon Mr. Cairns remarks: "You are wrong. You forget conscience."

# CHAPTER XIV

## DREAMS OF AVARICE

WITHIN a year of leaving the asylum I became medical superintendent of the Westmoreland Sanatorium. Thus, at the age of twenty-eight, I had free quarters, fire, light, board, horse, gig, coachman, and a salary of five hundred pounds a year. The work did not amount to more than four hours a day. Life in an institution, unless a man has a real interest in his work, is apt to demoralise. It is too easy. In my spare time I edited *The Control and Eradication of Tuberculosis*, a book to which the leading authorities in Europe and America contributed. This work occupied a year, and at last the book was published at fifteen shillings. I was to have half the profits on sales, which is perhaps a shade better than paying to have a book published. There are innocent people who write books and never reflect that if a publisher will not risk a penny on their immortal prose it is better that their thoughts should continue to blush unseen in manuscript. My book was sold for fifteen shillings, but the cost of printing, paper, and binding was not covered by sales. There were no profits to divide, and the translations and typing of the articles cost me nearly fifty pounds.

It is sad to be born poor but honest and with expensive tastes. I found an easier way to make money. There was a rubber boom. Before participating in this El Dorado I bought, for one shilling, a book which gave instruction on how to deal on the Stock Exchange. This book made everything clear. The next step was to find a stockbroker, and Providence provided for that. One of the benefactors of my sanatorium was a man of about forty-five, a bachelor with an income of ten thousand pounds a year. He was the only man I ever knew who actually found salvation on a golf links. Other men have reduced their weight and improved their health on a golf course, but this man saved his soul at the third green. In his unregenerate days he had, amongst the lesser vices, the habit of using bad language. One day at the third green the thought came to him: "If Jesus Christ wishes me to stop swearing, He'll make me stop." There was no more swearing at the third or any other green. Did this man join a church? He did not. Organised Christianity in any form was of no use. He organised his own variety, and addressed small gatherings of men, but never women. At these meetings the brand of Christianity revealed in short addresses was of the "brotherly type." He also gave large sums of money to one of the most useful and practical of the Protestant foreign missions. To me he gave his card to one of the largest firms of stockbrokers on the London Exchange.

The firm wrote to me. They would be very glad to act for me, and hoped to be favoured with my commissions. They were. I bought fifty Muhesa shares at thirty shillings, and two days later on the same account sold them for two pounds ten shillings. Fifty pounds profit in two days. All the profit was on paper, because as soon as one lot of shares were sold at a profit others were bought. There were few rubber estates in which, during these glorious months, I did not have an interest, if only for a few days. Being far from London and three miles from a post office, I arranged with an agency for the tape prices of the shares in which I was interested to be telegraphed to me twice a day. So it went on. I was on the way to make a fortune. At the end of six months I would be able to leave medicine, and go on the Stock Exchange myself. Then it might be millions. Did not Mr. Schiff, who left three million sterling, say that anyone could make a fortune on the Stock Exchange. He did; but subject to three conditions: (a) buy on a falling market;

(*b*) sell on a rising market; and (*c*) never be ashamed to take sixpence profit per share. Never have I heard of three commandments more opposed to the dictates of human nature. On the racecourse the bookmakers have a true saying: "The backer always beats himself." It is greed that defeats us. From the rubber market I extended my operations to American rails. Here the brokers gave me a warning. I had wired them to buy one thousand shares in an American railroad. In answer came a telegram, reply paid: "Please confirm buying order. Have you not mistaken pounds sterling for dollars. The price will be over seven thousand pounds sterling." They were wise brokers!

Yet I was not altogether foolish. There was a queer concern called the London and Paris Share Exchange, of which I had read in *Truth*. One day these people sent me a very friendly letter, the kind of letter that any country doctor, parson, or widow ought to welcome. The London and Paris Exchange were in touch with Wall Street, and had inside information as to what the biggest financial interests in the United States were doing. This valuable information they were anxious to convey to a select band of people, including myself. The information was to be sent free of charge. Lest lack of capital should hinder anyone from reaping certain financial advantages which would otherwise accrue, the London and Paris Exchange had arranged that for every one pound I sent they would buy in my name one hundred pounds of American railroad stock. If the price dropped one pound I would lose my deposit, but as the price would be certain to rise, each one pound invested might become five pounds or even ten pounds. A deposit of five pounds would likewise cover a fall of five points, and was perhaps a safer method of dealing than with a one pound deposit.

How different from my stockbrokers were these kind people! In place of making millions for themselves they

wanted to help me to make money. They made me feel
ashamed of myself. If I had, as twice in later life I have
had, inside information about shares, I would first of all use
it for my own benefit and then pass it on to my friends.
It would never occur to me to pass on my information to
total strangers. So I wrote the London and Paris Exchange
a nice, grateful letter of thanks, such as any country doctor,
parson, or widow might be expected to write. I said I would
like to know what Wall Street was doing, and, as American
stocks sometimes fluctuated more than one point a day,
that I would prefer to put up five pounds cover per cent. for
my investment. Two mornings later I had a wire from my
new friends: "*Buy* New York Centrals. Heaviest interests
on Wall Street about to operate. Immediate rise expected.
Five pounds covers one hundred stock up to five points."
At once I ordered my horse and rode into the town. At the
bank I drew out twenty-five pounds, and went on to the post
office, where I telegraphed twenty-five pounds to my new
friends with these instructions: "*Sell* five hundred New
York Centrals. Close option on a drop of five points."
They answered by post. They had sold five hundred New
York Centrals on my behalf. They mentioned the price,
and it was the lowest recorded on that day's dealings on the
Stock Exchange. Within three days New York Centrals
had dropped ten points, but it took me six weeks to recover
my twenty-five pounds, plus twenty-five pounds profit, less
a solicitor's charges which came to nearly five pounds. Yet
all the time my new friends continued to send me telegrams,
advising me as to how my "balance" of fifty pounds could
be employed to buy this or sell that. They never commented
on the fact that when they had advised me to buy I had sold.
But the game was too complicated for a second throw. A man
pursued by his enemies once paused outside an inn, and
thought thus: "They will think I have gone in there to hide,
and will go in to look for me. They know I realise that,

and they will think I have not gone in, and they will pass on. They know I will think that, and will come in to look for me." *Moral:* honesty is the least complicated policy.

Lest any reader should be deceived by my experience, I would add that I had never for one moment imagined that any dealings with the London and Paris Exchange were ever registered on the London or on any other Stock Exchange. These people were gambling with the criminal law of England, and I took them on. That was all. The sharks of finance rely on the cupidity of human nature, and on the widow and the orphan, "who pray for ten per cent." One of the truest sayings I ever heard came from the King of the Confidence Tricksters: "Blame me if you will, but do not waste your sympathy on any of my victims. I have never yet swindled an honest man." He spoke the truth.

You see a nice old gentleman walking in front of you in the street or in an art gallery. He drops a rosary. You pick it up and return it. He thanks you with tears in his eyes. It belonged to his mother, and he wouldn't have lost it for all the world. He has a nice Irish brogue, and takes you off to his hotel to have a little refreshment. There over a drink he tells you of his trouble, and why he was so glad to meet an honest man like yourself. An uncle in Chicago has died and has left him fifty thousand pounds on condition that he distributes ten thousand pounds amongst the poor of London. How is an old man like himself to distribute this money? He would like you, who are an honest man, to distribute the money on his behalf and he would like to hand it over to you.

At that moment another man enters, waving an evening newspaper, and hails the old gentleman as a long-lost friend. It is wonderful they should meet on this very day when a report of the legacy is in the "Stop Press" news. You all look at the paper, and there is the story in type. The old gentleman does not tell you that he has a little printing press in his lodgings. You have another drink, and then the old gentleman becomes a little suspicious about you. How is he to know that you are a man of substance? Have you any money at all? Yes, you have four hundred pounds in the bank, and you dash off in a taxi, draw the whole lot out, and return to the hotel. The old gentleman is glad to see you again and insists upon first showing his trust in you. He hands you his wallet, apparently bulging with bank-notes, and asks you to walk alone to the top of the street and back. You do so. Then you return the wallet, and hand the old gentleman your four hundred pounds so that he may walk alone to the top of the street. In this way a mutual trust will be established. The old gentleman walks to the top of the street and—does not return.

Why did you lose your money? I think you know. If not, I shall tell you what the King of Confidence Tricksters told me: "An honest man will say that he is incapable of distributing ten thousand pounds to the poor. If he be a Catholic, he tells me to go to the Society of St. Vincent of Paul. If he be a Protestant, he advises me to consult the Charity Organisation Society. The dishonest man hopes to get most of that ten thousand pounds for himself." The old gentleman has now retired, but the last time he went to prison the charge was that he had obtained four hundred pounds from—a Wall Street stockbroker!

For a time my speculations on the Stock Exchange flourished. My profits were all on paper, but had I closed my commitments at the right time my balance was as safe as if it had been lodged in the Bank of England. But I was going on. My last telegraphed order was: "Buy ten thousand Taipings at anything under five shillings." This Rubber Company had not yet made an allotment on their prospectus, but in those days one could deal in shares before the company was even floated. From the cost per planted acre I believed that after flotation the shares would be worth five shillings each. The brokers replied by telegraph: "Bought ten thousand Taipings at two shillings and sixpence." For once, even far afield, I had beaten the market. Next day Taipings would be five shillings. I felt sure of that.

It was a madness from which nothing, not even one of the most beautiful women in England, could distract me. Next morning she arrived to see over the sanatorium. She came in her car. She was certainly one of the most beautiful women I have ever seen, and assuredly she had one of the most perfect voices I have ever heard. As I showed her round the sanatorium my mind went back to other days. An awkward boy of thirteen, myself, was travelling with his mother from Edinburgh to Inverness in a first-class railway carriage. At Perth She entered, and her maid placed the jewel-case and hand-luggage on the rack. From the labels I read the name. She was married but looked little older than a schoolgirl. After a time she produced sandwiches and offered them to my mother. My mother declined a sandwich, but when the sandwiches were offered to me I helped to eat them. My mother thanked her for giving me sandwiches, and that, for some curious reason, displeased me. At Kingussie, where there is a tea-stall on the platform, my mother asked me to get a cup of tea, and then said to our fellow-passenger: "Won't you have one also?"

To which she said: "Thank you so much, but when I'm travelling I never drink anything."

And now I was seeing her again! Across the years I remembered the railway carriage and even whilst I was talking to her I was thinking of the sandwiches. She had changed very little. The years had been kind to her. It was the same girlish figure, the same hazel eyes, and the same voice. It was the voice that first recalled my memory. Having shown her all over the institution, I asked her to my sitting-room to show her the germ of tuberculosis under the microscope! Then I said to her: "I suppose it's too early to offer you a cup of tea?"

She laughed. "Much too early. It's only eleven o'clock."

"But I would like you to have something."

"Well, I would like a glass of milk."

I rang the bell and ordered two glasses of milk and a plate of biscuits. As she sipped the milk she said: "This is very good milk." I smiled, and she said: "Why do you smile? Don't you think it's very nice milk?"

"Yes, I do. But the last time I offered you a cup of tea you wouldn't have it. You were travelling."

"But this is the first time I have ever seen you?"

"No, it's not." And then I told her.

"Yes, in that year I did go to Scotland. But I don't remember anything about the train. . . . If you are keen on fishing come over and fish our river any time you like. I'll give orders this afternoon."

"It's dry fly fishing, isn't it?" I was not thinking of the fishing, but that her river was some distance away. To fish there would mean the best part of the day away from the sanatorium, and put me out of touch with—my telegrams.

"Yes, dry fly is best, but you can use the other. I have fished with both."

"Thank you very much. But your place is a good way from here?"

She looked surprised, as well she might. Any other man in my position would have jumped at the invitation like a fresh-run sea trout. "Yes, about ten miles, if you know the road. And now I must be going."

I saw her into her car and said good-bye. As her car went down the drive a telegraph boy on a bicycle rode up and handed me an orange envelope: "Taipings opened at three shillings and sixpence." I went back to my room and sat in my easy chair. My God, five hundred pounds profit in twenty-four hours! This was only the beginning. And yet what a fool I had been! How discourteous she must think me to be! I ought to have told her the true reason why I did not want to leave the place even for a day—not yet. It was no use now writing to her. That would make things worse. She would think I had weighed up her generous invitation and had decided to accept it. How uncouth I must have appeared! And she would never know the truth. In that last reflection I was possibly wrong, because it may be that the lady whom twice I met may read these lines. And her name is Moyra, Lady Cavendish, *née* the Lady Moyra de Vere Beauclerk.

I was tired. The excitement of speculation interfered with sleep. Why could not the hours pass quicker? I had to wait until eleven-thirty a.m. before I would know the opening prices. Another telegram arrived. A friend from overseas was in Glasgow. Would I join him and go for a week to the Western Highlands? Yes, I would go. I 'phoned to the chairman of my committee and obtained a week's leave. I told my assistant to take charge, and asked the matron only to forward telegrams. Then I wired the brokers: "Sell ten thousand Taipings at four shillings and sixpence. If price not reached before settlement, please carry over." That was all right. I would be content with a profit of one thousand pounds, and need not look at a paper for the next week.

In Glasgow I found my friend much depressed. On the way home he had met a girl on the ship. She was travelling with her mother. They lived near Glasgow. He had discovered their address, and had written to the girl asking if he might call. She had replied in a short note which contained the ominous remark: "My mother will be very glad to see you." He had gone to see them. The size of their place had appalled him. There were two entrances with a lodge-gate at either. He reached the main door. A bulldog came round the corner and sniffed him. A butler opened the door. My friend nearly forgot his own name. Both the ladies were out.

Next morning we boarded a steamer at Glasgow, and, in the evening, reached a beautiful bay where hills of heather, rocks and ferns came down to the sea. After dinner in the hotel we met two charming girls who amused themselves by guessing our occupations. One said that my friend was an accountant, and that I was a barrister. The other replied: "You are wrong. They are both doctors." Asked how she knew she said that doctors had a curious way of glancing at everybody whom they met for the first time. She may have been right. All the omens indicated that we were going to have a pleasant week.

Next morning I was down in good time for breakfast, and found a telegram awaiting me from the brokers: "Settlement passed. No carry over. Wire immediately what you are doing about account." My heart went cold. Something had happened. I asked the hall-porter for the morning paper. There would be no newspaper until noon. What a place! Where was the post office? I rushed off and wired: "Sell enough Taipings to meet account. Wire number sold, and the price." Then I returned to breakfast and met my friend.

"Look here," he said, "I don't want to pry into your affairs, but never in my life have I seen a man looking more the picture of misery than you do now."

"It's nothing," I answered. "I'm waiting for a telegram."

"Then you're not coming out with us after breakfast?"

"Certainly not. You can take those two girls out yourself."

I stayed about the hotel all morning waiting. Then the telegram came: "None sold. No market." Soon afterwards the morning paper arrived. The Rubber Boom was over. Men commit suicide on account of money; women on account of love. My brokers were Quakers.

There was only one thing to be done. I wrote to the brokers and told them I had been speculating and could not

meet their account. I would pay it off by monthly instalments
in eighteen months with five per cent. interest. Having
posted the letter I felt better, and set out to look for my
friend and the girls. The reply of the brokers was remarkable. They regretted to learn that I had been speculating.
My offer was accepted, but they declined to accept interest
on the money. They would hold the shares until such time
as they could sell them in my interest. This they did, and
at the end of four months the shares were sold at a price
which reduced my total loss by three-quarters.

Later on, when I came to London, I met several stockbrokers, and found them, for the most part, to be genial people.
One in particular heaped coals of fire on my head, because
he asked me out to lunch with his friends, although apparently
the only man who had ever swindled him had been a Scotsman.

"Yes," said the broker after lunch, "the only man who
ever did me was a Scotsman, and in doing me he made me."
He paused, and we all listened. "I'd just started on my own,
and things were slack. A few orders here and there. In those
days we had to watch our stamps. Well, I had one queer
client, or rather he wasn't a client. His name was James Ian
McQuilternach—a queer sort of name. But it wasn't only
his name that was queer. The man himself was queer. Not
that I ever saw him, but you could tell he was queer by his
letters. In fact they weren't letters. That was the queer
thing about them."

"Post cards?" I suggested.

"No," said our host, looking round the table, "they
were not post cards, and they weren't telegrams. I'll tell you
what they were—they were menus from restaurants of the
cheaper sort, old luggage labels—why, now I remember he
once even used a label steamed off a jam jar. Yes, McQuilternach was a queer fellow."

"Were they stamped? Of course they were stamped, or

I wouldn't have got them. On one side a halfpenny postage stamp and my address, on t'other his inquiries. No stationery expenses. Pen and ink provided by the post office.

"Oh, his inquiries were sensible enough. Was there room for capital appreciation in West Rands? What was the return on G.W. Fives compared to Midland Fours? Why were Tins depressed? Were Textile Possibilities fully discounted? That sort of thing. Interested in everything, was McQuilternach.

"Any orders? That's what I wanted to know. There were no orders. So I told my clerk that we couldn't waste time, paper and stamps on the fellow. I said his next request was to be brought to me, so that I'd write him myself and tell him we weren't a Carnegie free library.

"His next arrived all right—the damned thing, written on the cardboard circular cover of a jam jar. What d'ye say? Was it the same jam jar? How the devil do I know? Anyway this time it looked like business. He had come into ten thousand pounds and wanted to invest it in ten securities, having in mind safety, geographical position, dividends, and room for appreciation. What did I suggest, and would I give my reasons, likewise all-in cost, stamps, brokerage, and total income less income-tax, separately stated for each? Of course I thought he was a rich crank. Work! You people don't know what work is. You think it's something that grows on a tree."

"We do," said I, "and you have every reason to be proud of yourself." But the broker ignored the soft answer that usually brings on wrath, and continued his tale.

"That evening I carted home the office-books of reference. Borrowed a portmanteau to hold them. Taxi, then tips to porters. Cab at the other end. For five whole days and nights I worked at McQuilternach's income. Got it up to six hundred and fifty-nine pounds seventeen shillings and threepence. And that was pre-war, remember. Then I posted my reply, condensed on to five sheets of paper. Nicely typed, too.

"What happened? Nothing. At least nothing for a week or so. Then a man showed me a paper. He said it contained an excellent set of investments. It did. The paper had offered a prize of two hundred pounds for the best list of investments. McQuilternach had won the prize. He deserved it. His selections couldn't be beaten.

"How did that do me good? Well, I went round to the paper and made a row. Of course they were very sorry and only laughed. They'd paid McQuilternach. They couldn't publish my name as a broker, but they did put in a paragraph about what a certain broker thought of their competition. A lot of people wrote to the paper for the broker's name and their letters were sent to me. Then we began to get busy. And now I must be going. Where's that waiter?..."

# CHAPTER XV

## GOOD AND EVIL

FEW who have lived in London can be happy elsewhere. We are all snobs, but in London there is less snobbishness than in lesser cities, because whoever you are there is always someone better or better off than you are. Are you rich? In London an unmarried woman with an income of two thousand pounds a year told me that she was very poor. So she was, in comparison with people whom she knew with incomes of five, ten and twenty thousand a year. Are you intellectual? In London you may pit your brains against the greatest intellects of your time. Are you Prime Minister? In that event you will be much too busy to trouble about who or what you are.

It is not snobbery to wish to associate with your superiors in culture and intellect. No one improves their tennis by playing with inferior players. Any man of education who desires cheap success may become a King in the Saloon Bar or an Emperor in the Four-ale Bar. The only man who ever called me a snob was one whose friendship I declined after learning that his income was ten thousand pounds a year. I met him late one night at my club, which I named the Mausoleum. He was the first fellow-member who had spoken to me, and invited me to have a drink. We talked of the universities and of rugby football, and he said he was glad to meet me because it was his last night in the club. Some explorers were members of the club, so I remarked: "I suppose you are going abroad?"

"No," was the answer. "I have been expelled by the committee."

I changed the conversation, but he returned to it. "You never asked why I had to resign. The truth is I have told you my real name, the name under which I was elected to this club, but I have another name, and the committee discovered it." He pointed to a full-page advertisement on the back of one of the sporting papers. "That is my other name." I was surprised. One of the largest bookmakers in England!

"What on earth made you want to join a club like this?"

"Can't you understand? I get sick of the crowd I meet, and wanted peace, quiet, and the talk of educated men. Do you back horses? Never put a shilling on a horse: that's my advice, and I make ten thousand a year by laying them. A man came to me to-day, and asked me to lend him a fiver. He had lost hundreds to me. I refused the loan. Told him I would lend him four fivers if he gave me his word of honour never to back another horse. He refused, and I refused him. Why should I give him money to hand over to another bookie?"

Next week I dined with the bookmaker at the Ritz. Later, invitations became more frequent, and I declined them. The bookmaker sent me rather a rude note to say that I was a snob, since I refused to go about with him just because he was a bookmaker. I replied to his note and told him that if I went about with a man who had ten thousand pounds a year I would either be sponging on him or getting into debt. Having posted the letter I realised that I was worse than a snob—a prig.

In the Mausoleum I also met one of the most remarkable and erratic journalists who ever graced the Street of Adventure. In Fleet Street he was known as Charles, and was off and on the staff of the *Daily Mail* in Lord Northcliffe's time. Charles was a cockney, a small-built man, and a brilliant descriptive writer. He could turn the tear-taps on to paper to order. Technically this is called "the human stuff." He and no other could have written that wonderful account of the funeral of Edward VII:

"As the cortège passed there stood in front of me an old

flower-woman from Leicester Square, with her basket of flowers, and beside her a tall bronzed Australian. After the gun carriage came the riderless horse, and then a groom leading a little fox terrier. "E was fond of 'is dawg,' said the flower-woman, wiping her eyes. 'Yus,' sobbed the tall, broad-shouldered man from the great open spaces, ''e was fond of 'is dawg, 'e was.'"

There is genius in everything—even in bathos.

Charles was off and on the *Mail*, always being dismissed and then reinstated. A speech by Mr. Asquith at the Free Trade Hall in Manchester was the cause of one rupture. Charles was sent to Manchester to write a descriptive report of the meeting. He did not attend the meeting, but in a cosy public-house he wrote an excellent description of what happened. At closing time he took his work to the post office and telegraphed it to the *Mail*. Unfortunately, that afternoon Mr. Asquith had been taken ill, and there was no meeting in Manchester that night.

The coronation of King George V was the cause of another disaster. Charles was told to describe the procession, but after a late night at the Savage Club he awoke to find that the procession was over. But duty was duty, and he telephoned his description as seen from beside the triumphal arch of Canadian sheaves of wheat. Unhappily, on the previous night this arch had been destroyed by fire. Charles was also fired, and was forbidden to enter the office. This time the parting with the "Chief" was to be final. Many another man might have gone to the river, but in such moments Charles always showed the undeniable courage and resource of the London gamin.

He hired a cab and drove to a large orphanage. He presented his professional card to the secretary, who was delighted to see him. "Yes," said Charles, "the *Mail* wishes me to write up your institution. I would like to take five of the orphans out to tea, show them the shops, buy them a few toys, and study their reactions. I would like them to be in ordinary clothes, so that they won't feel self-conscious."

"Splendid," said the secretary. "Come along and choose the children."

Charles did so, and selected three girls aged five, six, and seven, and two boys, aged eight and nine. He packed them all into his cab and drove to a tea-shop, where he gave them an excellent tea. The children were wildly excited, and loved their new friend, because Charles was a very lovable man.

After tea he got them into the cab again, and drove—to the office of the *Daily Mail*. As Charles and the children entered the building the commissionaire forgot the order that Charles was not to be admitted. Charles knew the way upstairs and knocked at the Chief's door. Then he entered, each of his hands holding the hand of a child, and three other children holding on to his jacket. The Napoleon of the Press looked up from his desk in amazement. Charles produced his handkerchief and sobbed bitterly. "For God's sake, sir, do what you like with me, but don't take the bread and butter out of the mouths of these innocent children."

On beholding the sudden grief of their new friend all the children began to weep in chorus. Lord Northcliffe was speechless. He had made and destroyed governments. Tears trickled down his face, and he said thickly: "I never knew you had children. You may come back." Charles and the five children departed, leaving Lord Northcliffe with his head resting on his arms.

My first home in London was with a widow and her two daughters, who lived in a large house in Bloomsbury. I had known the family in Scotland, and in London I stayed as their guest for a month. The two girls—Flora and Violet, aged eighteen and twenty—were on the stage, the chorus at the Gaiety Theatre. They were hard-working girls, and spent most of the day in practising dancing, singing and elocution. In disposition they were generous. Their conversation was mostly of the theatre. At times their language was a trifle lurid, and their sense of humour somewhat boisterous. To stick an unused penny stamp on the pavement and to sit out on the balcony waiting for someone to try to pick it up was our usual Sunday afternoon amusement. And excellent fun it was. The neatly tied parcel lying on the pavement was an improvement on the stamp. When anyone tried to pick it up, it was jerked out of their hands by an attached string worked from the balcony. This was so successful that the police interfered and put an end to our simple pastime.

These girls knew all about sex, and their knowledge was a safeguard. I often went to the theatre to see them home, and around the stage-door was gilded youth and age. The chorus girl had two ambitions—to become a musical comedy star or to contract a brilliant marriage. She also knew that no girl is likely to marry unless she makes marriage her price. Thus sophisticated, the chorus-girl was better able to look after herself than her simpler sister, the shop-girl, exposed to similar temptations. If a married man told a chorus-girl that he was misunderstood by his wife—she had heard that tale before. The simpler shop-girl would as often as not believe the story, and think that she was falling into the arms of Romance. Neither of the girls I knew touched wine—they had seen others go that way.

My two friends had several admirers, and one reserved youth, when not in residence at one of the older universities, used to come to Bloomsbury for tea on Sunday afternoons. Then the widow would ask after his mother, whose indisposition had been reported in the society columns of the Press, and the young man would answer: "My mother is quite well now, thank you."

His mother never called at Bloomsbury, and when Flora did visit the young man's home it was to sing as a professional a few songs at an afternoon reception. I could never determine whether the young man was or was not in love with her. She was a very beautiful girl, and to take an actress out to supper or to a public dance was an essential part of a young man's education. Even had he been in love with her it would have made no difference. His lady mother and distinguished father had other plans. He is now a member of the peerage and married to a most capable wife, much interested in charities. Neither of the girls married, and some years later they left the stage.

The trees around the lawn of the Botanic Gardens were festooned with coloured fairy lights for the fancy dress ball on Midsummer Eve. I went as a matador, and soon realised that no matador could dance or fight with comfort in the heavy costume hired from the theatre costumiers. The girl whom I met there for the first time had a simpler dress—a nightdress—and her black hair fell half-way down her back. Her features showed breeding and she walked like a queen. As we danced I asked her name, and she answered: "I am the Sleepless Night." That shall be her name in this book, because even at the coroner's inquest her real name was suppressed.

We walked in the gardens and talked of books. She praised Shaw and H. G. Wells, and I said that each had destroyed more than he could ever create. The writer about whom we agreed was the half-mad George Borrow, but she took him literally and said it was her ambition to wander penniless through England from door to door begging for food. A strange ambition for a *débutante*—for so she was, having been presented at the previous Court. Society did not interest her, and, being of age, she was determined to lead her own life. At present she was trying to go on the stage.

A week later I was sitting in my consulting room at the St. Marylebone Tuberculosis Dispensary at four in the afternoon. There were no more patients to be seen, and the porter announced that a lady had called to see me. I did not like the grin on the man's face. "Show her in," I said, and a moment later the "Sleepless Night" entered my room. No wonder the man had grinned. Even for a chorus girl her face was over-painted, and her dress was untidy.

I showed her over the place and explained the work. Her comment was: "Don't you think you are wasting your time trying to help people? People don't wish to be helped. To give them money is all one can do."

"Let me give you tea," I said.

"I don't want tea, but I'd like a whisky and soda."

"You can't have that here, but we'll go out."

And out we went and walked the length of Marylebone Road and down Tottenham Court Road until we came to the Bedford Head. As we walked she saw that I had noticed a white scar on the right side of her face. "You've seen one blemish. I did that myself when I was twelve. A fit of temper, and I slashed myself with a carving-knife to spite my mother."

At the Bedford Head I brought two whiskies and soda to the table where we were sitting, and she showed me the book she was reading. It was Racine, and she knew French well. She had been educated at a well-known boarding-school in England, followed by six months in Paris. At the end of an hour she said: "You must have a pretty rotten time living in a boarding-house with your sister, and I've got an idea. There are cheap flats near King's Cross. Let's go there and live. I don't want any money, and we can each pay half. Think it over and write to me. No, not to-night. As a matter of fact I'm dining with another man to-night. You must think it over. I'm not an expensive girl, and at least I am educated. I know you won't write. You are too middle class. You are afraid of convention, although no one need ever know what you are doing."

I never wrote. It was neither morality nor convention that decided me, but the scar on her face. The girl was insane.

A year later I went to dine at Lincoln's Inn on a guest night. Along the Strand boys were shouting the sensation of the day. It was the death of the "Sleepless Night." Her requiem was an inquest, and the story occupied a couple of columns. As I entered the gates of Lincoln's Inn I was in a sober mood. I had done nothing to drag the girl down—and nothing to help her. We were ships that passed in the night.

My friend was a junior barrister, and we dined in the oak-panelled hall. On the walls are portraits of judges who once were benchers of the Inn. The benchers dine at a long table on a raised daïs at the end of the hall, and each, as he enters through a curtained doorway at the back, stops and bows gravely to the assembled company who are standing. Each barrister may bring one guest, and dinner is served at oak tables seating four. It is a well-cooked four-course English dinner, and the allowance of wine is generous—a bottle per man. With the joint you are also offered a tankard of ale. Thus two bottles of claret and two of port may be shared by four. The first glass of wine is raised to the man diagonally opposite, the second to your neighbour, and the third to your host, who is your *vis-à-vis*. These customs are very old, because the laws of England and the Inns of Court have survived revolutions and the fall of monarchies. Another custom is that the host is served with food before his guest. The meaning of many things is lost, but had I ever dined with the Borgias, I would have thought it the height of hospitality if Lady Borgia had been served first.

During dinner my companions discussed the inquest. I said nothing, and was startled when my friend asked: "Did you know her?"

"Over a year ago," I answered. "But why should you ask?"

"Well, it's curious that we both know her. I only met her once, a month ago. It was after the last guest-night here. Old Mac, the parson, was my guest. He was up from Scotland and wanted to see the night-life here. We went to a café where these girls go, and she came to our table. She was drunk, but anyone could see she'd been a lady. I told her that I was disgusted that any girl of her education should use such foul language. At the end we gave her a pound. She thought we meant business, and said: 'The tariff is five pounds.' I'm not surprised that she killed herself."

At the inquest the pathologist deposed that the girl was four months pregnant, and suffering from double venereal disease. Her mother told how she had sent four mental specialists to see her daughter in the hope that they could certify her insane. The girl's letter, written after taking eighty grains of veronal, was also read:

"My dear Mother,

This is my last letter as I have decided to kill myself. I am sorry you have had such a dull life. If ever you meet any of my friends, don't think too badly of them. Some were quite decent.—Your affectionate daughter."

# CHAPTER XVI

## DEATH ON THE MOORS

AT Christmas 1912 I went on holiday from London to the Highlands. My father had a house in Tain, a town which lies between red moors and blue inland sea. He had also the shooting rights over a small estate three miles away. I travelled by night and reached home at noon on the following day. My mother had lunch waiting for me, but my father had gone.

"He's oiled your gun, and left cartridges. He wouldn't wait, because the days are short, and he thought you might like to send some game to your friends in London. He said you could meet him at the far corner of the moors between half-past one and two o'clock."

During lunch a cart rumbled up to our gate, and I looked through the window to see what it was. The horse and cart were standing in the road, and a man was running up the footpath to our door. Without knowing why, I rushed to the door and opened it before the man had time to ring the bell.

"It's all right," he said. "It's not an accident. Your father was taken ill—a stroke, I'm thinking—and he's in the cart."

My father was lying there on his back, with a couple of empty folded sacks for a pillow. His two dogs, a spaniel and a Scotch terrier, were licking his face. The terrier had some blood on its neck. My father recognised me, but could not speak. It was apoplexy, with paralysis of speech and of the right arm and leg. With the aid of two neighbours we carried him to bed, and the shepherd who had driven him home told me all he knew. "I was minding the sheep when I saw him; he'd be two hundred yards away. The wee dog put a rabbit out of the whin. Your father fired, killed the rabbit, and wounded the dog. The dog started skirling; your father ran to it. Then he stopped, and fell back. When I got to him all he said was: 'I'm finished.' Not another word until he was in the cart. I went for help and to get a cart. We took the cart into a field and lifted him in. When we were about to start, he held up his left hand, the only one he can use, and said: 'Stop! Not without my dogs.' So of course I put the dogs in too."

Both the doctors who practised in the town were out, and I was faced alone with the question: to bleed or not to bleed. Although unable to speak, my father understood all I said, and showed signs of irritation when I mentioned bleeding. I went to the post office and telephoned to my father's friend, "old George," in Edinburgh. He also was out, on a consultation in the north of England. He would be home at seven, and could catch the north train at eight o'clock. That meant his arrival at eleven-thirty the next morning if the train was up to time. We improved on that. A fast car met the train eighty miles down the line at seven in the morning, and although the snow had fallen in the night, "old George" arrived two hours ahead of the train.

He was the leading consultant in Scotland—a tall, burly man, clean shaven, with keen, humorous features, quizzical eyes, and the grand manner. Some said that it paid practitioners to send for "old George," because his mere presence added lustre to his surroundings, but he had also common sense, kindness, and a great knowledge of medicine. He looked serious as he strode up our footpath, and I thought he looked old as I helped him to remove his coat. At the foot of the staircase he stopped me. "I'd rather see your father alone. We were fellow-students. He consulted me a year ago. I'll find his room."

I sat in an arm-chair in the dining-room and watched the clock. The spaniel sat in a cold corner of the room sharing the misery. He was an affectionate animal, and a year previously had done a remarkable act of kindness. A farmer, who lived a mile away, had been removed to the asylum. For two nights his dog—a collie—howled outside its kennel. On the third night there was no howling, and that night both our dogs had left the house after their dinner. The next day the people on the farm sent word that our dogs had sat by the collie's kennel all night. For four nights in succession these two dogs did this act of kindness—and kindness it was, because the collie was not a female.

The wounded terrier was staying with the hotel-keeper, who was treating his wounds. At the end of twenty minutes I heard "old George" coming downstairs. He entered the room, crossed to the window, and looked out across the fields. I said nothing. I was waiting for him to speak. He was considering his verdict, and in a moment I would know what he thought of my father's illness. At last he spoke, but without turning his face from the window.

"Sutherland, did I ever tell you that damned funny story about the parson on his honeymoon?"

In astonishment I rose, walked to the window, and looked at him. There were tears in his eyes. "Thank you for telling me that way," I said.

He nodded. "You see, there's nothing to say."

Six months later "old George" himself was dead. He died of the disease in which he had specialised—heart block. Many great physicians have died of the diseases in which they made their name—too many for the thing to be a coincidence.

The next day my father was worse. He was no longer conscious and his breathing had become stertorous. All the extra muscles of respiration were working, even the nostrils dilating as he drew breath. The vital centres in the brain were making a fight for life, but the strain on the body could not last very long.

That night after midnight I was wakened by my mother entering my room, holding a lighted candlestick. "Have you heard It?" she asked.

I listened and heard the howling of dogs around the countryside. "They are howling at the moon," I said.

"There is no moon to-night, and your father will pass to-day."

She was right. There was no moon, but a dark, snow-laden sky. On entering the warm sick-room, where a night-nurse sat by a shaded lamp, I saw that the character of the breathing had changed. It was now sighing breathing. Very short breaths, becoming deeper and deeper, and then gradually dying away. For a second or two the breathing would stop as if for ever, and then slowly begin again. The change from the laboured breathing of the day was like a ship entering harbour out of the storm. At seven in the morning he died, and the nurse, without a word, opened one of the windows. It was an old Highland custom—to allow the spirit to depart.

## CHAPTER XVII

## THE WHITE PLAGUE

WHAT is the lure of London? I left the sanatorium, worth seven hundred pounds a year, to take a post in London at two hundred and fifty pounds a year. It was a gambler's move. In London every man or woman must rise or sink to the level of his or her character and ability. Is it better to be the first man in a village or the millionth man in the capital of an empire? London is a kind and generous city. Paris is the city of light, but it is the hard light of the carbon arc. London welcomes all, and gives to each a fair deal.

The greatest romance which London ever gave me was the Romance of the Bandstand School in Regent's Park. From 1910 to 1929, in all weathers, a teacher led groups of children in Regent's Park to give them lesson in the bandstand near the Zoo.

She was Mrs. Fitzgerald of the Regent's Park Bandstand School, which ceased to be at the end of December 1929. And the closing of that school was the end of a romance.

In 1910, with the aid of friends at the St. Marylebone Tuberculosis Dispensary, I sought to found an open-air school on simple lines in a London park. A small meeting was held, at which the parents of a few children predisposed to tuberculosis were present. The parents were told that as they were living under poor and overcrowded conditions, their children would have a better chance of life if their days were spent in Regent's Park. They would have to provide their children with a dinner to be eaten in the park, and also contribute sixpence a week towards the services of a nurse-maid, a girl of sixteen.

The children were to be brought to the dispensary at

nine o'clock a.m. and taken home in the afternoon. And thus the school started with ten children, whose only shelter during the day was a tree in the park. Temperatures were taken in the morning and afternoon, and the children were weighed and examined once a week. As the children were of school-age, the school could never have started had not Dr. C. J. Thomas, then School Medical Officer of Marylebone, accepted medical certificates from me that the children's health would be prejudiced by attendance at an ordinary school.

There was also some opposition, and one elderly physician wrote to the local paper pointing out that the children would all die of pneumonia, and that the proper authority to deal with the scheme was the Society for the Prevention of Cruelty to Children. In point of fact, even when there were fifty children at the school there was never a case of pneumonia, and none of infectious fevers.

Our first difficulty was the nursemaid. One day on entering the park I found fifteen instead of ten children. The extra five were unknown to me. The maid of sixteen had been offering pennies to healthy children attending Council Schools to induce them to come to the park in the hope that her salary would increase by so many sixpences.

It was then that Sir Frank Morris, Chairman of the Charity Organisation Society, provided money whereby a certified teacher could be obtained for a period of three months, so that the idea might be given a fair test.

Then I saw the empty bandstand in which, during living memory, no band had ever played. An application to the Office of Works for the loan of this bandstand was made by the late Sir Eric Barrington. A week later a key was left at the dispensary, and on the back of the label were the words: "Key of the Regent's Park Bandstand."

Next morning the children took possession.

For a voluntary non-provided school funds are constantly

needed, and the bandstand could never have remained a school for all these years but for the devoted work of two ladies—Mrs. George Johnstone and Miss May Broadbent. It was also an undenominational school, and the only creed recited after prayers was that of the open air:

> I will always fear bad air;
> I will never fear good air;
> I will open the windows
> And save my life.

Having served its day and generation, the Bandstand School came to an end. As to this there could be no regrets, except those which were personal, because the idea it embodied is now universally approved, and larger and better open-air schools are provided by the public authorities.

From the dispensary I attended the consumptive poor of Marylebone. There was William James; at the age of thirty-five he was dying of consumption in a one-roomed house in a slum. He had been coachman to a rich man and had been dismissed for dishonesty without a reference. His wife was a handsome woman, ten years younger than her husband. She went out to work as a charwoman, kept the one-roomed home going, and nursed the dying man. I told her that the disease was too far advanced for her husband to be sent to a sanatorium, and she would not listen to the suggestion that he should be sent to a hospital. She would care for him to the end. I told her how their single room might be improved to his interest. Three days later I returned. She had stripped the paper off the walls and whitewashed them. She had sold some heavy, useless furniture, and that slum room now looked like a private ward in a sanatorium.

As I came to know him, William James told me that he had been wrongfully dismissed, and I believed him. From his wife I got the name and address of his late employer and wrote. Early next forenoon the rich man appeared at the dispensary, and I was sorry for him. A month after he had dismissed James he had discovered that it was his corn merchant and not his coachman who had swindled him. He had looked for James, but could not find him. What could he do now? Could James be sent to Switzerland? I shook my head. "No use at all. If he had fresh cream it would ease him, because the disease is now in his throat. And if you give his wife money she can nurse him all the time in place of going out to work." He departed.

That afternoon I visited James. He was lying in that dream-state between sleep and waking, gazing at the ceiling, his half-closed eyes apparently insensible, and muttering in a quiet delirium. It is called the *coma vigil*. At last he recognised that I was there, and smiled. "I had a wonderful dream, Doctor. I was dreading what will happen after death. It is going to be a long and pleasant dream—a dream from which we never wake up. . . . Oh, yes, my master was here this morning. He's going to look after my wife. He asked me to forgive him."

"And did you?" I asked.

"Oh, yes, but it's all too late now." He sighed, and once more dozed off into sleep. So far as I knew neither William James nor his wife had any religious belief, but they had what the theologians call Natural Religion, and that is something which ought to make thousands of Christians blush with shame.

Here is another case. An elderly grey-haired woman of sixty called at the dispensary with a boy of eight, to know if his chest was healthy. I thought she was his grandmother. "Oh, no, sir. I'm his mother, at least, his foster-mother. I had fourteen of my own, and my eldest girl is now forty. When all the children left home I took this one. At first his mother paid for him, but—then she went away. My husband and I had become that fond of the child we couldn't send him to the workhouse. So we adopted him legally. Here's the paper, sir."

These two people who had reared fourteen children of their own had freely, and without any money consideration, adopted this stray child. "What does your husband do, Mother?"

She brushed the tears from her eyes. "He was a labourer sir, but he fell from a scaffolding at Knightsbridge three weeks ago and was killed. The lawyers say I'll get three hundred pounds compensation, but what's that?"

"Mother, how long have you had that little lump in your neck?"

"For some months, sir; it began quite small, but it's getting bigger. I've never bothered about it. Yes, sir, you may feel it, but I never went to a doctor about it."

"The boy is quite healthy, Mother, but you must take this note round to the hospital. They may be able to get rid of that lump in your neck."

It was cancer of a cervical gland. And all that I have written here is true.

The case of Mr. Z and his wife did not occur in London. Mr. Z was an insurance agent, dying of consumption. As soon as I entered the dingy hall of his little house I had a feeling of impending evil. Some houses carry that impression, which is not related to riches or poverty. Mrs. Z was a tall woman, who had once been handsome, but was now untidy and unkempt. When she brought me to her husband's bedside I realised that no love was lost between them. The case of Mr. Z was hopeless, but at the end of a week he began to have attacks of sickness and colic, which apparently had no relation to his cough, but to—his food. After two days I found myself in the most terrible position in which a doctor can find himself—of suspecting poisoning. It was possible to have a chemical analysis of the product of the sickness, but that would cost money. These people were poor and mean, and they would want to know why an analysis was necessary. I remembered the advice of my old teacher, Sir Henry Littlejohn. "To save your patient and yourself there is only one thing to do—let the poisoner see that you suspect."

Before leaving the house I told Mrs. Z that I wished to speak to her, and we entered the dusty, frowsy sitting-room. I stood with my back to the window, and she stood at the back of a chair, facing me.

"I know what you want to tell me, Doctor. He can't last much longer. The sickness is making him weak."

"Mrs. Z, who cooks your husband's food?"

Her face went scarlet, then white, and she was gripping the back of the chair tightly. "Why do you ask a thing like that?"

"Because I don't think your husband's food is agreeing with him, and you might be able to find something that suits him better."

There was no more sickness, and a month later Mr. Z died, so far as I know, from natural causes.

From what I saw of the poor in London, it was clear that many of them were exploited, even in death. When Bill Smith was dying of consumption, the insurance agent came to the door, and suggested to Mrs. Smith that it would be a good thing to insure her husband's life. It was quite simple. All she had to do was to sign a paper stating that Bill Smith was in good health, and pay the weekly premiums. Then Bill Smith died, and I wrote his death certificate. On these certificates there is a space in which the doctor is asked to state the duration of the illness in years, months, or days. It is not obligatory to give this information, and I never gave it. A few days later the insurance agent called on me. "Sorry to trouble you, Doctor. Just a little matter of business. The company would like to know how long Bill Smith has been ill. They will pay you ten-and-six for the information."

"And they won't get it from me," was my answer. "You insured this man's life without a medical examination. Now you want to repudiate your contract, and stick to the premiums. Even if Mrs. Smith did make a false statement, the one who tempts is worse than the one who falls."

In other cases, when money was due on the death of an insured person, the insurance agent would have a talk with the undertaker, and it was curious how the funeral cost exactly the amount of the insurance money. The most scandalous funerals are to be seen in the East End of London. A house-to-house collection is made, and the whole street tries to give Bill 'Awkins a better funeral than the Widow Burton got last week two streets away. There is a hearse drawn by four black horses. The black horses are the only indication that the occasion is a funeral, because the hearse resembles a floral car in the Carnival at Nice. Attached to the back of the hearse is the design in flowers of a full-sized arm-chair—the Empty Chair. When watching one of these spectacles I overheard an old gentleman, obviously much impressed, say to a fellow-spectator, a boy of twelve: "Can you tell me who is dead, my boy?"

"Well, if yer asks me, I'd say it was the bloke under them flowers."

Poor Bill 'Awkins! In life you often were in want of money, and next week your widow will be destitute. For the first time you are driving in state, and to-day you are leading the only procession in which no one will ever bear us a grudge for having taken the first place.

The remedies for consumption are legion. They blossom and fade like the flowers in spring. There was one remedy much advertised in the medical press. It was prepared by a company, and the secretary called on me and asked me to give it a trial. He left enough of the stuff to treat three cases, and I selected three patients with advanced disease. A month later the secretary called again, and I told him the three patients were dead.

"You don't suggest, Doctor, that our remedy had anything to do with their deaths?"

"Certainly not. So far as I could see, your remedy had no effect on them one way or the other."

"Doctor, I have brought some more of the remedy. Could you not try it with more suitable cases, earlier and more hopeful ones?"

"That would be no test," I answered. "Give me a case sufficiently early, and I can cure it now with tuberculin, cod liver oil, and an open window."

"Yes, Doctor, but my directors are very anxious that you should give our remedy a further trial. Of course we understand the strict etiquette of the medical profession. It would not be possible for us to offer you a fee, but my directors would like to allot you one hundred shares in the company."

"Shares!" I said. "As I don't believe in your remedy I am not likely to take shares in your company."

"Doctor, you do not understand. You would pay nothing for the shares, and there would be an honourable understanding that if you wanted to dispose of them the directors would buy them back from you for one hundred pounds. I hope I make myself clear?"

"One thing is quite clear," I answered. "You and your directors think that I can be bought for one hundred pounds. The insult is not great enough. Clear out."

And yet at that time I wanted one hundred pounds. I did not want it for myself but for a lady. "What foolish things men do!" as a young girl said to me years later. At all events I went to the Jews. The Jew to whom I went had an office in Regent Street. He was a cultured, middle-aged man, with a country house near London, and his recreation was cricket. We had a talk, but when I gave him my London address, a boarding-house in Kilburn, he shook his head.

"You must give me your home address in Scotland, where you are known." I gave him the address, and he told me to return in two hours. This I did, and he said: "I suppose you wish the money in notes? Fives or tens? Just sign that promissory note. You promise to pay me one hundred and twenty pounds in three months' time. The interest is at the rate of eighty per cent. per annum. What inquiries did I make? A very simple one, and the people who answered it did not know the reason of my inquiry. I asked Stubbs' Agency for your reputation in that town in Scotland, and the answer was—'Trustworthy.' That was all. On that and on my own judgment of your character I am lending you the money. Sometimes I make mistakes. That is why the interest is high."

I paid him back, and did not grudge the interest. Nor have I ever joined in the outcry against moneylenders. When no bank will trust you, they will trust you. When prudent men think you are foolish, the Jews share your hope that in three months' time your ship will come home. They trust you—and they are gambling.

# CHAPTER XVIII

# THE SOUTHERN CROSS

ON the morning of Sunday, 2nd August 1914, I walked from Bideford to the fishing-village of Appledore. My companion was a lady, and, as we entered the village the postman was stopping at every door, and at every cottage he left a blue envelope. Then little groups of people appeared in the narrow, cobbled streets. Most of them consisted of a fisherman, his wife and children. The men were reading the notice which the postman had left, the women were crying softly, and the children were playing around them. England had mobilised her Fleet Reserve.

At noon we saw them go. They marched down to the harbour and embarked in boats which were to take them to the railway station on the other side of the River Torridge. The band of the local Boy Scouts led the procession. At the top of the harbour-steps was the vicar, wearing his surplice. He was a stout, elderly man, and was said to have a weak heart. He shook hands with each man as he passed down the steps. Once the men were all embarked there was silence, and the vicar prayed. Then the boats pulled off across the bay. Lining the harbour wall were women, children, and a few old men. There was no cheering. Those women could not cheer. Thus the men of Devon and of Appledore went to war, as their fathers had gone, over three hundred years before—to meet the Armada of Spain. Near the quay of Appledore and under a great stone are the remains of Hubba the Viking, who landed there in the ninth century and was killed in battle.

At eight o'clock on Tuesday morning, 4th August, my telegram arrived: "Report at Admiralty ten a.m. Wednesday for medical examination." I travelled by the morning train, and that night was in my club in St. James's Street. London was seething with excitement. Reservists in uniform were being fêted by civilians, and some were staggering about the pavements. At eleven o'clock that night the ultimatum to Germany expired. War was declared, and the enthusiasm of the crowds became unrestrained. Young men and girls drove about on the tops of taxi-cabs, waving little Union Jacks and blowing penny trumpets. Later on, thousands of those young men were standing in the muddy trenches of Flanders, awaiting the sound of a whistle which meant: "Over the top." Then they went out to die on barbed-wire entanglements, swept by machine-gun fire. That was war. Outside the German Embassy a crowd of three thousand Germans were singing "Deutschland über Alles." Armageddon was upon us, and that night I remembered how the men and women of Appledore had greeted war.

Next morning, with a batch of twenty other doctors I awaited medical examination. We all congratulated each other. We had all applied in good time to be taken on, in the event of war, as "emergency surgeons in His Majesty's Fleet." We discussed as to which of us had been the first to apply. I had written to the Admiralty on 25th July. One man had written on 24th July, the day after the Austro-Hungarian ultimatum to Serbia, regarding the assassination of the Archduke Ferdinand, heir to the throne of Austria, who was killed on 28th June 1914. At all events, we were all in good time, and the war would be over by Christmas. There was one pessimist who did remind the rest of us that in very small type, at the foot of the undertaking we had signed, was the statement that in the event of a war our service would be for the duration of that war. None of the others had noticed that. In any case the war would be over by Christmas! What did it matter?

After the medical examination I was called in to see the Deputy Director-General of Medical Services.

"Well, you have passed for a commission. Probably you will have your appointment long before your commission is signed by the King. The Pay Office will issue your grant for uniform. Go to the outfitters to be measured. The uniform may take three days to make. If you are appointed to a ship before your uniform is ready, join without it."

"Where am I appointed to, sir?"

"I don't know at present. We are working here day and night. You'll get a telegram. We may be able to give you a shore billet."

"I don't want a shore billet."

"In the Service you go where we think you are most useful. What is your present address? Your application was from the club in St. James's. Then you notified a change of address. Are you back at the club? Yes! Well, we'll telegraph you there."

"I suppose, sir, it's impossible for me to go back to Devonshire, pending my appointment?"

"Not impossible, but if you are appointed to a ship in the north of Scotland, London will be nearer your ship than Devonshire. But if there is any special reason . . .?"

"None, sir. I shall wait in London."

Within ten days I was aboard the "Comic Ship." That was what Jimmy the One, as the ratings call the first lieutenant, named her. The armed merchant-cruiser, *Empress of Britain*, was a very large ship, an ocean greyhound. Her speed was reputed to be twenty-three knots, as no doubt it was when she could be dry-docked every month and her engines overhauled. She was built to withstand the cold of the North Atlantic, and was sent to the Equator to cruise between Africa and the mouth of the Amazon. Our commission was to protect British commerce and to look for German raiders, which were mostly armed liners. We had eight 4·7 guns, twenty years old, and outranged by two thousand yards by the 4·3 guns of the German ships. There was one German ship we were not expected to engage—the *Karlsruhe*, a modern light cruiser who could have blown us out of the water in ten minutes. Fortunately she kept to the South American coast, although once she sent us a message *en clair*: "*Empress of Britain*, I am going to sink you next."

Number One joined us after we had been three days at sea. He left a cruiser and crossed to us in a boat. As he climbed on deck someone remarked: "There's temper, if you like." Next day he got busy, and we visited the stokers' quarters. "By God," said Number One, "I would not keep an animal here. They shall have the third-class cabins." The stokers liked the change, but grumbled bitterly when he stopped the "Black Pail." When the ship had been an ocean liner, the unused food from the first-class saloon had been placed in pails and sent down to the stokers. Be it said that in this way the stokers had very good food without the trouble of cooking it. That was not the way of the Navy. The stokers, like all other ratings, had to draw their rations and have them cooked. Number One was out to reform the stokers, and, at the end of the commission, one of the roughest of them said: "'E was fair, and acted according to 'is lights." They were degraded men. In times of peace when on shore between voyages they lived in a slum, and many went aboard drunk. Within twelve hours they were sober and stoked the ship. In Canada they were kept on the ship. Then home to be paid off, and return to a Liverpool slum and drink.

One forenoon, as we were cruising slowly in the tropical heat, the ship began to move at full speed, and on looking at the after-compass I saw that we were heading for our base, two hundred miles away. An hour later I was called to the bridge and found Number One white with rage.

"These damned stokers are throwing in their hands. Ten

are on their way to the Sick-bay now—to report sick. Tell them the Sick-bay is closed, and that if they don't go back to duty I'll call out the marines and have the ringleaders shot at sight."

I saluted. "Very good, sir."

On my way aft I thought of what I would say. In the Sick-bay I found ten sullen men, to whom I spoke: "I'm not going to ask you men to do anything for England. I don't think England has done much for you, but unless there is a head of steam, you and four hundred other people in this ship will be at the bottom within a few hours. I think it's five miles deep here. Also, if you don't obey, the marines will shoot the ringleaders at once. You know the marines have never yet disobeyed an order. Go back to the stokehold. If any of you collapse I shall come down."

They went. I returned to the bridge, and reported the result, but not what I had said. All that Number One said was, "Yah-ha." Two hours later we met a battleship, the *Albion*, who cruised with us for two days. So there had been urgency. It may have been the *Karlsruhe* on our track.

Number One and I became friends. He was to have been a gunnery officer with the First Battle-cruiser Squadron, but at the last moment he had been sent to this "Comic Ship." Yet we had a chance of action, and, if so, the ship would be fought to a finish. (That was certain, because all the ship's boats, bar four, had been smashed with axes and thrown overboard. A shell-burst is more dangerous when wooden splinters are flying about.) If successful, that might mean promotion. Long ago he had "married the Service." Only once had he been in love. The fleet was at Cannes. He was a midshipman, but in return for a dance on board, the most senior and junior officers were invited to lunch at a large villa on shore. So the junior "snotty" accompanied his captain. They had both seen the girl at the dance and were attracted. The captain pestered her to play tennis that afternoon, but she refused and asked the "snotty" to come for a walk. He went, and walked on air and dreamt dreams. She was only sixteen, but his love was hopeless, because already she was very near the steps of a throne. During their walk they met a middle-aged gentleman, who, to the "snotty's" annoyance, accompanied them. The girl afterwards became one of the most famous beauties in England, the middle-aged gentleman became Edward VII, and the "snotty" became Number One in the "Comic Ship."

The principal medical officer, or P.M.O., was an R.N. surgeon who had been retired to the Reserve in 1914. On the outbreak of war he was recalled, and he had twenty years' experience of the Service, as he always told me in his few moments of irritation. He was a wise man and within a week of our meeting he said: "There is not enough work on this ship for two of us. We are going to the Equator, and if we both attend the Sick-bay we shall quarrel. I shall do all the medical work. When I get tired of it, you can do it." Once again I had too little to do, so I wrote another book—*Pulmonary Tuberculosis in General Practice*. It seemed at times a useless thing to do, because none of us really believed that there was much chance of returning to England. It was the P.M.O. who helped me to write that book. Whenever he saw I was slacking he would entice me into a medical argument, and end by saying: "Well, why not get on with your book?" And back I would go to my writing. He drew all the diagrams for the book, and when it was published I thanked him in the Preface, but in more formal terms than I do now.

Naval officers in the main are very tolerant, and most of them are poor. The new-comer to a ship is accepted and judged on his merits, and if a man becomes unpopular in the wardroom, the judgment of the wardroom is usually right. They are slow to pass it, and, as the P.M.O. remarked,

"At the end of six months is the time to say whether or not you like a man." In this semi-monastic life it is necessary for peace that men should be tolerant and avoid treading on each other's corns. Even in monasteries there are rules for the prevention of quarrels and antagonisms. The Dominicans never speak at meals, and this rule of silence is only broken when a prince of the Church is their guest. Without such rules it may be dangerous for men to live alone. One who was with Scott on his last expedition told me how he and one other lived for six months in a hut throughout the Antarctic night. There came a time when he hated his companion and wished to kill him. Why? Because every night his companion, before going to sleep, ate a piece of toffee!

In the wardroom certain topics are not discussed in public: religion, women and politics. To the bones of contention it was necessary in our ship to add another—the War. Some of us who had joined for the War were firebrands who abused everything German. Permanent naval officers listened to these tirades at first without comment, and later with impatience. It was Number One who exploded against me. "Whatever you may think or say, the German Navy is the finest in the world—after us. They were the only Navy with whom we were friends. They were about the only people worth talking to about gunnery. Another thing to remember is this: in naval warfare men don't fight each other—they fight ships."

Politics were barred in the wardroom, but on board were a few earnest souls to whom in private I expounded the mysteries of the Marconi Contract, and the distinction between investments and gambling, according to Cabinet Ministers. One afternoon my audience and I were seated in deck-chairs in the shade of the lower deck. I had forgotten that the P.M.O.'s cabin was behind us, that his port-hole was open, and that he was trying to sleep in the great heat.

The heat had intensified the fervour of my discourse. "And what was the answer of Lloyd George to Lord Robert Cecil's question?"

Before I could tell them, there came from within the cabin a shout. "My God, is it not possible in this ship to escape from that story? I thought I was safe in my bunk, but you hold a meeting outside my port-hole. I've been twenty years in the Service. . . ." The meeting was adjourned.

In religion most of the officers I knew were like myself, vague Deists, and few believed in any particular Church. They respected the beliefs of others, and only one type of padre was despised—the type that is "hail fellow well met," even to the extent of including smutty stories in his repertoire. Of such a one a naval officer once remarked to me: "Why the hell doesn't he take off his uniform?" In that particular uniform they thought a man should at least try to live up to the ideals in which he, more than other men, professed to believe.

As wine-caterer for the wardroom I discovered that some of the officers cherished the delusion of being sound judges of the quality of the wine bought by me for the wardroom. Mine was a thankless task. Had I bought expensive wine they would have complained of the price, although all wines and spirits were duty free. When cheaper wine was provided they said it was muck. At last I found a plan which satisfied all concerned. I invited three grumblers to form a Testing Committee that would decide what wine should be ordered. At Gibraltar the wine-merchants sent on board samples of wines, numbered, labelled and priced. In my cabin I took a sheet of ruled foolscap and divided it into two columns. On the left I entered the particulars of each bottle in order of merit, beginning with the clarets, which ranged from a *vin ordinaire* to a vintage *Nuits St. George*. This accomplished, I re-gummed the labels and reversed the order—so that the *vin ordinaire* became the *Nuits St. George*. The right-hand column on the foolscap showed the apparent order of merit and price, and on the left was the truth about each sample. I did likewise with the ports and Marsalas—and kept the information to myself.

The Testing Committee enjoyed themselves. They began with the sample labelled *vin ordinaire*. This they pronounced to be absolute muck, almost indistinguishable from vinegar. The next they thought was a little better, and when they came to the *Nuits St. George* they excelled themselves. In reality this was, of course, *vin ordinaire*. One praised the bouquet, another the aroma, and a third the body of this noble wine. It was the same story about the port and Marsala—and all lived happily ever after. They were pleased with the wine, the moderate price at which I sold it, and by the amount of the rebate on their wine-bills. *Moral?* There is none.

All men except gluttons tend to grumble about their food, and at sea the fare soon becomes monotonous. Yet the Royal Navy has one royal dish—pea soup—in comparison with which the best *crème St. Germain* on shore is like thick or thin tasteless gruel. I sought for the secret of this noble soup, but the most I could ascertain was that everything, including sardine-tins, went into the stock! Alas, unless there be another war I shall never taste that soup again.

One evening we anchored near the southern Cape Verde Islands—islands of volcanic origin over which the sun sets in a blaze of kaleidoscopic colours. At night luminous fish appeared, like large electric globes under the water. Some, as they swam, left a trail of light behind. In these fish the luminosity is produced by two sets of secretory glands, which exist side by side all over the skin, and, as the fish swims, one set of glands secretes a substance called lucerifin and the other a ferment called luciferase. The two substances are not luminous, but unite to form a luminous compound. In other fish the light is produced by millions of luminous bacteria on the skin. This kind of fish is always lit up, and does not leave a trail of light in the water.

The next day the ship was at anchor all forenoon, while supplies of fresh water were brought from shore in a water-boat. There were plenty of sharks about, and the armourer had forged me a large barbed hook. On this I impaled a dead goose, obtained from the refrigerator two days previously. It was already so high that I used a gas mask when baiting the hook. The tackle was half-inch steel wire, attached to a stanchion aft. I threw the baited hook overboard, washed my hands in disinfectant, and removed the gas mask. In the clear water everything that happened to the bait could be seen, and I was joined on deck by a dozen stokers. A shark over ten feet in length approached the bait and stopped within about five yards of it. Two pilot fish, about the size of mackerels, swam to the bait, nosed it, and returned to the shark. These pilot fish accompany the shark, but I am ignorant of the nature of the partnership between them. On the top of its head the pilot fish has a sucker whereby it attaches itself to the shark when the latter is swimming. The pilot fish appeared to convey some information to the shark, because as soon as they returned he moved forward, grabbed the bait, and was hooked. The stokers shouted and wanted to drag in the steel rope. It is impossible to land a shark in that way, because the weight of the body tears the hook out of the jaw. I told them to fetch a running steel noose, which could be run down the tackle, passed over the shark's head, and drawn taut around the tail. In that way only could the shark be got aboard. The stokers were shouting and swearing with excitement when a messenger arrived. "First lieutenant's compliments, sir; he will see you on the bridge."

On the bridge I was greeted by Number One.

"What the hell do you think you are doing?"

"Fishing for shark."

"Why?"

"Well, I heard that if you kill a shark and take the heart out, that the heart will go on beating until sunset. That ought to be verified. In normal saline one might keep it going for days."

"You don't kill a shark on this ship. Damn it, the deck would stink for weeks! I know the stench of a shark. Anyhow these stokers you've collected aft wouldn't kill it. They'd hack off its fins, wedge its mouth open with a stake, and throw it back into the sea—to watch it, defenceless, being attacked and eaten by other sharks. Bloody cruel, I call it, and by God I won't have it here. The shark can't help its nature."

I turned to go, when he relented. "Look here, I don't want to stop your experiment. I'll give you a boat, and you can drag your shark to the beach and kill it there with hatchets. The boat's crew will obey you, and the stench will make you sick. If you bring the heart aboard—keep it in any place except my bath."

On returning aft I found that the stokers and my shark had disappeared. In their impatience they had tried to drag it up on the hook, and the shark had broken from the hook. The hook had become unbent, and I did not rebait it.

Amongst our captures was one of the strangest ships that ever sailed the seas. We discovered her at dawn, three hundred miles from shore. She was a steamer and carried wireless. She was flying the red ensign, and the paint had been scraped off her funnel. To the flag-signal in the international code, "What ship?" she made reply after some delay, "British ship." But her name was not in Lloyd's Register, and our next signal was: "Stop your engines." Her engines were stopped, her helm put hard over, and this suspicious craft went round in two short circles before coming to a standstill.

We came to within half a mile of her, launched a boat,

and Lieutenant Stockwell, with a boarding party of marines, were rowed over.

They were on board for an hour, and when Stockwell returned he told a story which most of us thought was incredible. As our boat approached, sounds of singing were heard, and on the deck of the vessel they found over a hundred negroes—men, women, and children—singing "Onward, Christian Soldiers" to the strains of a harmonium. Stockwell interviewed the negro captain in the latter's cabin and asked for the ship's papers. There were no papers. These people were negroes from Carolina who had subscribed for and bought the steamer. They had sailed from the United States without permission. The captain had no mariner's certificate.

"Then who," asked Stockwell, "navigates this ship?"

"Professor Lewis, sah. He was Professor of Astronomy in negro university."

"Let me see him," said Stockwell.

The negro captain thrust his head out of the door and shouted: "Professor Lewis, come up at once and see British officer."

From below a voice answered: "Yes, sah, when I get my collar on."

In due course Professor Lewis appeared. He knew astronomy and some navigation. His reckoning as to the ship's position was only wrong by two hundred miles. Where were they going? They had bought a concession of land from the King of Liberia, and were going there to found a Christian Republic. When Stockwell made his report, the captain decided that the story was so extraordinary that the negro ship must come into harbour. This she did. A Naval Court of Inquiry was held, and every word of the story was proved to be true. Professor Lewis was given charts of the African coast which he did not possess. A coloured mate with a certificate was signed on at Freetown. The ship was allowed to proceed on her way and as she left harbour all the negroes sang "Onward, Christian Soldiers." And this happened in the middle of a European War between the Christian nations of Europe. At the time I wrote an account of the affair to a friend in London, and asked him to send it to one of the daily papers. He replied that unless I had written it he would not have believed a word of it. In any case, it was no use sending it to the Press. No newspaper would ever believe it.

At one time we became a pirate ship. This was during an interregnum between the departure of our first captain and the appointment of another. In the Royal Navy a pirate ship is any ship in which the officers grow beards. We all grew beards, and mine was one of the best. It was a red, square beard. In a white drill uniform and a topee I looked like a disreputable African explorer, not above dealing in "black ivory." I had a photograph taken and sent a print to my mother. She replied that it was not very humorous to send a photograph of someone else as my own.

One day Captain E. Wigram, R.N., arrived and dined that night in the wardroom. He was clean shaven, immaculately dressed, and had great charm of manner. In fact, when he invited you to have a drink you felt as if you were having two. Years later he became an equerry-in-waiting to the King. That evening I looked at myself in the glass. What must this man think of my appearance! With a pair of scissors I cut off the beard, and next morning appeared clean shaven. To my astonishment all the other officers were likewise clean shaven. We had all thought alike. The captain made that breakfast amusing. Turning to Number One, he asked: "Is this ship running a double watch of officers? No? Well, it's very curious. Last night I dined with most interesting officers, and they have all disappeared." Then he described each one of us as we had appeared the night before.

"In your place, Surgeon, was the image of an elder of the Kirk whom once I saw when shooting in Scotland."

It was Commander G. B. W. Young, R.N., who brought the ship back to Liverpool. We zigzagged up the Bristol Channel, and at three a.m. were at the mouth of the Mersey. No pilot was awaiting us and to wait for a pilot in that submarine-infested water would have been courting disaster. Our R.N. captain had never sailed the Mersey, but he navigated the great ocean liner up the river and into dock. Only sailors know what that implies.

At Gibraltar the Secretary of the Mediterranean Club once made a signal—"Oysters tonight." He had ordered them from the other side of the world for an American heiress who had a house on the Rock. Some of the oysters she had presented to the Club, and there that night I dined. E. Wigram had been appointed to the *Inflexible* and our Captain was now Commander G. B. W. Young, R.N. He and the P.M.O. joined me at table, and I invited them to share my oysters.

"No, thanks," said Young, "ten years ago I lost my best friend through his eating oysters."

"Same here," added the P.M.O., "I remember two men who died that way."

I smiled, put an oyster in my mouth, and swallowed it. In the midst of what happened next I heard the P.M.O. say to Young—"I ought to have stopped him. They don't even look right." My shout to the waiter was for half a tumbler of neat whiskey. That and a tablespoonful of castor oil completed my dinner, and next morning in place of breakfast I had an anti-typhoid inoculation. A few days later I enquired about the American heiress and learned that she was apparently in perfect health, but it was six years before I could once more face an oyster in its shell.

# CHAPTER XIX

## NAVAL OCCASIONS

FOR my sins I was appointed censor of all letters written from the ship. We had been three weeks at sea when a notice appeared that there would be a postal collection, and that the censor would be Lieutenant Stockwell. He was a Royal Naval Reserve officer, holding a high position in the Merchant Service. He was one of the most conscientious and least assuming men I ever met. He did his work and did not talk about it. He was a pleasant shipmate, and on Saturday nights took a single glass of port, when the old toast was given: "Sweethearts and wives," to which someone is expected to add: "May they never meet." Years later, when he received a high honour, I knew that he had deserved it by a life of self-discipline. Number One said his only fault was that he sang in his morning bath, and that anyone who did that should be shot at sight. I felt that Stockwell had no sense of humour, and therefore dropped into the post-box the following letter:

"DEAR VON RECKLINGHAUSER,

It is some time since we met, and I hope that by now, according to plan, you have reached a neutral country. On that chance I am writing. It is not possible for me to see A, but, if all goes well, I hope to meet B in a few weeks' time.                    H. S."

The letter was addressed to a street in Geneva. Next morning at breakfast Lieutenant Stockwell looked really ill. At eleven o'clock I was called to Number One's cabin. On his table lay my opened letter.

"Did you write this damned rubbish?"

"Yes."

"What the hell did you do it for?"

"To pull Stockwell's leg."

"It's damn silly. If people didn't know you, you could get into a hell of a mess. Fact is, you've too little to do. You can censor the letters yourself, and the P.M.O. can censor yours."

He tore up the letter and threw it out of the port-hole. Later on in the day Number One and I had a walk. "Yah-ha! Not a bad leg-pull. Old Stockwell was as white as a sheet when he brought me your letter."

Thus I came to censor the letters of four hundred people, officers and men. From that experience I learnt a great lesson—that humanity was far better than anything I had ever thought it to be. There were a few exceptions, such as the boy who wrote this:

"DEAR GRANDPA AND GRANDMA,

I hope this finds you as it leaves me, in the pink. We are having a hard time, but it's grand to be fighting under the dear old flag. Yesterday we had a brush with the enemy. They came alongside, threw their grappling irons and boarded us. We drove them back with our cutlasses, and I can tell you the decks were dripping with blood. Both our surgeons should have the V.C. The way they looked after the wounded amid the shot and shell. I am quite well.    YOUR LOVING GRANDSON.

P.S.—It's quite safe to send postal orders, and the Paymaster will cash them."

In the confident belief that no editor in England would publish such a letter, I let it go. Another letter, from a boy to his sister in an orphanage, was this:

"DEAR MAGGIE,

Before I left I gave the Matron 5/- to give you at Xmas. I am very happy. The Officers and men are nice. There is no bullying. You will soon be leaving the Orphanage. It would be nice if you could go into service with nice people. We have no parents, and our relations are best left alone. When you leave the Orphanage you will be more alone than ever. If ever you are tempted to do wrong, remember you have a brother in the Navy. We have only ourselves."

That was the only letter whose contents I ever divulged, and I only disclosed them to Number One, who said, "Yah-ha." Three days later he said: "I've inquired about that boy. Good lad! I've recommended him for a step in promotion. Yah-ha."

Amongst other work I was given was that of decoding. The first captain we had would send for me at all hours, unlock his safe, produce the A Code and watch me decoding messages taken in on the wireless. The A Code was a five-number code, and the book was the size of the *London Telephone Directory*. It was bound with *lead* covers, because, in the event of a ship's going down, it was the captain's first duty to throw the code overboard. No human being could memorise that code, but, as I discovered for myself, it was possible to memorise certain combinations of figures. This saved time when I was decoding, with an impatient captain waiting to know what the message was. Can a code be deciphered without the code being known? Yes, it can. You have only to notice that a certain combination of sounds, figures, or letters precedes certain happenings. Unless the code is changed the same combination will mean that the same thing is ordered to happen again.

The most secret code is not proof against stupidity,

treachery or capture. As soon as there was any suspicion or risk that the A Code was known to the enemy, the Admiralty altered the code. That takes time. If the alteration—say in place of 1 read 7—were sent out in code by wireless to all our ships on the seven seas—the enemy would also receive the alteration. To fleets in home waters the information could be sent by King's Messenger, but in the South Atlantic I have seen a sealed bag, containing a new copy of the A Code delivered by the skipper of a collier!

Once a code has been discovered, numerical changes cannot altogether replace the lost secrecy, because the enemy knows the principles on which the code is built. This knowledge aids subsequent deciphering. Thus, early in the War the German cruiser *Magdeburg* went ashore in the Gulf of Finland, and a copy of the German naval code was captured by the Russians. We sent a special cruiser to bring the code to England, and, by October 1914, the code was at the Admiralty. In a room at the Admiralty some of the cleverest men in Britain sat day after day and month after month. The *Magdeburg* Code revealed the principles on which the German code was based, and so enabled our experts to decipher more easily the subsequent German codes. Thus we knew beforehand whenever the High Seas Fleet was coming out.

In all probability the Germans, although they have never admitted it, could read our A Code with equal facility. Of a certainty they must have known our B or Consular Code, because before the War we had at times allowed Germans to act as British vice-consuls. The B Code was used by warships when communicating with our consuls. There was the story that Admiral Craddock, on his ill-fated voyage, suspected a leakage of information through the B Code, and sent an officer to interview a British vice-consul in a South American port.

"Where do you usually keep the B Code?"

"In my safe."

"When you are on leave has your deputy access to the safe?"

"Yes. But when I go on leave I send the code to my bank."

"Which bank?"

"The Deutsche Bank. But Herr Smitz is all right."

To my knowledge the Admiralty A Code was changed twice during the first year of the War. For one change I was responsible. The ship called at a foreign port, and I had to take certain papers to be signed by the British consul. By the ship's time it was eight-thirty a.m. when I reached his house. By the shore time it was seven-thirty a.m. The garden gate was opened by a very pretty girl, who, at first glance, I thought was English. She was quite frank: she was the German governess. The consul was not up, but she would tell him I was there, and showed me into the dining-room. In one corner of the room was the small wireless installation which enabled him to get into touch with our ships within a radius of fifty miles. Lying open on his desk I saw—the A Code. I had breakfast with the consul, his wife, two little girls, and the governess. After breakfast I remarked to the consul's wife that she was fortunate to have such a nice governess.

"Yes, in a place like this. And, do you know, all we pay that girl is twenty pounds a year. Of course she's a German, but it's wonderful."

It was—most wonderful. Late that afternoon in London the A Code was changed, and next week the pretty governess went home via Holland. And yet I may have been wrong! In any case, nobody was ever either thanked or blamed.

Pride goes before a fall, and the A Code nearly got me into trouble. We were in harbour and near us was a battleship, the *Vengeance*, in which one night I dined. It was a "wet" ship. There were cocktails before dinner and champagne at dinner. Opposite me was a rather cocksure young lieutenant, who remarked that it was a pity the "big ships" had been recalled to the Grand Fleet. The big ships were the *Invincible* and the *Inflexible*. They had been detached from the Grand Fleet to go south to meet Von Spee's fleet and avenge the disaster which befell Admiral Craddock and his squadron off Coronel. The big ships had not coaled at Gibraltar. Then came the rumour that the big ships had been recalled to the North Sea. In answer to the young lieutenant I said: "On the contrary, at this very moment the big ships are half-way across the South Atlantic."

From the head of the table came a roar from the black-bearded captain. "Silence, sir! You have said enough. I shall see you after dinner."

At a table in the captain's cabin sat the captain and commander, looking very grave. I was asked my name, ship, and date of commission. This he verified from a Navy List. "And now," said the captain, "I have to ask you a very serious question. Have you access to the A Code?"

"Yes, sir. I do decoding at times, but the only interesting thing that I learnt from the A Code during the past week is that the *Highflyer* wants a ton of potatoes."

There was no laughter in court, and the captain proceeded. "If that be so, can you give me any explanation for the statement you made during dinner about the big ships?"

"Yes, sir. For the past five days there has been a persistent rumour on shore that the big ships went back to the north. Last night I dined in the *Electra*, the cable company's ship. She had just returned from cutting the German cable to Pernambuco. I put two and two together. It was brilliant strategy of our people to spread a rumour on the coast. It would reach Von Spee via Pernambuco. Then the cable was cut. If the rumour was false, the contradiction would never reach South America. That was my mental deduction."

"Quite so, but as long as you are in the Service, especially in war, I hope you will cease from making mental deductions, or, if you do, that you will keep them to yourself. To-night you divulged something which I had concealed, even from my own commander."

The commander looked at me reproachfully.

"I am very sorry, sir, but I would never have made such a statement except to officers. I said nothing in the *Electra*."

"Officers! You forget the Maltese servants, who also heard it. Now I have no wish to spoil your evening, and shall not announce the upshot of all this until the morning. Your ship by that time will be at sea, but all shore leave from this ship will be suspended. All the cables to South America have not been cut; you forgot that. No one shall land from this ship until—certain other news arrives. As to what that is, you are no doubt capable of making another mental deduction! And now, before you go back to the wardroom I think we might have a glass of port."

"Thank you very much, sir." Thus we squared yards.

On returning to the wardroom I was met by my two hosts, the major of marines and the P.M.O. of the ship.

"What did the old man do to you?"

"Gave me a wigging for trying to discuss the movements of ships and then gave me a glass of port."

"How like him!" said the major. "But how absurd! What could you know about the movement of ships?" ·

"Nothing at all," was my answer.

The others were playing roulette. The stake limit was sixpence, and the rule was that the heaviest loser was allowed to take the bank the next night, because the bank usually wins. As the croupier was about to spin I put sixpence on zero, and zero won! That night my luck was in.

At ten-thirty we ceased play, because a beautiful girl in full evening-dress entered the wardroom, sat down at the piano, and sang to us in a rich soprano voice. As the ship was a mile from the shore I was surprised, and said to the man next me: "Who is she?"

"She is the governor's daughter, and she comes out occasionally to cheer us up. Would you like to be introduced? Come along."

The beautiful girl was most gracious, until I told her that it was delightful to see an English girl again. Then her voice changed, and, in a deep bass, "she" said: "Don't be an ass, old man. Have a drink with me!"

A marine entered. "Your boat is alongside, sir." The "girl" went to the piano, and the wardroom sang as I said good-bye to my hosts:

> We don't want to lose you,
> But we think you ought to go.

Next morning I awoke at eight o'clock to find that the ship was moving at full speed, and that the P.M.O., fully dressed, was standing in my cabin. He looked very annoyed, and was very annoyed.

"I have been twenty years in the Service and am not yet aware that it is any part of my duty to inform you that the ship is about to go into Action."

"Action!" And I was out of my bunk in a second. "Then why the devil did they not sound the bugles?"

"The first bugle was sounded half an hour ago."

"Are we having breakfast?"

"Yes, if you go to the bridge and ask them to delay Action until you have had your breakfast. A couple of marines can easily be taken away from their gun to get your breakfast. I have been twenty years in the Service. . . ." And he left my cabin. Good old P.M.O.!

I dressed hurriedly, and went to my station. There was

no time to act on the Admiralty instruction that when the exigencies of the Service permitted, all officers and men, prior to Action, should have a bath and put on clean underclothing. As I walked aft I noticed that all the pumps were on, and cascades of water were pouring down from the upper decks. To prevent fire! That was a good idea. My place in Action was to stand on the deck between the two aft guns and at the top of a companion-ladder. In all armoured ships the doctors go in Action to the most protected part of the ship, on the assumption that a live doctor is of more use than a dead one. In our ship no one place was safer than another, and I had told the P.M.O. that I would be much happier on deck where I could see what was happening than I would be down below listening to the noise. He agreed, and this arrangement also suited Number One. Standing at the top of that companion-ladder I was a breach of the Hague Convention. On the left lapel of my jacket was pinned the morphia syringe, but round my waist was a belt and holster in which was a loaded Service revolver. If during the action the stokers panicked, their nearest way to the gun-deck was up that companion ladder. A panic on deck would demoralise the guns' crews, and in that event I had promised Number One to do what he wished me to do.

Fear is a strange emotion. The word Action always caused me to have a sinking feeling in the region of the stomach, but in truth my real fear was that I would show fear and not behave decently. The religion of the Royal Navy conquers fear, and that religion is to do your duty. If you have something to do, especially something very exciting, you have no time to think of yourself; or if you do think of yourself you will remember the hundreds of men, better than yourself, who are literally in the same boat.

There is a third emotion which sustains the mind—that it is a privilege, in however humble a capacity, to exercise the executive power of England.

In charge of one of the after guns was a chief petty officer, who saluted as I arrived.

"Morning, C.P.O. I'll be glad when this is over, and we're back home."

He smiled. "I'm thinking, sir, that you're not the only one in the ship that's thinking that."

"Where is your home, C.P.O.?"

"Appledore, sir. In Devon, you know."

"Yes, I know. What's this four-funnelled thing we're chasing?"

"God only knows, sir. Some say she's a German raider. But if so be, why doesn't she engage? Maybe she's leading us on to the *Karlsruhe*. They've been morseing her for the last half-hour in the international code, 'Stop your engines or I fire.'"

"Then why don't we fire?"

"The range, sir. But it's closing every five minutes. We'll get her—if the boilers don't burst. We must be doing nineteen. Look at the paint on them funnels."

A boy, listening to a telephone beside the gun, turned and said: "Down two hundred, closing." At that moment one of our for'ard guns fired. We watched for the fall of the shell. It was at least four hundred yards short. I watched for the answering flash of flame, but none came. There was no more firing. A wireless message arrived addressed to our ship from a brand-new French liner: "Come to my immediate assistance. Am being chased by German raider. She has opened fire. I have four hundred passengers on board." The French liner gave her exact position, from which it was clear that—we were the German raider.

Again our searchlight blinked a message. We told her who we were, ordered her to stop, and to stop using her wireless. For the first time her searchlight flashed an answer to our demands: "If you will stop, I will stop." As soon as that message was known, dozens of hungry men on our decks laughed. We stopped, and smoke and steam poured from our funnels to the sky. She also stopped and morsed again: "Let us both talk." To that we answered: "Come into harbour for recognition." Her reply was: "If you go first, I will follow." We did, and she followed. Then we had breakfast.

A few weeks later I saw the "big ships" on their way home from the Falklands. The *Inflexible* and the *Invincible* coaled at St. Vincent, and we were also in harbour that day.

The big ships came in at dawn and sailed at five p.m. They were coaling, and therefore were not at home to visitors, so none of us went on board. When they sailed we said good-bye. All our men manned the rigging and officers stood by the side. In each of the big ships over a thousand officers and men did likewise, and their rigging was decorated by hundreds of men, every man apparently standing upon the head of another. All this was done in silence. The big ships weighed anchor, and in the silence we heard their engine telegraphs tinkle. They began to move dead slow out of harbour, and we stood at attention. As the first ship came abreast of us, our Number One called through a megaphone from the bridge: "Three cheers for *Invincible*—hip, hip, hip," and with each hooray every officer and man raised his cap aloft. Again a moment of silence. From the bridge of *Invincible* came the order: "Three cheers for *Empress of Britain*," answered by over a thousand men. Again silence, until the *Inflexible* passed, when once more the greeting was given and returned. The next silence was broken by music as our ship's band on the quarter-deck played:

> Will ye no' come back again?
> Will ye no' come back again?
> Better lo'ed ye canna be,
> Will ye no' come back again?

Only one verse, and silence again. From across the water the bands of the big ships echoed:

"Will ye no' come back again?"

So for a few minutes music was answered by music across the water, until at last we could no longer hear the bands on those steel giants, now moving at thirty knots back to the Grand Fleet. In those few minutes I saw the symbolism of the Royal Navy *in excelsis*—ships that pass in the night.

At last Action came, or we thought it was coming. I had decoded this message: "From a source, hitherto reliable, *Kron Prinzessin Cecilie*, commerce raider, will meet a Swedish store-ship for ammunition and supplies in Lat. . . . Long. . . . on the night of . . . . D Squadron will meet her. As far as is known, *Kron Prinzessin Cecilie* will not be supported." In other words, they did not know if the *Karlsruhe* had crossed the ocean to support the *Cecilie*. Even so, we had a chance. We would be three to two. There was the old light cruiser, the *Highflyer*, which, with the senior naval officer on board, was our leader. She had for'ard one six-inch gun. That was something, but she was not in the same class as the *Karlsruhe*. At the beginning of the War she had been re-commissioned from the scrap-heap. She had a copper bottom, which could be scraped at sea by the crew, and thus she could remain at sea for long periods without going into dry-dock. At this time she carried as a Royal Naval Reserve officer a man I would have liked to meet. His name was Erskine Childers, and he had written a great novel about sailing. It is called *The Riddle of the Sands*. It was not a novel. As I know now, it was a true story. When a squadron, even of three ships, are sailing together but are never in harbour at the same time, it is difficult to meet those whom you wish to meet on another ship. One day, as the three ships were cruising, I reported to my captain that I had an idea. In the middle of the South Atlantic is the loneliest island in the world. It is not inhabited and is called St. Paul's Rock. I suggested that as we were near this place, we should land a search-party, because Germany might have established a secret wireless base on the island. The captain liked the idea, and sent it by morse to his senior officer. Within half an hour the reply came that the rock would be searched next morning. Next morning three ships were around the island. Then I learnt that only the leading ship was to land a search-party. In vain I submitted that the idea was mine, and that I should be allowed to join the landing-party. They searched that island for four hours and found nothing. I never met Childers. After the War he went to Ireland in search of new adventures and joined the rebels. The Irish Republican Government captured him and shot him as a spy. I am glad that England did not shoot him, because he was one of the greatest Englishmen whom I have never met. Had I had the responsibility of defending him at his drumhead court martial, the defence would have been to hand to each of his judges a copy of *The Riddle of the Sands*, and to ask them to read it. That book explained all. He was a spy, but an amateur spy, and long before the Great War he had risked his life, his liberty, and his ten-ton cutter amidst the Frisian Islands—for England. And he discovered the Secret of the Sands—how the invasion of England had been plotted out—and he told it in the form of a novel. It may be that the British Government did not believe his story of that famous cruise. Yet to my knowledge, in 1917 they realised that there was the plan for a coastal raid, under cover of a bombardment from sea, to land troops from motor barges which had crossed the North Sea.

Our squadron consisted of the *Highflyer* and two armed ocean liners—the *Marmora* and the *Empress of Britain*. For two days we steamed to our destination. In the Royal Navy, as soon as a thing is inevitable and there is no chance of leakage of information, the facts are usually made known to all concerned. It is better that men should know what they are expected to do than rot their minds in vain speculation. To know the worst is always best. Once our destination was known the reactions of the wardroom were interesting. Our wine-bills ceased. We became very polite to each other. The man who had sat opposite to you at meals for months, and whose stories and conversation bored you, was a very decent fellow. And he thought the same of you. I noted these facts more than once. Everybody realised the brotherhood of men, and the nearer to death the better men become. It is only when we are some distance from death that we say: "Eat, drink, and be merry, for to-morrow we die."

The second afternoon was spent in "capping" lyddite shells—that is, in screwing fuses into shells, hoisted from the magazine to the deck. It is a rule in the Royal Navy that in all unpleasant tasks the officers work with the men. When coaling ship every officer, except the captain, is expected to put on old clothes and help to carry coal. So also in the case of putting fuses into shells. We squatted on deck—a fair distance apart—with a lyddite shell between our knees, and screwed in the fuses. At first my idea was—who could screw in the most fuses in the least time. Then the master-gunner, who was supervising, checked me: "Not so fast, sir. If you feel a bit of grit in the thread of the screw, don't screw it down. Because if you does, the shell may go off, and then where would you be?"

I answered with humility: "Master-gunner, that is a big question, and I don't know the answer."

After that warning I screwed in fewer fuses than anybody else. My fingers are delicate of touch, and I was on the look-out for the slightest particle of grit in the thread. By tea-time all the shells were capped and stacked neatly beside their guns. We had arrived at our destination in good time, and the three ships stopped in line, about a mile apart. The *Highflyer* was in the centre.

After tea, "Sparks," the wireless officer, entered the wardroom. "We're getting hot. Within the last hour I've taken in the same message three times: 'Are there any British warships in the vicinity? I have news to communicate?' What ship? That's just it. Name of British ship, registered at Liverpool. There is an English ship of that name. They found that out top-sides—but the real ship has got the Marconi and this ship was using the Telefunken. Yes, I think we are getting hot."

At the start of this expedition we had orders: "Under no circumstances is the wireless to be used for sending. Only for receiving." Wireless is a great boon, but in war, on the sea, it has this disadvantage—it betrays the fact that you are there.

At eight o'clock that night, "Sparks" gave us more news: "Hotter and hotter. There are two of them talking. Of course I don't know, but it's the German four-figure code all right. How near? Damn near. From the strength I'd say within fifty miles. Wish to God we had the new Directional Finder. Then I could tell you almost exactly where they are. God only knows. They may be north, south, east, or west, but they are—damn near." And we were one thousand miles away from the nearest shipping route!

At eight-thirty the *Highflyer* morsed on the searchlight her final orders: "If any ship or ships approach during the night, open fire without challenge. Your station in action must depend upon circumstances. Great care must be exercised not to mask my guns. We are receiving enemy signals very strong." Then darkness fell on the ocean, and none of our ships showed any lights.

As I went to my cabin, the door next to mine was open, and the P.M.O. asked me in. He was sitting at the table in his pyjamas, and had finished writing a letter. He smiled and said: "Looks like it to-night, doesn't it?"

"Yes, I think it does."

"Finished your book?"

I laughed. "That's a damn funny thing. I wrote the last page this morning."

"Well, you didn't waste your time. By the way, do you believe in God?" he asked.

"Yes, but I'm not religious."

"Neither am I, but I have always carried about a prayer. I got it over twenty years ago from a Red Indian in Canada. It's quite short. To-night I made a copy for you. I think you'll like it." He handed me a folded paper. "No, don't read it now. Read it in your cabin."

"Thank you very much. Good night."

"Good night, old man."

In my cabin the MS. of my book was lying on the table. On another sheet I wrote the publisher's name and address in London, and beneath: "If found, please forward to above address." I placed the lot in a dispatch-box. Round the box I wrapped my oilskins, and corded it carefully. The last covering of the package was my lifebelt, and more cord. It was certain to float, and if the worst happened I hoped to have time to fetch it from my cabin and throw it overboard.

The Red Indian's prayer began: "O Great White Father." I read it and said it. It was curious that the P.M.O., who had been brought up in the Church of England, and that I, who had been a Presbyterian, should find comfort in a prayer composed by a Red Indian. Then I turned in and was soon asleep. That night I believed in the Fatherhood of God. As I slept, the *Kron Prinzessin Cecilie* crept up from the south. None of our ships saw her, but, as became known after the War, she recognised that there were three of us, turned, and went south again.

## CHAPTER XX

## THE WHITE MAN'S GRAVE

OUR base, for a time, was Freetown, on the south bank of the Sierra Leone River, six miles from the sea. The river, four miles broad at Freetown, is the best natural harbour on the West African coast, and, as a naval base, guards three ocean lines of communication: to South America, to Australia and New Zealand, and to the Cape.

From the river the land looks like Paradise: a luxurious undergrowth of coolest green sprinkled with blossoms of white, scarlet, blue and gold, reaching to the edge of the water or to bays of yellow sand with dull red rocks; trees of kola, coconut, orange, lime and banana; tall palms with motionless green feathery leaves against a deep blue cloudless sky; and beyond, in a great half-circle, the purple mountains of Sierra Leone. A vision of almost unearthly beauty.

> Charm'd magic casements, opening on the foam
> Of perilous seas, in faery lands forlorn.

On our first visit we steamed up the river at dawn, and after breakfast I went ashore. The streets of Freetown are wide, bordered by grass plots, and shaded by trees; but most of the houses are small, with wide verandahs. From the town a broad white road leads uphill. On this road I overtook and passed an officer in khaki, who called to me: "Excuse my saying so, but you are walking too fast." I stopped, and joined him at an easier pace. He was young, tall, and bronzed, and his eyes were bright, but rather sunk—as are the eyes of those who have had malaria many times. "You are just ashore here? Well, if you walk fast in the heat you won't last long. Come with me to the barracks. The major will be glad to see you."

At their Mess I found the major at breakfast. He was not late nor was I early, because on board we kept Greenwich time, which is well ahead of shore time. After his breakfast the major apologised that he had to leave me for an hour. "I've got a sad job on hand: to take a snapshot of a boy's grave for his mother in England. What did he die of? Malaria, of course, or rather blackwater fever, which seems to be the same thing. The conquest of malaria! How can you pour paraffin over thousands of miles of swamp; how can you make natives take quinine, or how can any of us live for years on quinine? Look here, in the past three years I've buried five boys—clean-living boys, straight from England. Oh, yes, this place is still the White Man's Grave, but I'll take you to the swimming-pool."

Behind the Mess, on the top of the hill, was a rectangular, marble-lined swimming-pool, in which the water was as blue as the sky. In this pool I swam, attired in my topee, because one dared not to swim bareheaded in that sun. In the corner of the pool a little fountain was playing, but the water was warm, and the illusion of coolness was melted by the reality of tropical heat. I thought of the woody shade around Highland burns, where boulders, moss and ferns are drenched in cool spray from cascades in the hills.

From the barracks Freetown looks like a wood filled with houses, and on the other side of the river are the mud flats and islands of Bullom. From these islands natives cross, even in rough weather, by paddling the trunks of trees, burnt into the shape of large canoes, each carrying a dozen men. Often they are capsized, and the swimming crew empty their craft of water in midstream and re-embark. Beyond the river, seventy miles away, the Blue Mountains rise in the clear air.

After lunch I went to the military hospital, and found an overworked major, R.A.M.C. The British troops were long overdue for change to England, and the routine had become two weeks on duty followed by one week in hospital. There, for the first time, I saw blackwater fever—six cases. A mysterious disease. Some said it was a form of malaria, and others that quinine was the cause. Having nothing else to do, I went to the hospital every day whenever the ship was in port, and did some work in the laboratory, where it was necessary to use a microscope in the shade lest the eyesight was blinded by the glare of light. I searched blood films of the blackwater patients for a new organism—and found nothing except malarial parasites. The major had made a therapeutic discovery. To stop the otherwise intractable vomiting the patients took copious draughts of water with one teaspoonful of bicarbonate of soda to the pint. That dissolved the poisonous mucus lining the stomach, and eased their distress. Apart from malaria, this major had strong views on another aspect of the West African coast. Over the mantelshelf of his sitting-room hung a strange device. Glued to a wooden panel was an empty gin bottle, surmounted by a glass with two straws rampant, and below this effigy were the words: "The bad West African climate." Be that as it may, the major had carried on where other men would have dropped. That I know.

That night, before going aboard, I dined at the Garrison Club, and shared a palm-oil chop with the Commissioner of Police. Palm-oil chop is worth a visit to the West African coast. It consists of portions of meat, game or chicken, with foufou balls, ground nuts, fresh capsicum pods, green leaves, oysters, and breadfruit—all cooked together and served in boiling palm oil. It is strange that the great dishes of tropical countries should be hotter than those of temperate climates, as witness also the curries of India. Moreover, these dishes cannot be produced in their native splendour even at the most expensive restaurants of Europe. Some say that a taste for such dishes is acquired, but I appear to have been blessed or cursed with an inborn liking for the best food and drink of every country in which I have lived. Yet there is one collation of composts which I loathe with all my soul and gastric plexus—the English Sunday dinner!

In the morning I was again ashore—to buy cigarettes for the wardroom and a bottle of cod liver oil for an officer who used that beverage as a tonic. My money was sovereigns, and I changed one at a *brasserie* which purported to sell lager beer, receiving in change the beautiful silver coinage of the colony, which has a palm tree on the reverse side. At a chemist's shop I bought the bottle of cod liver oil, and paid four times the London price. The chemist was a Syrian, who explained that the increased price was due to the War. From the chemist's shop I carried my parcel to an English store, where I began to buy a stock of cigarettes. This transaction was interrupted by the entrance of a piccaninny aged about eight, who came in smiling, and holding up a shilling in his fingers, said to me: "Massa say no good."

To which I answered: "Run away, little boy, I'm busy."

A few minutes later the chemist entered the store and announced that I had given him a bad shilling. He demanded a good shilling in exchange. This I refused, and told him he ought to have noticed the mistake at the time. His next demand was for the return of the bottle of cod liver oil, and in reply to that I pushed the bottle across the counter and told the English assistant to pack it with the cigarettes and send it to the ship. Whereupon the chemist left the shop saying: "I fetch de police."

The English assistant looked worried. "No, sir, it's not all bluff. These people are very independent."

Soon the chemist was back with a little native policeman, who came up, clicked his heels, and saluted. "I arrest you, sar. Charge of passing bad money in de colony."

This most polite policeman listened attentively as I explained that my silver had been obtained in the town, that I did not know a good shilling from a bad shilling, and that the chemist should have noticed the mistake at the time. The policeman must have admired my uniform, because again he clicked heels and saluted. "I arrest you, sar. You come to de police station!"

This was more than I had anticipated. "You listen to me, policeman. You cannot possibly arrest me. No person, other than an officer of my own or senior rank in either Service, can put me under arrest. Also I do not come to police stations: I go to police stations. You and this chemist will walk in the middle of the road one hundred yards ahead of me, and neither of you will look round. You will lead the way to the police station where I am going." Again the little policeman saluted, and marched off with the chemist.

On reaching the police station I followed my advance guard into the charge-room, where a black sergeant rudely said: "Put out dat cigarette." There was a placard on the wall, "No Smoking Allowed," and I threw my cigarette out of the window. The sergeant continued: "Serious charge, ver' serious charge! Passing bad money in de colony."

To which I answered: "Silence, sergeant, I shall see the Commissioner."

My accuser and the little policeman were about to lead the way upstairs, but I called them back and explained: "When I go to police station I walk behind, but in police station I walk in front." They fell back, and I led the way upstairs, where I knocked on a door marked "Commissioner of Police." As I entered, the commissioner rose from his desk. "Hullo, Doctor, glad to see you. None the worse of our palm-oil chop?"

"Hist! I'm under arrest!"

He looked dubious. "Is this meant to be a joke?"

"No joke about it. Wait until you see the procession coming upstairs!"

My two captors entered the room, and the commissioner became very official. He sat at his desk, gave me a chair

252

on his left, and said to the little policeman: "What is your report?"

The policeman gave an accurate account of what the prosecutor had told him: that in buying a bottle of cod liver oil I had tendered and passed a bad shilling.

Turning to me, the commissioner said: "What have you to say?"

I repeated my defence—that if I had passed a bad shilling I had done so unwittingly, and that the shopkeeper had not noticed the mistake at the time.

This so angered my accuser that when asked for his version of the affair he told a brand new story. "You want de truth, sar? When dis officer buy de bottle of cod liver oil, he pay me in good money. Den, when my back is turned to wrap up de bottle, dis officer lean over de counter, take a good shilling out of de till and put a bad shilling in de till. I swear dat is de truth, sar."

"What's your answer to that?" said the commissioner to me.

"A damned lie."

"All right, but do leave out the damns for the moment." And he turned to the prosecutor. "This officer says that your story is a lie. I believe him and I do not believe you. You have told lies. You told one story to the policeman, and in this room you have told a totally different story to me. You have made a false and wicked accusation. If your story to the policeman were true it means that you are not fit to look after a shop. If your story to me were true, your story to the policeman was a lie. There is a law against passing bad money, but there is also a law in this colony against perjury. For the future you had better remember the law about perjury, and now go back to your shop."

*Moral:* in all judicial proceedings stick to your original story!

I stayed to smoke a cigarette with the Commissioner, and

he drew my attention to twenty-five microscopes in their cases on the floor along one side of the room. Our squadron had taken as prize a German steamer, the *Professor Woermann*. Only Germans could have given such a name to a ship, and any ship with a name like that was fortunate in escaping from the high seas by being captured. The microscopes had been part of her cargo for German West Africa. The Naval Prize Court had sent them to the Commissioner with a view to selling them to the medical services in the colony. I examined one. It was a new Leitz, with oil immersion lens, condenser, movable stage, and dark illumination. The Commissioner wished to get rid of them. "I've wired to the Colonial Office, but have got no answer. I expect they'll lie there for months. What are they worth?"

"Not much out here," I said. "But I'll buy one for five pounds."

"All right," he replied. "I suppose I had better get rid of them." He took my cheque for five pounds, and I left the police station with a brand new Leitz microscope.

On board, in my cabin, I displayed the microscope in all its beauty to the P.M.O., and that evening after dinner he invited me to a glass of port.

We had always been friends, and he diffidently reminded me that it was not every Fleet surgeon who did all the work on board, and allowed the surgeon to go ashore so frequently. Not that he grudged these concessions, because they had enabled me to write a book. Had he himself been ashore that morning he would have had the microscope, whereas I had already one microscope in London. With a microscope a man could do research. . . .

The appeal was irresistible. "You can have the microscope for what I paid, and I'll go ashore in the morning and get another one. There are lots more."

The P.M.O. was honest. "But the ship sails at eleven o'clock in the morning."

"That's all right. Number One will give me a boat, and I'll go ashore after breakfast."

The P.M.O. rose, went to his cabin, returned with a cheque for five pounds, and collected the microscope.

At ten o'clock the next day I entered the room of the Commissioner of Police with a cheerful "Good morning," but soon realised that the atmosphere had become tense.

"Well, what is it now?" he asked.

"Oh, I just came for another microscope."

"I dare say you did, and you won't get one. The Colonial Office have bought the lot at twenty-five pounds apiece. They seem to think that twenty-five pounds is a fair price for a new microscope!"

There are moments in life when even the best of us must close our ears like the camel and silently fade away. As I hurried back to the boat I felt sorry for the Commissioner of Police. He was probably now reflecting whether after all there might not have been some truth in the story of the bad shilling.

## CHAPTER XXI

## BILLOW AND BREEZE

ON returning to England, I was appointed bacteriologist to the naval hospital at Pembroke Dock. There, in October 1915, I discovered the ætiology of cerebro-spinal fever, but it is of other matters that I am now writing.

In the dockyard town, one of the hotels had a bar-parlour, and here in the evenings a few naval and military officers sat, drank, and heard each other's grumbles.

In this pub I met a sad, silent man named Armstrong. He was a major in the Territorial Army, never drank more than two glasses of beer, and never by any chance ordered a round of drinks. There were rumours of domestic trouble and of an invalid wife who henpecked him. She had appeared one evening on the tennis court and ordered the major home, publicly announcing that it was "his bath night." No wonder the poor man was said to be in love with someone else! Yet these stories did not move me. If they were true, had he never heard of divorce? Little did I know of the fires of hell that were burning in the mind of that silent man. Some years later the river of hate overflowed and he poisoned his wife with weed-killer, was convicted and hanged.

One night there was local news of interest. A Russian armed yacht had anchored in the Haven below the dockyard, and twelve of the crew had been ashore in the town. At this time the town was placarded with a Royal Proclamation entitled "Notice to Aliens," and the police had acted on this notice by arresting the Russian sailors and detaining them for some hours. It was also stated that the admiral in command of the dockyard had not visited the yacht, whose captain was a Russian prince. We all agreed that these incidents were a deplorable insult to an allied nation, and that something must be done to put things right.

Next day I visited the yacht. On the quarter-deck the Officer of the Watch received me, and we conversed in French. I was a surgeon in the British Navy, and had come to visit the surgeon on the Russian yacht. There was no doctor on the yacht, but three of the crew were sick, and would be grateful if I would see them. This I did, and found one poor fellow in the last stages of consumption. Afterwards the officer gave me Russian tea in the wardroom and apologised for the absence of the captain who had been called to London. The yacht was palatial, and had belonged to the American millionaire, Gordon Bennett, who had left it on the outbreak of war at Marseilles. It had then been bought by the Russian Government, who sent officers and a crew to bring it to St. Petersburg. It was now a unit in the Czar's Navy. A two-inch gun was mounted on the fo'c'sle. That evening I scrounged a supply of medicines from the naval hospital and sent them out to the yacht.

A few days later two Russian officers, resplendent in cream and gold, with swords complete, visited the naval hospital. The principal medical officer turned out to meet them, and they courteously explained to him that their business was with me. They found me in the laboratory, and came as envoys from the Prince, who thanked me for my courtesy in calling and for my kindness to his sick. He would be honoured if I would lunch on the yacht next day. A steam pinnace from the yacht would await me alongside the dockyard jetty at noon.

At noon next day I was at the jetty and found that I was not the only guest. In the launch were five soldiers: the colonel, major, captain and two subalterns of an infantry regiment encamped in the neighbourhood. Like myself, the colonel had already paid a courtesy call on the captain. On the way out the colonel said to me: "I have heard these

Russian lunches are rather remarkable affairs, and if the Prince wants to take anybody on at drinks you are the Senior Service and ought to respond!''

On the quarter-deck of the yacht we were received by the Prince and his officers, in cream and gold. In the wardroom we adjourned to a buffet where we had caviare and vodka. Next to absinthe, vodka is the most unpalatable drink I have ever tasted. The wardroom had been the dining-saloon on Gordon Bennett's yacht, and was one of the most palatial rooms I have ever seen. The walls were of carved mahogany panelling, and the floor was covered with a deep, rich Turkey carpet. After this prologue we sat down to table and were served by Tartars. Of all races of mankind the Tartar has the most forbidding appearance, and, to English eyes, looks like a potential Houndsditch murderer.

We began with oysters and drank Chablis. After each course in this Gargantuan feast there was an interval of at least ten minutes during which each wine served was finished. Then came hare soup, with which we drank a golden sherry, Oloroso Magnifico; the fish was sole Morny, with which we drank a still Moselle. As an entrée there came a Russian dish—small portions of garnished meat wrapped in pastry, reminding one of miniature Cornish pasties. This was followed by the roast beef of old England—in point of fact, a prime sirloin of Scotch beef—served with Yorkshire pudding and horse-radish sauce. With this we had each a bottle of Bass XX. Then a Russian cigarette and a water ice to pave the way for the game—roast pheasant to the accompaniment of Heidsieck, Dry Monopole 1909. The sweet was a pineapple ice, followed by a mushroom and bacon savoury. With the fruit we drank Cockburn 1892. With the coffee there was offered an amazing selection of liqueurs. Lunch finished at four o'clock, and the Prince then asked: "And now, gentlemen, what will you drink?''

After the royal toasts the Prince rose to propose the toast of the Royal Navy. He spoke in French, and I, being the only representative of the Senior Service, rose to reply in the same language. Never was my French more fluent! In the course of his speech the Prince had referred to that "Deplorable Notice to Aliens," and had produced a copy of this Royal Placard, which had been served on his ship by a policeman. This I asked him to hand to me, and amidst tumultuous cheers tore the thing in pieces. I stated that such proclamations were never intended for our allies, and concluded by quoting a verse of doggerel:

> Aux Alliés. A bas le Turque,
> A bas l'Autrichien
> Et tous les autres chiens.
> A basso i Boche.

This immortal toast brought every man not only to his feet but on to the table!

The Prince was not to be outdone, and made yet another speech. He invited us all to remain to dinner, which was to be served at seven o'clock. As for the "Notice to Aliens," he knew that such mistakes happened, and he on his part wished to offer an apology for the deplorable conduct of the Russian Embassy in London. It was true that the Embassy had arranged for this lunch to be sent by train from the Savoy Hotel, but to his astonishment they had refused his other request that women should be sent from London for the entertainment of his guests.

The colonel and I were the first to go ashore. As I left the wardroom I noticed in a corner of the room a flickering flame in front of an ikon of the Virgin. On the journey we said nothing, and I had qualms of conscience. The hospitality I had received was the hospitality of barbarism, and I wondered at whose cost.

I was an ungrateful guest! As we walked through the

dockyard the colonel spoke for the first time. "One thing is clear to me. You and I are perfectly all right."

"Absolutely, sir." I affirmed.

"Whose house is that?" asked the colonel.

"The admiral's," I replied.

"Well, look here, it's nearly tea-time. What about calling on the old bird to tell him what he's missed and what we think about his conduct in not calling on the Prince?"

"No, sir, not to-day. He couldn't touch you, but he could eat me."

"Well, what are you going to do now?"

"I'm going to my bed. I've eaten and drunk enough to last me for a week."

On reflection the next morning I came to the conclusion that the admiral probably had his own reasons for not calling on the ship.

Next week a British armed yacht, flying the white ensign, entered the Haven, and I was instructed to see the sick on board. I was warned to mind my p's and q's, because her captain was "pukka R.N." and "one of the old school." On the yacht I was received by a short, square-built old gentleman with four gold rings and the curl on his sleeve. He had white hair, a red face, and fierce blue eyes—and I appraised him as a regular quarter-deck bawler.

"This way, Doctor, you'll see the sick in my cabin."

He led the way to a large cabin on the upper deck where five sick men were paraded. The men looked a little anxious as we entered.

"Now then, Doctor," shouted the captain, "no objection, I suppose, to my being present? No? That's right! Ha, ha; I'm treating them, and can tell you all about their cases." He went up to the first man, and, in a gentler voice, said: "Well, Smith, how's the throat? Better? That's right. Case of tonsillitis, Doctor, but he's been gargling his throat every hour. I see to it myself that every man has his medicine."

I looked at the man's throat, and it was perfectly normal.

"The next one, Doctor, is anæmia. I spotted he was looking rather pale, and put him on arsenic and iron. Feeling stronger, Jones? That's right." So this clinical lecture proceeded, punctuated by my examination of the patients. At the end of the inspection I was in a quandary. I had come to the conclusion that none of these men was ill, and moreover that none of them wanted to be ill. Yet the last thing I desired was to have a row with this extraordinary old martinet, so I hazarded the remark: "You must have plenty of medicines on board, sir?"

"Ha, ha; of course I have. You come with me. I'll show you medicines!"

We entered another cabin—the complete replica of a druggist's shop—and in astonishment I asked: "What was this yacht, sir, before you took her over?"

"Belonged to a French millionaire. Carried his own doctor and dispenser. What do you think of it?"

The situation was difficult, but had to be faced there and then.

"You wish my opinion, sir, about your sick?"

"Of course I do, sir. Do you think I'd have sent for you unless I wanted your opinion?"

"No, sir, and my opinion is this. I don't think the medicines you are giving these men are agreeing with them."

"What the devil do you mean, sir? Do you suggest that I know nothing about medicine? By God, sir, if you do you are the first of your cloth . . ."

"Not at all, sir. You know a great deal about medicine. But that's not the point."

"Then what the devil is the point? Out with it, sir. No shilly-shallying with me!"

"The point is this, sir. These are French medicines, and I couldn't dispense them myself. They were meant for French people, and they don't agree with English sailors!"

He paused. "By God, I never thought of that! I think you are about the cleverest doctor I've met. Come along, and we'll have some tea."

Back in his cabin and over tea he continued a pleasant monologue:

"You're at the hospital ashore? Well, the beach is all right, but not in war. That's the time to be afloat! When war was declared, I told my daughter: 'I'm going afloat.' She's a most sensible woman, and of course she agreed. Impossible to sit through the War talking to old fogeys in the club! There were difficulties at the Admiralty—too old! By God, sir, would you believe it that one man said that to me! He didn't repeat it. And that it was impossible for me to fly my flag at sea! Who the devil wanted to fly my flag at sea? I told them I'd go with the rank of post-captain in any craft they gave me. And I threatened them. Suppose I'd joined up as a rating, eh? That would have given the Service something to talk about!

"They gave me this yacht as a submarine-chaser. I've made her shipshape. There's a useful gun on the fo'c'sle and two depth charges aft. If the submarine submerges before you get her with gunfire you sail over the spot and let go the depth charges. At three fathoms they automatically explode. You know all about that? These are the new ideas, but if they don't work I've still got a shot in my locker. The old way—ram the submarine. Run her down, sir! If this yacht strikes a submarine amidships you know what will happen to the submarine?"

"Yes, sir, but what about the yacht? Would her plates stand the collision?"

"The yacht! What's a yacht to a submarine? And I've enough boats on board for everybody. Now, Doctor, I've told you all about the yacht. How would you like to sail with me?"

"Nothing better, sir."

"Very well, I'll write to-day. I'll tell them that you wish to come. I've been applying for a surgeon these past three months. Always the same answer: not enough surgeons, and the exigencies of the Service. Exigencies of the Service! Often used the words myself! And there was a time when I could have taken you and told the Admiralty afterwards."

Three weeks later the yacht was back in the Haven, and word was passed that she had got "a fish." That afternoon I went on board to congratulate the captain, and to ask what the Admiralty had said to his request about myself. On the quarter-deck I met the commander. He was a very tall and slightly bent old man, and his face, eyes and voice conveyed an impression of sadness. As a "snotty" he had been in the Navy at a time when Her Majesty's ships were under sail. And upon my soul, if either of these old gentlemen had told me they had served under Nelson I would have believed it.

I congratulated the commander about "the fish," but even that did not cheer him. "Yes, we got 'the fish' all right. At least, the 'old man' got her. She came up ahead within a hundred yards of us. The 'old man' was on the bridge, took the wheel, and went full speed for her. The gunner missed—she was too near. We caught her amidships. There was no doubt about it. The shock threw some of our men on to the deck. The 'old man' reversed the engines, shouting to everybody to stand by and look out for the oil. I was on the bridge with him. Oil came up all right, and the 'old man' danced about like a lunatic, and pulled two blasts on the whistle. That nearly killed me. How? Because two blasts is the signal to let go the depth charges—and the ship was going astern. By God, I had to sprint aft as I've never sprinted in my life. I was only just in time. The rating in charge had his knife half-way through the rope holding the depth charges. The yacht would have been blown out of the sea! I rather think he knows what he nearly did."

In his cabin I congratulated the captain.

"Oh, yes, Doctor, we got one, and the Admiralty have admitted it, and I'm going to get a lot more. I've also at last got a doctor."

"Me, sir?"

"No, not you. They turned that down, but they can't defeat me. Sit down and have some tea, and I'll tell you about it. My daughter put an advertisement in *The Times*. Here it is: 'Wanted. Fully qualified doctor to act as medical officer in a yacht now cruising on the west coast. Pleasant life. Salary, four hundred pounds per annum.' She got a dozen applicants. She interviewed them at Kensington and selected one. She told him what the billet really was, and he agreed to come. She says he's a tall, quiet, middle-aged man. The Admiralty could say nothing. I told them that as they couldn't find me a surgeon I'd found one myself, and that the least they could do was to give him a commission. They did it, and he arrives at six o'clock to-night. What are you doing to-night?"

"I'm on duty at eight o'clock, sir, at the hospital."

"H'm! He's never been afloat before. I'd have liked you to meet him and put him up to the ropes."

"Well, sir, I'll be very glad to meet his train at six, take him to the hotel for an hour, and your boat could meet him at the jetty at seven-thirty."

"I'm much obliged to you, Doctor." He shook hands, and thus I said good-bye to an Admiral of the Fleet, retired.

One afternoon the senior naval officer made a signal instructing me to proceed by motor launch to a ship lying off the mouth of the Haven. "Captain ill," was the only medical information in the message. The journey occupied over an hour, and outside the Haven the sea was choppy: there was a strong breeze and plenty of spray. I got chilled and drenched. As we approached the ship I saw that she was a tramp steamer flying the red ensign, and my blood boiled. It was scandalous that I should be sent out to a steamer owned by some private company. Vast fortunes were then being amassed out of shipping, such fortunes as enabled Cardiff to become known in the reign of Lloyd George as the City of Dreadful Knights. What was the S.N.O. thinking about? Why had he not ordered this ship to come into harbour? The whole affair was nothing more nor less than a public scandal, against which I would enter a protest both afloat and ashore!

As I climbed the rope ladder against the side I determined on what I would say to the mate, who would be awaiting me on deck. On the deck there was no mate, only four passengers. And what passengers! Young men in lounge suits and tweed caps. It seemed years since I had worn a lounge suit. I knew what kind of passengers they were.

To my annoyance the passenger nearest to me came up and said: "It's the skipper who wants to see you."

"Yes," I replied bitterly, "and it is the skipper I want to see." The fellow actually looked surprised, but I kept my temper, and as we walked for'ard I continued: "No one has any blasted business to get me out to this steamer in a wet sea. Even if the captain is ill, any damned fool could have taken the ship in. It's deep water all the way. Damn it, I've steered a mine-sweeper in myself, and God knows they're tricky enough on the helm."

There was no need to tell this landlubber that I had run the mine-sweeper aground on a shoal of shingle, and so suddenly that the rating who was with me on the bridge was moved to say: "Now, sir, wot 'ave you gone and done?"

Fortunately the tide was rising. I moved the handle of the telegraph to "Full Speed Astern." It was glorious to hear the tinkle and ring of the bell in the engine-room. The engines were reversed, and I put the helm hard aport, lest the tide swung her round and smashed the propeller on the shingle. In a few minutes she was once more afloat in the channel. No entry was made in the log, no court of inquiry was held, and their lordships of the Admiralty were spared the pain of learning how a surgeon came to be navigating a mine-sweeper in the early hours of the dawn.

In reply to my tirade the miserable scrimp on the steamer only smiled, and remarked with aggravating sweetness: "Very true, surgeon, very true indeed. But if I were you I wouldn't say that to the skipper. You see his foot is giving him gyp, and in these cases I've heard that the slightest excitement may prove fatal."

I stopped and stared at the fellow. This cool assurance and choice of words was the language of the Service—all over the world! As to that there was no shadow of doubt.

"Then you are . . ." I began slowly.

He laughed, and finished the sentence for me. "An N.O. as much as you are, but I'm glad you didn't spot it at first."

"And the skipper?" I asked.

"Lieutenant-commander."

"And the—others?"

"All R.N. The whole show is Navy."

"And what's the meaning of it all?"

"You'll probably know before you leave us. But do come and see the skipper."

As I entered his cabin I was glad to know at least that there was some mystery. An uncouth figure hobbled on a stick to greet me. He had a week's growth of hair on his face and was dressed in a soiled plain blue reefer, a grey shirt without collar or tie, and flannel trousers. On his left leg was a sea-boot, and on the right foot a large red carpet slipper. In his right hand was a stick by the aid of which he limped. He transferred it to his left hand as he stood on one foot to shake hands. "Take a pew, surgeon." I sat down, and he settled himself with a grimace in a chair. Obviously he was in pain.

"Now, look here, surgeon," he began, "there's going to be no nonsense."

"Certainly not," I replied, but my mind was racing to escape from what appeared to be Alice in Wonderland.

"Under no circumstances am I going into hospital."

"Certainly not," I said.

"Look here, surgeon; I don't want to be personal, but do you always answer questions in that way?"

"Certainly not."

"Now you've said it again! We've only just met, and we don't want to part brass rags, do we?"

"Certainly not."

"By God, man, can't you listen to what I'm saying?"

"I am listening," I protested, but was wondering if such a thing could possibly exist as a floating naval mental hospital, manned by patients.

"Very well. Listen. You know that they don't appoint crocks to these ships? You know that?"

"Yes."

"You know that the Admiralty take note of everything?"

"Yes."

"Very well! The point is, I can't afford to have any more sick leave."

"No."

"All right. A fortnight ago I was kept for a week in hospital at Queenstown. The bloody fools said it was gout. Now, there's no gout in the family, and I've never had enough money to get gout. It's not gout, but it's giving me gyp. I want you to patch me up without putting me in hospital. That's why I kept the ship out here."

I examined his right foot. The great toe was red and swollen. There were red lines running up the leg, and a tender, swollen gland in the groin. His temperature was 102 degrees F.

"It's not gout," I said. "You've had a corn in the pad of the right big toe. There's pus underneath, and unless it's let out you'll probably get blood poisoning. I absolutely refuse to open that toe here, and without at least a local anæsthetic. You must be reasonable! Come with me to the hospital. I'll freeze it with ethyl chloride and let the pus out. Then, as you refuse to go on the sick list, you can have it dressed on board at your own risk. No one can keep you in hospital against your wish. What about it?"

"Right ho, surgeon. I'll tell them to take the ship in."

That skipper was taking a risk, but he recovered and gained promotion. On the way in I learned something about this mystery ship. The after deck-house was not a deck-house, but a painted dummy of wood and canvas. On pressing a spring the whole thing fell flat on the deck, revealing a gun. In the wardroom the officers showed me their wardrobe. There were skirts which fitted round the waist with a half-hoop of iron spring, blouses padded in the bust, wigs, and Dutch headgear. When a submarine appeared, the Dutch flag was hoisted, and the passengers rushed about in a state of panic. On the bridge was a Dutch skipper waving his arms in the air, and the submarine came alongside to make sure there was no deception. A Dutch matron, hugging her baby to her bosom, leaned over the ship's side, the very picture of a distracted mother. To the horror of those on the submarine the demented mother raised the baby in her arms and threw it down the open conning tower. The baby exploded, and there was the end of a submarine. The officers shook their heads sadly. Those happy days were over. The enemy knew all about those babies, and the newer stunts were more difficult.

Some time later, during a week-end at a seaside resort, I met a lieutenant-commander in the hotel. He was a Highlander, and we forgathered and went for a walk. He was in command of ship Q. —, and told me something of his work. When a submarine appeared, officers and men took to the boats and apparently abandoned the ship. The submarine would open fire at a thousand yards, and the boats would pull away out of the range of fire. As the ship made no reply to this gunfire, the submarine was satisfied that there could be nobody on board, and came nearer to make certain of sinking the steamer. Once the submarine was near enough, four men rushed from the chart-house of the steamer to unmask a gun and engage the submarine. It was trying to sit waiting under gunfire for perhaps an hour, but these men did it, and encouraged each other by holding out their hands after each shell burst—to see whose hand was the steadiest. A rubber of bridge was another distraction.

When the War was over this lieutenant-commander was going to retire from the sea. He was going to provide himself with an oar and carry it on his shoulder into the very heart of England. He would walk until he came to some hamlet where people would run out of their houses to ask him what the thing was that he was carrying on his shoulder. There he would stop, buy a farm, and live happy ever after.

At eight one morning I reported for a day's duty on a new destroyer moored in the Haven. She was going out for a speed trial, and, by regulations, had to carry a doctor. Her skipper was reported to be a "full out" fellow, and so he was. His greeting was: "Hullo, surgeon, coming for the speed trial? Well, I think the best spot for you will be an arm-chair in the wardroom."

"As you please," I answered, "but I'd rather be on the bridge."

He laughed. "All right, but it's pretty filthy outside, a full gale. Come along, and I'll tog you up in my second sea-boots and oilskins."

It was a full gale. The bridge in front of the chart-house was covered in with glass in front, top and sides, and even at half-speed a great white sheet of water was thrown up from the bows every five seconds, and crashed against the glass, which leaked like a well-made conservatory. There was constant tremor, and the thud of heavy seas on the deck. Amazing how she stood it, for her plates were little more than one-eighth of an inch in thickness. At the end of two hours she was worked up to full speed, over thirty knots, and the skipper spoke to the engineer lieutenant-commander. "All right below? Good. Stand by: I'm going to put the helm over." He gave the order to the steersman, the ship shuddered violently, listed until the starboard scuppers were submerged, and raced through half a circle. "Not so bad," said the skipper when she righted herself, and it was once more possible to stand comparatively upright on the bridge.

Apart from the intermittent spray, visibility was good, and I saw some black things like large bladders in the water. "Dead mules," said the skipper, "decomposing and blown up like balloons. Some mule transport." Later on I saw something else in the sea. It appeared for a few seconds bobbing like a cork between the trough and crest of the waves. As we raced past it was not more than twenty yards away. It had a lifebelt round its body, the face was that of a skeleton, but the scalp was intact and the sodden tresses of hair were black and very long.

"Did you see it?" I asked.

"Five minutes ago."

"Not going to take it on board?"

"Christ, no! It would demoralise the men." After a pause, he added: "The *Lusitania*."

At lunch-time I made my way aft from the bridge to the wardroom, and the journey occupied a good ten minutes. There were no side-rails, but a life-line was stretched along the centre of the deck. In places the deck was awash, and it was necessary to pause and cross in moments when the deck was horizontal. In the wardroom I made a rush for an arm-chair screwed to the floor, got into it, and hung on to it. I watched the side of the wardroom rising to where the upper deck should have been, stopping there for a moment, and falling back to below the level of my chair. It was hard work to avoid being thrown out of the destroyer by centrifugal forces. The skipper joined me, reached the other arm-chair and laughed. "Well, what do you think of this? How would you like being a surgeon in a destroyer all the time?"

"One of the things I asked for. It can't be like this all the time, and there's plenty of shore leave if you are friends with the skipper."

"And there ought to be plenty of leave and better pay for the skipper. Just listen to the row!"

"Yes," I agreed, "Kipling was right—mixture of switchback, waterchute, and hell continuous."

Our lunch was a mug of cocoa. No other meal could be served, and the messman showed great dexterity in managing to reach us with the cocoa. After lunch we returned to the bridge, where things were somewhat easier, as the ship was only going half-speed. The door of the chart-room opened and a messenger appeared with a signal for the skipper. He read it, moved the engine-room telegraph to full-speed, and handed the paper to me. This was the signal, which had been sent *en clair*: "Q. — to all ships. Have engaged submarine for two and a half hours. Lat. . . . Long. . . . I am sinking. This is my first and last signal."

"Q. —!" I exclaimed.

"Yes. Do you know the lad?"

"Went a walk with him two weeks ago."

"Well, come into the chart-room and we'll see where he is."

After measuring with a pair of compasses, the skipper continued: "A goodish way off. One hundred and twenty miles ahead. Take us four hours. There are bound to be lots of people nearer, but I'll make the course until I hear." He gave an order to the steersman, and returned to study the chart. The messenger also returned with a decoded signal. "Just what I thought," said the skipper. "There are two destroyers within twenty miles of him, and they are on the way now. Let's go on the bridge."

In the evening we were back at our moorings in the quiet waters of the Haven, but the Skipper refused to say good-bye. "Look here, I gave you a rotten lunch, come and dine with me at the pub."

I have met three V.C.'s—two in the Navy, one in the Army. They were all unassuming men who gave an impression of strong moral character, although the Army V.C. was the most irascible man I ever knew. He had been crossed in love, went out to France, and returned with wounds and the Military Cross. The girl still refused him. Off he went again, only to return with wounds and the Victoria Cross. After the War I met him in a bar near Piccadilly. He was as irascible as ever, and two days later his name appeared in a short news paragraph. A woman had thrown herself from one of the bridges over the Thames. My friend, who was passing at the time, jumped off the bridge, brought her ashore, gave his name without rank or decorations to the policeman, then disappeared. As I have said, he was a most irascible man, and wild horses would not induce me to set his name in print.

# CHAPTER XXII

# THE INVASION OF ENGLAND

IN the first week of February 1916 I was transferred to the
Royal Marine Depot at Deal. There was plenty of
excitement in the air, as enemy aircraft were in the habit
of crossing the coast at this point. Zeppelins passed on their
way to London, and Taubes on their way to and from the
bombing of Dover. Our air defence was weak, and more
than once I saw a dozen planes bombing Dover. Not until
the last had gone did our own planes reach a height at which
counter-attack was possible. Any unused bombs were
reserved by the enemy for the Depot. For defence we had
two Maxim guns, and on one occasion I borrowed a rifle from
a protesting sentry—an innovation which was not encouraged.
When enemy aircraft were about, the blinds of most of the
houses were lowered, and this suggested a corpse in every
house.

On a bright, cool Sunday morning I was walking along a
quiet road, smoking a cigarette and thinking of nothing in
particular. A sharp "crick-crash," a gust of wind striking
me in the face, glass falling out of the houses on either side,
I jumped about a foot from the earth, and for a moment
thought that I was killed. Twenty yards ahead was a smoking
crater in the roadway. My first thought was to run at full
speed in the opposite direction. It was not my uniform that
stopped me, but the sudden recollection of a booklet called
*Sutherland's First Aid to the Sick and Injured*, and I ran to
the smoking crater.

In the roadway were the remains of a man who had
literally been blown to bits. The details of such a sight
should only be described by those who have never seen it.
There was also a lad on the ground with a shell wound in

273

the right thigh. Later I learned that he was only seventeen, and, being under age, had been bought out of the Royal Marines the previous day by his mother. As I rose to my feet an elderly sergeant appeared. He was shaking his fist at the rapidly departing Taube, tears were streaming down his face, and from his lips came a well-selected string of oaths and abuse. I began to laugh, and laughed so much that the sergeant stopped, stared at me, and exclaimed: "You're laughing, sir?"

"Yes," I laughed, "and look, man, look at that!" I pointed down the roadway. There, on the doorstep of a large house, the blinds of which were lowered, stood a very fat sergeant. With his left hand he was hammering the knocker on the door, and with his right almost pulling the bell out of its socket. Within the house the bell was ringing furiously. The fat sergeant was seeking shelter, and rightly so, because, although he was not seriously injured, the force of the explosion had completely blown away the seat of his trousers.

The Zeppelins, on their way to London, came at night, and the only warning we had of their coming was when the electric light was suddenly cut off. Once this happened towards the end of dinner on a guest night. In the darkness the mess president apologised to the guests, and within a minute the servants had brought lit candles in silver candlesticks. Once the guests had departed, the officers rushed to their rooms to change. They had to distribute two thousand men along the inside of the wall enclosing the depot, so that in the event of a direct hit there would be as few casualties as possible. I alone did not change because I had nothing to do except to wait for casualties, and I sat alone in the ante-room in naval dress uniform. Within ten minutes the row began, and I walked out on to the lawn to see what was happening. One Zeppelin had been picked up by a searchlight. She looked very beautiful—a silver cigar floating in the dark sky. Everything was firing at her. Dover was firing and warships anchored in the Downs were firing.

On the lawn Captain Syson passed and stopped to talk for a few minutes. He was the coolest man I ever knew. On the Marine Reserve of officers before the War, he was recalled from being gym. instructor at Eton. He was in the retreat from Antwerp, and led his marines—not into Holland, but to the French lines. "Not much use firing from the ground," he remarked. "Aeroplanes are the only thing." A terrific explosion followed which shook the earth. "That's the monitor in the Downs," he continued. "A fifteen-inch gun. I doubt if it can do the elevation, but we'll see in a minute." A great red circle of flame appeared in the sky behind and below the Zeppelin, followed by the concussion of the burst. "A good mile off her I would say, and—hullo, they've picked up the other one." We turned, and over the Mess was a second Zeppelin in a searchlight. The depot was the objective, because a little later she dropped four bombs into a marsh some miles away.

From behind us on the grass came a dull thud. "What's that?" I exclaimed.

"Well, I've got a fairly good idea what it is, but we'll see." He produced an electric torch and flashed it on the grass. "Yes, there it is; a fairly large piece, too. Probably from that fifteen-inch shell. Well, I must be getting along to see the men along the north walk. Half of them are only boys, you know." Off he went, and I returned to the ante-room.

The whole place was shaking, and the noise was hellish. I pressed the bell, without much hope of it being answered. Within a minute the Mess sergeant appeared, as imperturbable as if it were noon on a Sabbath morning. He and I were the only occupants of the Mess.

"A double whisky and soda," I said, "and, sergeant, have one yourself."

"Thank you, sir." He returned with one large whisky and a siphon. I put in the soda. "Where's your drink, sergeant?"

"In the pantry, sir."

"Well, good luck, sergeant."

"Thank you, sir."

I pulled an arm-chair to the fire and thought what wonderful people these marines were. I had wanted to talk to someone, but the sergeant was right. What would the Mess president have said had he known that I expected the sergeant to have a drink with me in the Mess? Could nothing disturb their equanimity——not if the whole damned place was blown to bits? What a perfectly hellish noise! Then there was my servant. Where would he be? Perhaps at the north wall. And what a fuss we'd had before dinner when he put out my dress clothes.

"I think we'll have a clean shirt to-night, sir."

"No; the old one will do. I've only worn it once."

"Excuse me, sir, but this is a guest night, and I'd get the blame."

"Who on earth is going to blame you even if I wear a tennis shirt?"

"Well, sir, it's the Mess sergeant. If an officer isn't properly dressed it's his servant that gets the blame."

"All right, put out the clean one, then."

Wonderful people! If ever I had enough money I'd have an ex-marine servant. Would I ever have enough money, and would this blasted noise and vibration ever cease? At that moment the Mess sergeant entered. "Excuse me, sir, but there's a sergeant in the porch. Perhaps you'd see him, sir."

"Certainly." And I went into the hall.

An elderly sergeant was leaning against the wall of the porch. He was as white as a sheet and trembling from head to feet. I knew the diagnosis. But for Syson and the

276

whisky I might have felt like that myself. As I came up to him he stood at attention. "Don't blame me, sir. I can't help it. I swear to God, South Africa was nothing like this."

"Of course not," I answered. Not that I'd been in the Boer War. I told the Mess sergeant to bring a double brandy neat, and while he was getting it I asked the other: "What are your orders?"

"To deliver this message at the north wall, sir." He was holding an envelope.

"Well, you'll get there all right in a few minutes." The brandy was brought, as usual on a silver salver, and I told the man to drink it straight away.

He did so and replaced the glass. "Thank you very much, sir." He saluted, and went off into the noise of the night.

At Deal I assisted in the defence against the invasion of England. No news of this episode was ever published in the Press, and it is not recorded in the official history of the Great War. Nevertheless the thing happened, and the truth is known to several thousand people. For that reason the story is now to be published for the first time—Official Secrets Act or no Official Secrets Act—with all copyright reserved and reproduction forbidden. The major had shooting rights over a marsh a few miles from the depot, and one forenoon he and I were out after snipe. We had reached the end of the marsh when a marine appeared, running, in the distance. Splashing his way through pools and mud, he was making straight for us.

"Why can't the fool keep on the dry?" said the major.

"Looks like a cinema show," I replied.

Ten minutes later a breathless, soaked and mud-bespattered marine saluted, and from his tunic produced a message. The major read it and passed it to me. "Return at once," was the message, signed by the adjutant. We returned in a two-seater car, and found the gates of the depot closed. At the orderly-room was another message—to report at the general's house on the sea front.

The general was sitting at the dining-room table, around which were officers seated and standing. The major apologised for our appearance in mufti with twelve-bore guns in our hands.

"As every one is now present, I shall read the orders received from the Central Army: 'Enemy wearing our uniform and speaking our language expected to land between North Foreland and Dover. The Royal Marines will hold the coast from a point one mile north of Deal to a point one hundred yards south of Walmer Castle. Landing will probably be covered by bombardment from the sea. As soon as bombardment begins civilian population will leave the town, using fields and bye-roads, leaving all main roads clear for military operations. Ten thousand troops will proceed to the point of attack as soon as this is known. The position is to be held at all costs and under no circumstances will a retirement be permitted." The general paused, and I had a sinking sensation in the epigastric region. He continued: "It is unnecessary, gentlemen, for me to add anything. You all know your duties, and the traditions of the corps will be maintained."

Within half an hour the adjutant had allotted to me thirty-six raw recruits as stretcher-bearers. They would be of no use in the trenches as they had not yet learned to handle a rifle. I marched them to the hospital, and obtained nine horse-hair mattresses to be used as stretchers. There were only two real stretchers in the whole establishment. The mattresses were carried to an empty garage, where we fitted rope handles to each corner so that they might be carried like stretchers. I gave the recruits twenty minutes of stretcher drill—all that I could remember out of *Sutherland's*

*First Aid to the Sick and Injured.* After that I dismissed them, telling them to fall-in at the garage when the corps paraded to march to the trenches already dug on the foreshore. These trenches were only to be fully manned during the night, as in daylight we would have ample warning of the raid. I told the recruits to wear double underclothing as the night would be cold.

The line of trenches for which I was medically responsible reached from a hillock at the south end of the town to the point beyond Walmer Castle. My next task was to commandeer a house to serve as a casualty clearing-station. At random I chose one in a terrace behind the hillock, as this hillock might give some protection against bombardment. The house selected was occupied by an elderly lady, a widow, with two daughers in their twenties. I explained my business. They were delighted, and offered there and then to move the furniture out of the drawing-room into the garden. I said this was unnecessary, and that nothing need be done until something happened. Even then it would be sufficient if arrangements were made for an ample supply of hot water in the kitchen. The three ladies were so pleased that I said I would do my best to look after their house when they left it.

"What perfect nonsense!" said the mother. "Whatever happens, we're not going away."

"No," added one of the girls, "and if we went away I wouldn't be here to drive you about in my car."

That settled the matter.

In the late afternoon I marched my stretcher-bearers to positions behind the lines. On the way, I led them past the house behind the hillock, so that they would know where the casualty clearing-station was situated. I left them in three groups more or less equi-distant, and about one hundred yards behind our trenches. I reported in the trenches where the stretcher-bearers were to be found if wanted. I was leading the third lot towards Walmer Castle. The light was failing, rain was falling, and a mist was blown in gusts from the sea. As we came to a bend in the road I saw a column of troops marching like a phantom army out of the mist. They carried their rifles at the slope, and my heart thumped when I saw at a glance that they were not wearing our uniforms, but the field-grey of the Prussian infantry. But for the twelve lads behind me I would there and then have bolted inland. As it was I halted my stretcher-bearers, and, with as much assurance as I could muster, shouted to the advancing army: "Halt! Who goes there?" They halted, and the next moment I expected to be riddled with bullets. My challenge was answered by a shout of: "Friends. Volunteers from Dover." With great cordiality I replied: "Advance, friends, for recognition." An elderly gentleman marched briskly forward and explained that the volunteers were to occupy the line to the south of ours. He had over-marched the distance by a quarter of a mile. This was the first I had seen of the volunteers, and in colour their uniforms resembled those of the German troops. Leaving my stretcher-bearers on the road, I showed him the place where our lines ended. These volunteers were all old and mostly retired professional or business men. Three of them died of pneumonia in consequence of their vigil that night on the coast.

On returning I found some of the stretcher-bearers shivering. It was a cold night with half a gale of wind, and the sea was a swirling vortex of white-ridged waves. Any Germans crossing the North Sea that night in motor barges deserved the Iron Cross and anything else they could obtain. Under my naval greatcoat I was wearing a çamel-hair dressing-gown and yet I was cold.

To one shivering recruit I said: "How old are you?"

"Eighteen, sir," was the answer. "That's your army age," I said. "What I want to know is your real age."

"Excuse me, sir, but I'm nearly sixteen." I marched them to the front door of Walmer Castle, and rang the bell. It was then the country residence of the Prime Minister, Mr. Asquith. He was not there that night, and his butler readily agreed to my request that these stretcher-bearers should spend the night in the kitchen. I arranged that two of them would be on duty outside on the road. This they did by pairs every hour, and the butler gave them cocoa and sandwiches throughout the night.

I returned to the casualty clearing-station and there had supper. Afterwards the girl got the car out and drove me to inspect the stretcher-bearers. It was a dark night of rain and wind, the car had no lights, and I had some difficulty in finding the places where I had left my men.

Once something large loomed out of the darkness on the road. The girl ran her car on to the sward and braked, as an enormous motor lorry thundered past without lights.

"What's that?" asked the girl.

I told her. "Twenty thousand rounds of extra ammunition from the Central Army."

"But how thrilling!" she said.

At dawn the troops returned to barracks, and most of us slept all forenoon. In the late afternoon the trenches were again occupied for the night. Next day the Marine Office in London telephoned to know why certain routine reports had not been received. They were not yet aware of the state of emergency on the coast, and full particulars were forthwith sent to London by motor dispatch rider. Marine headquarters telephoned to the Admiralty. The Admiralty knew nothing about the threatened invasion, and telephoned to the War Office. The War Office knew nothing about it, but the Admiralty insisted that the War Office must know something about it, and two hours later the War Office made a discovery. Two days previously they had transmitted the following intelligence to the Central

Army: "Enemy spies wearing our uniform and speaking our language expected to land between North Foreland and Dover." During transmission the word "spies" had been omitted, and the Staff of the Central Army had done the rest—very effectively.

# CHAPTER XXIII

## ULTIMA THULE

AFTER the War I went on holiday in Lewis, the most northern island of the Outer Hebrides. The north end of the island is known as Lewis, and the south as Harris. My companion was "young George," or rather George Herbert Rae Gibson, D.S.O., M.D., F.R.C.P.(Edin.). In the Great War he had risen from captain to be D.A.D.M.S. of the Canadian Corps in France, and was now Deputy Commissioner of the Board of Control in Scotland.

On reaching Stornoway, the seaport, we were on an island about fifty miles long and twenty-five miles broad, where three of the greatest controversies in the world could be studied on a small scale. These were religion, alcohol, and big business.

The only Catholic church on the island was in Stornoway, and all the windows were smashed. During the previous year a handful of Catholics had attempted to hold a service in the church and a crowd had pelted the building with stones. In the main, the people of the island are Calvinists and regular churchgoers. Dressed in the deepest black, they go to church on Sabbaths and sometimes on week-days. Whenever I saw these little groups coming along the roads on their way to worship, the thought always came to me: where is the corpse? For the youth of the island, dancing, music, or gay dresses were taboo. These things were sinful. Many of the old women would sit in their chairs groaning aloud for hours. That was sanctity. Apart altogether from dogma, this attitude towards life is the antithesis of Catholicism. The Catholic Church knows and has named every sin that the human heart can commit, and there is one sin defined as "Accidia"—taking a delight in being miserable.

In South Uist, one of the islands of the Outer Hebrides, are people of the same race, but there the girls wear coloured dresses, and there is dancing, singing and bagpipes. South Uist is Catholic, and I do not think that the extraordinary difference between the people of these two islands can be explained otherwise than as a difference in their faith. At its worst Catholicism is human; at its best Calvinism is inhuman.

In Lewis it was not possible to buy a drink in any of the hotels, and all the hotels in Stornoway were closed. Whilst there we lived in lodgings. The women of the island, when the men were at sea, had voted for no license, whereby all the public-houses were closed. It was possible to buy whisky from a licensed grocer, provided one bought half a gallon at a time. Men would club together to buy this amount and carry it down to the foreshore, where they drank it. Consequently drunkenness was not unknown, and for the twelve months following the veto of local option the amount of alcohol imported into the island had increased. In the more remote places private stills were working.

The greatest war on the island was against Big Business, as represented by Lord Leverhulme. I say "Big Business" rather than capitalism, because the crofters who opposed Lord Leverhulme were capitalists in a small way, inasmuch as they held the secure tenure of land. Otherwise they would have been incapable of opposing him. Lord Leverhulme had bought the island. The price of land, mostly peat morass, was about fourpence per acre, and the rates in the island were twenty-five shillings in the pound. It was a poor island. Lord Leverhulme had the best intentions. He wished to build at Stornoway a large factory for canning herrings, which his fishing fleet would provide. This would give employment to the people. Secondly, he desired at his own expense to replace the little black houses costing about twenty pounds, in which most of the people lived, with modern houses costing about four hundred pounds. He also proposed to start a large dairy farm on pasture land at the north end of the island, in order that the people might have a pure milk supply.

When I reached Stornoway I found a half-built factory on which work had been abandoned, a derelict small-gauge railway, and thousands of pounds' worth of machinery rusting on the shore. The pasture-land had been seized by raiders or squatters, who built little huts upon it and had dug it up into allotments. Lord Leverhulme had been driven out of Lewis and had retreated to Harris, where he was attempting to put his ideas into practice. It was an extraordinary situation, and I think Lord Leverhulme failed because he was badly advised. Had he sought the advice of the school teachers or the Inspectors of Poor on the island, he might have been more successful or have saved his money. He was a self-made Lancashire millionaire, then aged seventy-three, and rather deaf. He failed to understand the mentality of the people with whom he was dealing, and to realise why he failed it is necessary to know something of the Lewis men and their black houses.

Most of the men on the island, outside the small town of Stornoway, are fishermen-crofters, and belong to the Fleet Reserve. In January they go south to one of the large naval bases, join a ship, and undergo their annual training. They return to Lewis, visiting their friends in Edinburgh or Glasgow on the way home. Their next work is the early spring line-fishing off the coast of Lewis. When that is over they dig up their crofts and sow their crops, mostly potatoes and corn. That done, they join the herring fleet for the early summer fishing. They are home by midsummer to harvest their crops. Then comes the late autumn herring fishing, and, when that is over, they return home and do nothing until the time comes for their annual training in the Royal Naval Reserve. That is their life—a varied and interesting one, which engenders independence of character and also at times laziness.

Three-quarters of the houses on the island were black houses. This is a generic term to distinguish a primitive dwelling from its modern rival, the white house, built of stone and mortar and roofed with slates.

A black house is a low, rectangular building of flat, uncemented drystone, thatched with turf or straw. The walls, about seven feet high, are double, and the space of six inches between the two tiers of stone is filled with earth. The thatched roof overlaps the inner but not the outer wall, and has a slight incline from the middle. A high-pitched roof would not withstand the winter gales, and the whole house appears like a mound stuck to the earth. In the great gale of March 1921, which swept the outer isles, the roofs of many modern houses were blown off, but none of the black houses was damaged. In a few black houses there is a low chimney in the middle of the roof, but in most the peat smoke percolates through the thatch. The only entrance, and the small, closed windows, are on the lee side from the prevailing wind.

To me the black house was something strange and new. On entering I was in a dim, windowless cow-byre. Through a grey haze of peat smoke, smarting to unaccustomed eyes, I recognised the cow, and startled hens flew upwards from the ground. The floor was the earth, covered with dung and cow bedding. This bedding is renewed but not removed, so that after a time the floor is raised some feet above ground level. Once a year, in spring-time, the byre is cleaned out and the manure is placed on the land.

A wooden partition, rising nearly as high as the thatch, separates the byre from the living-room, entered through a loosely fitting door in the partition. In the living-room a peat fire burns on the centre of the floor, which is the earth. The atmosphere is a thick grey haze of smoke, rising and percolating through the thatched roof, from which hang long stalactites of black peat tar. This tar differs from coal tar because when the thatch is so saturated with tar that no more smoke can escape, the roof is taken off, and makes the best dressing for potato crops. Despite the smoke in the room, there is no dust nor dirt on the white-scrubbed wooden table, nor on the white crockery on the clean wooden shelves. Alongside one wall is a broad wooden bench on which at least four people can sit in comfort, and here in the evening the old men have their gossip. There are no chairs, but a few stools around the fire, and hens which roost in the byre wander about picking up what they can find.

In the living-room was the patient whom we had come to visit. He was an epileptic, but his relatives and friends remembered the time when my father, as Deputy-Commissioner in Lunacy, had visited this house. The patient, now an old man, had suffered greatly from fits in his youth, and these fits had continued throughout life, despite the fact that a white cock had been killed and buried under the fire. In the Western Isles that was the recognised cure for epilepsy until nearly the end of the nineteenth century.

The living-room is larger than an outdoor view of the house would suggest, and despite the closed windows and haze of smoke is well ventilated. The heat of the fire, the porous roof and walls, ensure that air is continuously leaving and entering the room. This is obvious, because the smoke rising from the fire is constantly wafted from all sides by unfelt currents of air.

Another wooden partition with a door in the middle separates the living-room from the sleeping-room. All the family sleep in this room in three box beds arranged along the back wall and facing the windows. These are not the unwholesome closet beds of the Lowlands and of Wales, built into the wall. They are large, rectangular boxes, placed on their sides, and standing against the wall three feet from the ground. The box-bed is thus a protection against unwanted shower baths from the porous thatch in rainy weather. Alongside the front wall are large wooden chests, in which food, clothing and fishing tackle are indiscriminately stored. There is no fire in the sleeping-room, but it gets its fair share of smoke coming over the top of the partition.

George Gibson * regards the black house as "an example of specialised development devised to meet certain positive needs: the Scottish equivalent of the tee-pee of the Red Indian, the mia-mia of the Australian aboriginal, the snow-hut of the Eskimo."

Over a thousand years ago, when the Highlands and Islands of Scotland were covered with forest there were probably wattle huts and wooden cabins as in England. With the burning of the forests new problems and conditions arose. As the trees vanished, a house requiring the minimum amount of timber for its construction became a necessity. When he lost the forests, man also lost nature's protection against storm. A gale may be raging over the tree-tops of a forest, but on the ground all is as calm as in a submarine five fathoms below the waves. "It was to compete with these two factors that the black house was evolved. Everything in its structure is indicative of this. The only portions of the building where wood is employed are the rafters, doors and partitions. Low-lying and round-shouldered, it hugs the ground without an angle or a flat surface to catch the wind."

Thus does the black house stand for the survival of the fittest, and yet it might evolve into something better, although never, please God, into a white house. In the humblest black house there is nothing to suggest the cramped space of a doll's flat or the squalor of a slum. The cattle might have a house of their own, the peat fire might be better on a hearth and the smoke in a chimney. Another blemish is the

* *Caledonian Medical Journal*, August 1924, p. 208.

dampness. For three years my friend * had sought a remedy for the structural defect arising from the damp earth lying between the double walls. He was sure there was a solution if only it could be found. "Like the old songs and pipe music, it was probably almost forgotten, and as with those departing melodies only the old people would remember." He was right, and at last, in Dunvegan, he found an old man who told him the lost secret of the houses.

"In a properly constructed black house both the outer and inner walls were constructed of flat stones, all set at a slight slope downwards and outwards. This Venetian-blind effect provided a means by which the moisture in the intervening space could drain towards the outside, and was at the same time prevented from soaking inwards.

"Anns na h-aosda tha gliocas (Among the ancients is wisdom)."

Are the black houses healthy? Most of those who live in these houses are verminous and carry head and body lice. If typhus fever came they would be decimated, because the typhus germ is transmitted by the louse from one person to another. At this time the public health authorities had started a de-lousing campaign in the islands. This was opposed to the ideas of the people, who believed that lice came out of the blood and were a sign of health. At first glance that view is sheer superstition, but I discovered that it was merely a wrong deduction made from the *correct* observation of facts. More than once typhus fever had decimated the population, and during the fever the temperature of the body rises. When the temperature rises all lice leave the body. This fact these people had *observed* and remembered, and from that observation had concluded that lice were a sign of health, as, in logic, they are. The prevention of body vermin is merely a matter of bathing facilities.

* George Gibson, *loc. cit.*, p. 217.

When attending the London poor I was often infected, and would have remained infected had I not had a daily bath. In the time of Marie Antoinette this de-lousing problem exercised the minds of the physicians attached to the Court. In the Court of Queen Elizabeth it was worse.

Now comes a most extraordinary fact. Children are born in the black houses, and until they can walk—at nine months to a year—they do not cross the threshold. Outside Stornoway there are no perambulators. And yet, in 1923, according to the registrar-general's report, the infantile mortality in Lewis was twenty-eight per one thousand births—one of the lowest in Europe. For the same year the rate in Edinburgh was eighty-two, in Glasgow ninety, and in Aberdeen one hundred and four. Rickets was unknown, and never have I seen healthier or more beautiful children. The food of these people is rough, but pure and unadulterated: milk, potatoes, dried fish, salt herrings, oatmeal, butter, and, very occasionally, meat. When the men go out to the line-fishing they take two bannocks or large scones. As soon as a cod is caught, the liver is cut out, sliced and placed between the two bannocks. These are placed on a seat in the boat, and the man sits on them. At the end of an hour a good deal of the oil has been expressed from the cod's liver into the bannocks, which the man eats; and he is eating bannocks plus the purest and freshest cod liver oil.

Amongst the people of the black houses there is a curious custom in courtship, and, like all primitive sex customs, it is based on economic conditions. The time for making love is during the long winter nights when the young men are at home. On that bleak windswept coast it would be difficult for two people to make love out of doors. So the young man goes to the girl's house. Again, with one living-room where the family are sitting, it is difficult to make love. The girl goes into the sleeping-room. There is no fire there, nor any light, because the burning of tallow candles and oil is a consideration to people who are poor. So, for warmth, the girl goes to bed. Once in bed, both her legs are inserted into one large stocking, which her mother ties above her knees. Then the young man goes into the sleeping-room, and lies beside her. It is called "bundling" and was a practice in New England during the early part of the last century.

At the back of each black house is a small croft or farm of two or three acres. On such a croft I saw two old men working, and I asked one of them about the Lord Leverhulme feud. The old man gave evasive answers until he realised that I was Highland.

"Why won't I let Lever build me a four-hundred-pound house? See that black house! It cost me twenty pounds, and is rated at twenty pounds. A four-hundred-pound house would be rated at four hundred pounds. Who is going to pay the rates? Me and my brother. Where are we going to get the money? Not out of this land. At present it keeps me and my brother and our old sister. We live all right. But to pay the rates on a four-hundred-pound house there would be only one way: to answer a whistle at six in the morning and work for wages in Lever's factory. No damn fear. Poor as I am, I'm master here, and could order you off this croft. Why did some of us raid his pasture-land? A dairy farm for the island it was to be! I've another name for that—a monopoly in milk. No damn fear. We are poorer now than we were. Why? Because the line-fishing in the spring has failed. Why? Because of these damned trawlers that spoil the spawn, and half of them are Lever's English trawlers. He makes us poor, and then wants us to work for him. No damn fear!"

Such were the forces opposed to Lord Leverhulme—forces of which he knew nothing. Could the condition of the island have been improved in any other way? A lady on the island said it could. She had been to the Frisian Islands, and had seen what Germany had done for islands such as

Lewis. The peat bog had been drained by great trenches, and the land treated for three consecutive years with artificial fertilisers. Then wheat would grow. To protect the wheat from the fierce winds of the North Sea a variety of pine had been found which sent its roots down through fifteen feet of peat to the rocks below. These trees along the coast formed a wind-screen. Then farm-houses were built, and farms on the instalment system were handed over to approved tenants.

On going south to Harris I found Lord Leverhulme at Obe, a beautiful hamlet at the foot of the mountains overlooking the Sound of Harris. There he was, constructing, at what cost I know not, a breakwater, a harbour, and a factory. There were not enough people in Obe to do this work. So he imported Irish labourers, who worked under the supervision of English and American overseers and engineers. In vain the local sailors—and they are amongst the most fearless I ever knew—told him that the Sound of Harris with its thousand rocks could not be navigated at night in winter. The persistent old man replied: "If the Harris men cannot sail my ships, I will get English sailors, and, if necessary, I will put a light on every rock in the Sound of Harris."

At the entrance to a beautiful glen at one end of the village I saw three new model little houses, with iron palings round their gardens, and on the palings of the first house was affixed a galvanised iron plate: "Lady Leverhulme Terrace." There was to be a cinema in Obe, but no public-house. Amongst the staff engaged on this great work were half a dozen attractive English typists, with bobbed hair, short skirts, and silk stockings. These girls aroused the ire of one of the preachers in the island, who denounced Lord Leverhulme and all his works: "Woe is me, woe is me! Oh, my dear friends, it is something awful to see the harlots and the concubines of Lever running about the streets of Obe." Lord Leverhulme had antagonised an island. It was left for him to antagonise a nation. On the first of December, 1920, the local Parish Council had asked the Postmaster-General to change the Norse name of Obe, centuries old, to—Leverborough. Hitherto no one on the mainland had troubled about what was happening in Lewis. As soon as the change of name was announced, quiet old gentlemen all over Scotland rose from their chairs and said: "What the devil is the meaning of this?" Poor Lord Leverhulme! He was trying, at the age of seventy-three, to buy one of the things in this world which money cannot buy—an immortality for his name. He had bought an impoverished island from that Highland chief, who was Lord of the Western Isles, but other things he could not buy.

The morning came when I had to clamber over the slippery seaweed on the rocks of Obe to reach a small boat in which I was rowed out to the steamer for the mainland. My friend clambered after me, and, as I stood up in the boat to say good-bye, he said: "You will come back to Obe, and, when you do, all this will have disappeared."

I answered: "That is a prophecy, but I believe it."

Within a year Lord Leverhulme was dead and the scheme for making Obe a centre of modern industry was abandoned. And now George Gibson has gone too. The wild winter seas in the Sound of Harris are smashing up that half-built harbour. Alternate gales and sunshine are cracking up the little modern houses, but the old black houses stand. The dream of a millionaire is fading like mountains in the morning mist. But the witchery of the islands is now upon me, and once more the Atlantic is breaking on the rocks of Ultima Thule.